IMPLEMENTING CITIZEN PARTICIPATION IN A BUREAUCRATIC SOCIETY

IMPLEMENTING CITIZEN PARTICIPATION IN A BUREAUCRATIC SOCIETY

A Contingency Approach

Mary Grisez Kweit
Robert W. Kweit

PRAEGER

PRAEGER SPECIAL STUDIES • PRAEGER SCIENTIFIC

Library of Congress Cataloging in Publication Data

Kweit, Mary Grisez.
Implementing citizen participation in a bureaucratic society.

Bibliography: p.
Includes index.
1. Political participation—United States.
2. Bureaucracy—United States. I. Kweit, Robert W. II. Title.
JK1764.K85 320.973 81-11879
ISBN 0-03-056113-2 AACR2

Published in 1981 by Praeger Publishers
CBS Educational and Professional Publishing
A Division of CBS, Inc.
521 Fifth Avenue, New York, New York 10175 U.S.A.

123456789 145 987654321

Printed in the United States of America

To Our Parents

PREFACE

As political science students during the turbulent sixties, it is probably not surprising that as soon as we completed our studies and obtained our "union cards" we began to study citizen participation. Certainly there was an increasing distrust for, and alienation toward, government as we entered the decade of the seventies, but the federal government was taking steps to give government back to the people. As programs continued to proliferate, and more and more discretionary authority was transferred from our elected representatives to unelected professional bureaucrats, citizen participation was mandated as a means of maintaining democratic responsibility. In other words, citizens were guaranteed a voice in government decisions. Elected officials could use citizen advisory boards as a means of obtaining information and opinions while divesting themselves of some of the responsibility for overseeing the bureaucracy. Bureaucrats could use citizens as sources of information, sounding boards, and presumably supporters, as they attempted to serve the public. Citizens, of course, gain by the ability to influence decisions that affect them also also develop the feeling that they are part of the system.

Unfortunately, to no one's surprise these ideal goals were seldom realized. Our research was aimed at finding out why citizen participation worked some times, in some places, but failed in others. It is easy to be cynical and say that citizen participation fails when elected officials and bureaucrats refuse to give up power and works when they cooperate. It would be nice if things were so simple. Many "evil" government officials have been forced to yield to well organized, intense, informed citizens. On the other hand, many well meaning officials have been distressed by public apathy or the self-interested activities of a few. We have been pleased in our studies to find that most government officials are extremely well intentioned. In this book, we present a discussion of the importance and development of citizen participation in the United States. We investigate some of the problems and conflicts that make ideal citizen participation an elusive goal. Finally, using two data sets, we examine some of the factors that affect the ability of citizen participation to cause policy impact, increase citizen trust and satisfaction, and bring new participants into the system.

We hope this study will be useful to government practitioners, citizen participants, scholars, and interested citizens.

ACKNOWLEDGMENTS

We have spent seven years doing various studies of citizen participation. In that time one builds up many debts. Financial help from Clifton McCloskey, former Director of the Institute of Government, University of Virginia, allowed us to do case studies in Richmond and Norfolk, Virginia. Summer research grants from Hamilton College allowed us to gather data in Syracuse and Utica, New York. Summer research professorships from the University of North Dakota enabled us to begin this manuscript.

Many students have helped in various capacities along the way. Mark Rosenbaum and Guy Sibilla did the bulk of the interviewing in New York and Virginia, respectively. Dana Frey, Joan Flynn, Rich Bailey, and Edie Lowery aided us in finding sources, sharing ideas, and reacting to our formative thoughts. We also appreciate the assistance of Ron Grimm and Marcie Parker.

We wish to thank all those who participated in our interviews and the government officials who assisted us by providing background data. Two bureaucrats who deserve to be singled out for the stimulating thoughts they've shared with us are John Staley, City Forester of Grand Forks, North Dakota, and Mary Lou Bingham, Principal City Planner, Norfolk, Virginia.

Bruce McDowell, of the Advisory Commission on Intergovernmental Relations, assisted us in obtaining ACIR-ICMA survey data. Bob Stein, Rice University, did more than bend over backwards in getting us that data.

Betsy Brown, political science editor at Praeger, has been a delight to work with. We appreciate her friendship and guidance.

We have saved our greatest debt of gratitude for last. We sincerely want to thank Irene Wagner for her cheerfulness, her typing skills, her concern, and her ability to read our minds and transcribe what we meant, even if it isn't what we said. Thanks, too, to her family for sharing her time with us.

CONTENTS

LIST OF TABLES

LIST OF FIGURES

IMPLEMENTING CITIZEN PARTICIPATION IN A BUREAUCRATIC SOCIETY

1

INTRODUCTION

In April of 1979, Grand Forks, North Dakota was inundated by the "flood of the century." When the flood waters receded, it was discovered that one of the victims had been the old pool in Riverside Park. The flood waters had cracked its walls to the extent that it was no longer usable. There was not immediately much consternation about the damage. The pool had been flooded before and had been leaking for years. There had already been some discussion of repairing it or building a new one, either in the same park or in one of the newer, growing areas of the city. The 1979 flood simply forced the issue.

As soon as the flood damage was assessed, the Superintendent of the Park Board was quoted as saying that no new construction should take place on the same site since the frequent flooding would only mean constant damage.[1] On June 5, the Park Board was entertained at its monthly meeting by a film demonstrating the wonders of a pool with simulated ocean-like waves and decided to make the construction of such a new pool "top priority."[2] The only question left seemed to be where to put it. But the residents around the Riverside Park had not yet begun to fight.

To get citizen opinion on the placement of the new pool, the Park Board held a public hearing on June 28. The Superintendent presented six options for consideration. He was greeted by approximately thirty residents, most of whom were from the Riverside area. (The Riverside area had been organized into a Riverside Neighborhood Association prior to this and this organization was to play a major role in mobilizing the area residents.) The citizens nixed the idea of a wave pool and demanded that the Riverside Pool be renovated. The Park Board responded that a decision would be made at its July or August meeting.[3]

By the time of the July meeting, the Riverside area had mustered more forces to lobby for the pool. The Superintendent moved that funds should be made available to enlarge the other public pool, which was in a new and growing section of town. But the Commissioners voted to table his motion in the face of opposition expressed by the large numbers of Riverside residents who attended the meeting.[4]

When the August meeting took place, the politicking was in full swing. On the day of the meeting, the *Grand Forks Herald* ran a picture of Riverside children picketing the Park Board office carrying placards demanding that the Riverside Pool be repaired. Meanwhile, the Riverside residents had been going door-to-door to drum up community support.[5]

The August meeting, which was held in a senior citizens' home in the Riverside area, was attended by approximately 150 residents, mostly from Riverside. Not only did the Riverside residents have power in numbers, they also came armed with expertise. They were accompanied by a pool design consultant who contradicted the conclusion of the Park Board engineers that the Riverside Pool "was not worth repairing." He estimated that repairs could be made for $250,000. In the face of this, the Park Board Commissioners decided that the safest route was to order a full-scale study and agreed to hire a local engineering firm.[6] As the study was progressing, the Park Board also set up a ten-person City-Wide Swimming Pool Study Committee, composed of representatives from neighborhood associations, including Riverside, and of such groups as the Chamber of Commerce.[7]

In November, the engineers presented the Park Board with four options, ranging from $136,254 for renovating the Riverside Pool to building a new pool at an alternative site for $363,000. The Board waited for the Study Committee's report before deciding,[8] and at the January Park Board meeting, the report was made public. On a four to one vote (half the group's total membership), the Study Committee recommended that Riverside should be abandoned and the other city pool should be expanded—the same recommendation made by the Superintendent of the Park Board.

But the Riverside residents were not defeated. Approximately 75 Riverside residents attended the hearing despite the fact that the temperature was nudging -20°. In the face of this, the Commissioners voted not to accept the recommendation, and on a three to two vote agreed to restore the Riverside Pool to a usable condition.[9]

The decision on the Riverside Pool was quite clearly a product of citizen participation. Despite the recommendation of the Park Board Superintendent, the organization of the Riverside residents forced the Park Board to agree to rebuild the Riverside Pool. But the efforts of the Riverside residents were aided in no small measure by the city's willingness to provide access to the citizens' demands through the public hearing, the city-wide study committee, and the open Park Board meetings.

The Riverside Pool decision is by no means unique. In virtually all journals designed to be read by government officials, articles abound in which experiments with citizen participation are described and the successes and failures are analyzed. For example, in a June, 1978 issue of *Public Management*, officials from areas as diverse as Guilford County, North Carolina, Janesville, Wisconsin and Dayton, Ohio discussed their experiences.[10] In Guilford County, fifteen local community councils were included on a county "umbrella" council. In Janesville, the city manager described a process of deciding where to locate a city pool that included public hearings and citizen petitions. In Dayton, neighborhood councils were formed into a system of six priority boards with representatives elected from each neighborhood.

Obviously the Riverside pool decision is typical of the degree to which citizens are now participating in decision making at all levels of government. In some cases, the participation results from demands by citizens for access. The Riverside Neighborhood Association would no doubt have become involved in the pool decision even if the city had not facilitated their access. But in many cases, the governments themselves have stimulated participation by mandating it and requiring that participation structures be established.

The structures of participation have assumed a bewildering variety of forms. The city-wide advisory committee and public hearing used in Grand Forks are two of the most common structures. But other techniques used include neighborhood or county councils, citizen surveys, public information programs, neighborhood city halls, hotlines, and ombudsmen,[11] and the list could be extended. Citizen participation has even entered the electronic age through the use of interactive cable television to provide instantaneous citizen referenda.[12]

What has happened in the past two decades has been an explosion in both the amount of citizen participation and in the types of structures and procedures used by citizens to participate. The Riverside Pool decision illustrates some of the best and the worst aspects of this explosion in participation. The effect of the participation was to prolong the process of decision making. The plans for rebuilding the pool were not approved until May, 1980—a full year after the issue arose. In fact, the pool was not reopened until June, 1981. In addition, the decision may not have been the best in terms of rational allocation of funds. That, at least, was the conclusion of the Superintendent of the Park Department, as well as the City-Wide Study Committee. The decision may not have reflected rationality as much as the intensity of the concern of the Riverside residents, yet the Riverside residents, of course, were very pleased. And the city may well have benefited from the citizen satisfaction the decision produced. A Riverside resident quoted after the January Park Board meeting said that, "It is a thrill to us to see that the city government is so responsive to the people." Of course those citizens on the Study Committee might have been dissatisfied that their work and recommendations went for nought. "Successful" citizen participation may be in the eye of the beholder.

The focus of this book is to examine some of the problems of citizen participation as well as to consider the prospects of what citizen participation can produce.

PERIODS OF CITIZEN PARTICIPATION

The explosion in participation that has occurred in the last two decades in the United States is not unique in U.S. history. Lucian Pye has argued that when ". . . there is uncertainty over the appropriate rate of expansion and when the influx of new participants creates serious strains on the existing institutions," a participation crisis exists.[13] Twice before in our history such participation crises have occurred. The role of citizens in government, as initially defined by the Constitution, was to be solely indirect. Citizens were to participate by electing representatives who would then filter and refine public opinion in making the final decisions of government. Not all officials were to be elected, and state laws determined that only a small proportion of the citizens were to have the right to participate in choosing them.

This limited access, while liberal for its time, contradicted basic experiences and beliefs of Americans. As occupants of a new land, Americans had had nearly 200 years of experience in forming governments by a social contract of the whole community. The Mayflower Compact is a prototype of that democratic process.[14] This contradiction between a history of self government and constitutional and legal limitations has created the tension that has given rise to periodic participation crises. Although the Constitution may have seemed to close the door on anything but minimal citizen participation, throughout U.S. history the citizens have periodically pushed the door open. In essence, U.S. political history can be seen as a process of democratizing a republican governmental structure.

The settlers moving westward beyond the close confines and norms of the eastern establishment provided the impetus for the first participation crisis. The atmosphere of the Age of Jackson resulted in an assault on the legal restrictions on who could vote and hold office. Jackson, via the spoils system, even opened the bureaucracy to citizens in the process of democratizing the national government. The second crisis occurred at the end of the nineteenth century as part of the reformist Progressive Era. The party structures, which had initially acted to broaden participation, were a major target of Progressive reformers because many local party structures had become dominated by machines. The resulting corruption provided the impetus for reforms that simultaneously broadened participation in some areas and narrowed it in others. The parties' control over staffing the bureaucracy was eliminated on the national level by the civil service system, thus limiting popular access to public jobs. Nevertheless, attempts were made to increase the role of elections by instituting initiative and referendum in many states.

The third, and current, participation crisis was initiated by a complex set of social changes. The movement by blacks to achieve political and social equality, the decline of the traditional family structure, the increase in the role of government in our lives, and the growing sense of distance from government, all contributed to demands to alter the structure of citizen participation. The party structure, weakened by the reforms of the Progressive Era, grew even weaker. In addition, participation in elections decreased. As party and electoral activity declined, interest group activity increased. And as government increasingly was personified by the bureaucrats who administer policies, the bureaucracy became the focus of citizen participation. All of these changes in participation signaled that traditional electoral forms of participation were no longer perceived as adequate. People wanted more direct forms of access that were not mediated by such intermediaries as parties or representatives chosen in elections.

DEVELOPMENT OF MANDATED PARTICIPATION

The government has traditionally responded to participation crises by attempting to grant access to those demanding it. In the current crisis, the government has gone beyond granting access to mandating that citizen participation be part of government decision making. There was some historical precedent for this. As early as 1912, Congress chartered chambers of commerce to provide them with information on the views of the business community.[15] Two years later Congress provided funds for county agricultural agents and in many states the locally chosen farm bureau was recognized as the county operating organization. In the Agricultural Adjustment Act of 1938, this practice of using locally chosen farm groups to implement the program was continued.[16] The Tennessee Valley Authority encouraged the participation of the people in the target area. Those who became active were the farmers, the businessmen, and the agricultural extension officers. Finally, the early urban renewal legislation required that citizen participation be part of the planning process. The first Housing Act required only public hearings, but the second act specified that citizen participation be part of a "workable program." This was usually implemented by establishing a citizens' advisory board, staffed most often by representatives of the business community.[17]

Although mandated citizen participation had existed previously, what distinguishes the third participation crisis is the sheer number of federal programs that now demand that citizen participation be part of the process of implementation on the local level. The first, and unquestionably the most controversial, federal program in this era was the Economic Opportunity Act of 1964 which created the Office of Economic Opportunity (OEO). The goal of this program was to eliminate poverty. But an important assumption of the act was that the most effective way to end poverty was to mobilize the poor and involve them in making policy decisions in areas relevant to them. This was the famous "maximum feasible participation" requirement.[18]

The attempt to implement this program on the local level resulted in a significant amount of conflict and unrest, unlike the prior mandated participation. The reasons for the difference are clear. The prior participation had basically done little more than provide access to those groups who were already organized and active: the chambers of commerce, the local farm bureaus, the businessmen, and others. The War on Poverty aimed at mobilizing those who had not previously been active, but local officials were often unwilling to face the mobilization of another group that would have to be considered. At the same time, other active citizens' groups could be expected to be concerned about the increased competition for the community pie.

Despite the fact that OEO did result in improved service delivery in some areas, the acrimony surrounding the program led Congress to pass the Demonstration Cities and Metropolitan Development Act of 1966 (Model Cities). This program essentially combined the goals of renewing the decaying sections of U.S. cities with the social welfare goals of the War on Povery. To avoid the conflict engendered by the initial poverty program, the Model Cities legislation gave local governments control over the program to tailor it to their own needs. Although the act provided for "widespread" citizen participation, it was made clear from the outset the final authority rested with local governments. Model Cities citizens' boards representing target areas were required to work through City Hall. This contrasted with OEO in which the community action agencies were often encouraged to become alternative, conflicting power bases.[19]

These two programs were the apex of citizen participation mandates in the sense that the government was assuming the role of political mobilizer. The requirements for participation that followed these programs were, in most cases, significantly less ambitious than the "maximum feasible participation" of OEO or the "widespread participation" of Model Cities. A few examples should illustrate the difference. The Housing and Community Development Act of 1974 requires only "adequate opportunity for citizen participation."[20] Coastal Zone Management Act of 1972 "includes encouragement of the participation of the public."[21]

Although many of the mandates may be less demanding, there are significantly more of them now than at any other time in our history. The Advisory Commission on Intergovernmental Relations surveyed federal agencies which administer grants-in-aid programs on the state and local level. From the 95 percent of the agencies on which the ACIR managed to gather data in 1978, they found that 155 federal grant programs have citizen participation requirements that are mandated either by legislation or regulation. Perhaps more significant than the number is the fact that these 155 programs accounted for more than 80 percent of the grant expenditures in the previous year. It is also important to point out that the ACIR also discovered that 124 of the total, or approximately 81 percent, were enacted after 1970.[22] It is perhaps equally significant that these federal mandates have often altered the structure of state and local decision making even in those programs not controlled by federal grants. As Robert Wood wrote, the genie of citizen participation has been let out of the bottle. Citizens now expect to be provided access to decision processes.[23]

These figures indicate the extent to which citizen participation requirements in federal grant programs have mushroomed in the past decade. This participation is different from past participation in three fundamental ways. In the first place, more is mandated. Secondly, it is a mandate from one level of government to another. The federal government is essentially dictating that state and local officials provide access to citizens. This represents an increase in the impact of federal policy, and on policy directives on the state and local level. Thirdly, since the mandates require involvement of citizens in the implementation of policy, this participation brings the citizens directly into the policy process, rather than providing them indirect access through the electoral arena. This in turn inevitably brings the citizens into direct contact with local bureaucracies.

PROBLEMS OF CITIZEN PARTICIPATION

This new participation creates a major and fundamental anomaly. The idea of citizen participation arises from the classical theory of democracy, yet the structure of our government is not that of a pure democracy but that of a republic. Citizen interests are to be realized indirectly by actions of elected representatives, and the policies they determine are then to be implemented by bureaucrats acting in organizational structures that are the very antithesis of democracy. Bureaucracies are designed to maximize such values as expertise, efficiency, hierarchical authority, routine, and impersonality, which are in direct contradiction to the democratic values of equality, freedom, and individual human dignity.

In essence, the anomaly of citizen participation is that democratic expectations have been imposed on governmental structures that were never designed to function democratically. If citizens are to make policy directly, what is the role of the elected representative? Perhaps even more problematic is the relationship between citizens and bureaucrats. If bureaucrats are to carry out policy designed by elected officials, they should be shielded from other pressures; that is, decisions should be made apolitically. In fact, that is one purpose of the merit system of appointment and promotion. If bureaucrats are to implement policy in ways that their expertise would determine to be best, then citizen demands would seem to be irrelevant.

This conflict between the structure of government and citizen participation is one fundamental problem in implementing citizen participation. A second problem arises from the expectations that accompany citizen participation, which is often seen as a panacea for the ills of society. The expectations that accompany it are often too high to be realized; for example, citizens expect to increase their control over the government. This greater influence is desired for reasons that vary from the search for greater self-fulfillment to the desire for better garbage collection. Government officials expect that citizens who participate will become more understanding of the officials' plight and therefore will become more trusting—out of this process both expect society to be transformed. Not only are the expectations that accompany participation often too high to be realized, they are also often implicit. The participation mandates do not always specify what goal participation is to achieve. When citizens and officials are left on their own to devise what each expects from the process, there is fertile ground for conflicting expectations to arise, which a single participation experience may not be capable of fulfilling (none of these expectations may be explicit, but all of them must be considered as a basis for evaluating individual participation).

In sum, there are two major sets of problems in implementing citizen participation: first, there are the problems of imposing democratic expectations on government structures that were never intended to function democratically, and second, there are the unrealistic and conflicting expectations. This book investigates the dimensions of both of these problems and attempts to determine what goals can realistically be expected from citizen participation and under what circumstances these goals can be maximized.

A major argument made here is that the goals of participation differ to such an extent that a different set of factors affects the attainment of each. It will be argued that there are three goals that citizen participation is expected to produce: redistribution of power, improvements in citizen attitudes, and improvements in service delivery. It is, therefore, believed that there are three models of participation impacts, one for each of the three expected goals. The categories of variables that are believed to affect the outcome of participation include characteristics of the environment in which the participation occurs, characteristics of the organizations toward which the participation is targeted, and characteristics of the participation structures established.

OUTLINE OF THE BOOK

The next chapter examines the history of citizen participation in the United States and sketches the dimensions of the current participation crisis. The following three chapters examine the problems of implementing citizen participation: Chapter 3 identifies the three goals posited for citizen participation and investigates the conflict among the goals; Chapter 4 examines the dilemmas of structuring citizen participation in a republican form of government, and Chapter 5 focuses on the special need for and problems of citizen participation in bureaucracies.

The sixth and seventh chapters review the current literature on citizen participation: Chapter 6 examines the evidence concerning what impacts citizen participation has been found to produce, and Chapter 7 focuses on the factors that affect what impacts participation will have. Based on this review of the literature, Chapter 8 will develop three models of participation. The following chapters will use two sets of data to test the accuracy of these models. One set of data was a survey of budget officers in cities over 10,000 and counties over 50,000 conducted by the Advisory Commission on Intergovernmental Relations and the International City Managers Association. The second set of data consists of surveys conducted in four cities by the authors. The final chapter summarizes the findings and evaluates their implications for the future of citizen participation.

Citizen participation is an essential component of any system that considers itself a democracy. For the past decade the opportunities for citizen participation have expanded greatly, yet citizen participation that is considered successful by participants and observers does not happen automatically, even when opportunities are provided. This book is an examination of the problems of implementing citizen participation and of the factors that affect what impacts citizen participation will produce. Its goal is to provide a basis for a realistic understanding of what can and cannot be accomplished by participation in U.S. government in the eighties. It is hoped that this realistic appraisal will be of benefit both to the citizens who will participate and to those officials who are both the implementers and the targets of the participation policy.

NOTES

[1] Ryan Bakken, "Riverside Pool in Bad Shape, May Not Open," *Grand Forks Herald*, May 9, 1979, B-1.

[2] Ryan Bakken, "Choppy Pool May Be Wave of the Future," *Grand Forks Herald*, June 26, 1979, D-1.

[3] Ryan Bakken, "Riverside Residents Ask for a New Pool," *Grand Forks Herald*, June 29, 1979, A-2.

[4] Ryan Bakken, "Decision on Pool Delayed," *Grand Forks Herald*, July 11, 1979, D-1.

[5] "Riverside Kids on the March," *Grand Forks Herald*, August 7, 1979, B-1.

[6] Ryan Bakken, "Riverside Pool Wins Reprieve," *Grand Forks Herald*, August 8, 1979, D-1.

[7] Sue Ellyn Scaletta, "Study Shows Riverside Pool Plan Costly," *Grand Forks Herald*, January 6, 1980, B-1.

[8] Jim Durkin, "Board Hears Pool Options," *Grand Forks Herald*, November 4, 1979, C-1.

[9] Sue Ellyn Scaletta, "Board Votes to Save Riverside Pool," *Grand Forks Herald*, January 9, 1980, B-1.

[10] "Commentary-Public Appetite." *Public Management* 60 (June 1978):8–10.

[11] For an overview of techniques, see Judy B. Rosener, "Matching Method to Purpose: The Challenges of Planning Citizen-Participation Activities," in *Citizen Participation in America*, ed. Stuart Langton (Lexington, Mass.: Lexington Books, 1978), pp. 109–122.

[12] Ibid.

[13] Lucian W. Pye, *Aspects of Political Development* (Boston: Little, Brown, 1966), p. 65.

[14] Daniel J. Boorstin, *The Americans: The Colonial Experience* (New York: Vintage Books, 1958), pp. 66–67.

[15] Advisory Commission on Intergovernmental Relations, *Citizen Participation in the American Federal System* (Washington, D.C.: ACIR, 1979), p. 109.

[16] Ibid.

[17] James Q. Wilson, "Planning and Politics: Citizen Participation in Urban Renewal," in *Urban Renewal: The Record and the Controversy*, ed. James Q. Wilson (Cambridge, Mass.: The M.I.T. Press, 1967), pp. 407–421.

[18] Peter Marris and Martin Rein, *Dilemmas of Social Reform: Poverty and Community in the United States,* 2nd. ed. (Chicago: Aldine, 1973); Bernard J. Friedan and Marshall Kaplan, *The Politics of Neglect: Urban Aid From Model Cities to Revenue Sharing* (Cambridge, Mass.: The M.I.T. Press, 1975).

[19] Ibid.

[20] *Housing and Community Development Act of 1974* (P.L. 93–383), Title I, Section 104.

[21] *Coastal Zone Management Act of 1972* (P.L. 92–583).

[22] ACIR, *Citizen Participation in the American Federal System*, pp. 112–127.

[23] Robert Wood, quoted in Friedan and Kaplan, *The Politics of Neglect*, p. 74.

2

THE PARTICIPATION CRISIS IN THE UNITED STATES

In 1966 Lucian Pye warned that one of the major challenges that developing nations would face in the decades ahead would be a participation crisis caused by their need to determine how citizen participation could be structured in a way that would not threaten the stability or the effectiveness of the government. As Pye warned:

> The participation crisis occurs when there is uncertainty over the appropriate rate of expansion of political participation and when the influx of new participants creates serious strains on existing institutions. As new segments of the population are brought into the political process, new interests and new issues begin to arise so that the continuity of the old polity is broken and there is the need to reestablish the entire structure of political relations.[1]

It is ironic that one of the major participation crises to occur after Pye's warning was in the United States. This irony is partially due to the obvious fact that the United States is not a new or underdeveloped country faced, for the first time, with defining and structuring relations with its citizens. At the time of Pye's warning, it appeared that the United States had long ago survived its participation crisis. Despite its high levels of citizen participation, the United States had managed to maintain stability. Political scientists believed the successful melding of participation and stability was due to the development of mediating structures such as parties and groups that aggregate demands and channel them to the political system. Pye argues that "The question in many new states is whether the expansion in participation is likely to be effectively organized into specific interest groups or whether the pressures will lead only to mass demands and widespread feelings of anomie."[2] What Pye is implicitly arguing is that developing countries could successfully weather their participation crises by following the U.S. model and developing such buffering institutions.

What then constitutes the participation crisis in the United States and what are its origins? On the surface, the current participation crisis revolves around attempts to resolve three basic dilemmas concerning the structure of citizen participation. The first considers the question of who will be given access to participate in politics. This refers primarily to the issue of restrictions (both legal and extra-legal) on the participation of certain individuals or groups. The second dilemma concerns direct citizen participation in the government: should it be permitted in addition to indirect participation through representatives. The third dilemma concerns at what stage of the government's decision making process citizens should be permitted to participate. For simplicity, the decision making process can be conceptualized as having three stages. In the first, which may be called the stage of pre-decision, issues are raised and various positions are articulated. (It is at this stage that the agenda is set.) In the second, the stage of decision, choices are made between alternative resolutions to the issues on the agenda. The implementation stage is last, where the decisions are carried out, usually by the bureaucracy.

The dilemmas concerning how citizen participation should be structured are by no means new in the United States. As this chapter will demonstrate, there have been other participation crises in U.S. history during which one or more of these dilemmas have forced new national contemplation of how citizen participation should be structured and that have resulted in major changes in the structure of citizen participation. Each of these participation crises has resulted in an expansion of participation. Legal barriers were removed, more direct access to government was provided, or access to more stages of the decision process was ensured; however, these changes ended the crisis only for the moment. The battle had been won, and yet the war was temporarily suspended, only to be resumed in the future. Thus the current participation crisis can be seen as only the latest in a series of crises which, in all probability, will recur.

The reason for the continuing debate on participation is not solely due to the lack of consensus on how participation should be structured. An additional reason, one that is more fundamental, is the lack of consensus on what impact citizen participation should have and on how much impact participation should have. This is not to say that the structural dilemmas are unimportant. In fact, the structural questions of who should participate, how, and when are intimately related to the question of impact of participation. It is precisely from this relation that the structural dilemmas derive their importance; yet, it is the expectations concerning impact that are the major source of problems in implementing citizen participation.

As will be discussed more fully later, the expectations that surround citizen participation often include such basic and contentious political issues as the distribution of power in society and the allocations of government benefits. Such fundamental issues should be expected to generate conflict that is not easily resolved in any absolute or final way. It is for this reason that creating structural changes in citizen participation has, throughout U.S. history, provided only temporary resolutions to the participation crises that faced this country. When the structural changes did not produce the impacts desired, or produced those impacts for only certain segments of the society, a new crisis arose.

Thus, the debate over structure masks more fundamental debates concerning who will be winners and who will be losers in political battles. It is for this reason that despite the rhetoric that eulogizes citizen participation, there remains significant ambivalence concerning the role of citizen participation in the United States.

This ambivalence has roots deep in U.S. history. The immigrants who were the founders of the modern United States had their origins in countries that lacked any tradition of citizen participation as it is perceived today. Although England had developed a recognition of the "rights of Englishmen" since 1215, these rights seem minimal when viewed from the perspective of the twentieth century. The major thrust of the English Bill of Rights, like the U.S. version that followed it by almost 100 years, was the protection of citizens from capricious and arbitrary governmental action rather than the provision for active participation by citizens in their government. The right to such active participation was limited to a small segment of British society while the common man was granted the right only to petition his government.

Nevertheless, as Daniel Boorstin has argued, foreign institutions were subject to major transformations when attempts were made to transplant them to American soil.[3] As the migration to the United States transformed the vocations of law and medicine, so did it transform the avocation of citizen. In Europe the governments existed and citizens were born into an established political order. In the United States, however, with few exceptions, communities existed before their governments and the people were required of necessity to participate in constructing their own government structures and the laws that would be enforced. The prototype for this is the Mayflower Compact, but Boorstin argues that this creation of government would be repeated constantly as the highly mobile U.S. residents continued to move beyond the jurisdictions of existing political authorities. "A kind of Mayflower Compact, then, was made by each group as it formed for its westward trek."[4]

In such a construction, of government by the community, there was the genesis of the Lincolnian ideal of "government of, by, and for the people." As Boorstin writes:

> There was seldom any hint of a doubt that final control on all matters rested with the majority, who had so recently made the constitution and laws, and could alter or abolish them. The majority

> chose all the officers and decided in each case whether an alleged crime deserved punishment.[5]

Citizens not only participated in government, they *were* the government.

Here then were two conceptions of the role of the citizen, each of which is part of U.S. political history. The traditional image (portayed in the British Bill of Rights) was that of a passive citizenry, permitted only to petition an existing and sovereign government with the hope of redressing grievances. The new image was that of an active citizenry that itself is the sovereign.

Although there is an obvious conflict between these two images, both have existed simultaneously in American thought. In the early days of the new republic, it was Jefferson who trumpeted the call for the people as sovereign. What had been the practice in the New World since the Mayflower Compact was given legitimacy, if not legality, by the Declaration of Independence, which recognized the right of people to alter or abolish governments with which they were dissatisfied.

A decade later, however, the men who gathered in Philadelphia to construct the structure of the new U.S. government were in no mood to give legal status to Jefferson's ideals. The chaos that had characterized the country under the weak Articles of Confederation had convinced most of the representatives to the Philadelphia convention that stronger centralized governmental control was necessary—and such control was to come at the expense of direct citizen involvement in government.

The predominant mood of the convention was illustrated by the apprehensive way in which James Wilson suggested the possibility of election of the chief executive directly by the people rather than reliance upon some indirect means of selection. James Madison's *Journal* records that "Mr. Wilson said he was almost unwilling to declare the mode which he wished to take place, being apprehensive that it might appear chimerical. He would say, however, at least that in theory he was for an election by the people."[6] Wilson, of course, did not get his way.

For the most part, the constitution waffled on the role of citizens, leaving most of the decisions to the states; but, where a stand was taken, it downplayed the direct role of citizens in government. Citizens were only to elect the House of Representatives directly and were to have no other direct input to government. If there were any doubt about the goals of the Constitution, Madison put them to rest, at least for the moment, in *Federalist #10*. In unequivocal terms, he wrote:

> . . . it may be concluded that a pure democracy, by which I mean a society consisting of a small number of citizens, who assemble and administer the government in person, can admit of no cure for the

> mischiefs of faction. A common passion or interest will, in almost every case, be felt by a majority of the whole; a communication and concert result from the form of government itself; and there is nothing to check the inducements to sacrifice the weaker party or an obnoxious individual. Hence it is that such democracies have ever been spectacles of turbulence and contention; have ever been found incompatible with personal security or the rights of property.[7]

Direct participation in this government would certainly be quite limited:

Madison continues, in *Federalist #10*, to illustrate how the multiple structures and overlapping authorities of the new government would protect it from the vagaries of the people. The Electoral College and the indirect election of Senators were provisions specifically intended to blunt the impact of citizen participation. Yet the question of citizen participation was by no means laid to rest permanently. What resulted from this new government structure was the creation of a gap between the rhetoric and the reality of citizen participation. The ideals of the Declaration were invoked in the initial words of the Preamble: "We the people . . . do ordain and establish this Constitution." Yet the reality of the structure created therein provided little role for "the people," and what little access was provided was extended to only a small segment of the population.

The gap between the rhetoric of "the people" and the reality of limits on citizen involvement remains. This gap has resulted in a constant tension that, in turn, has led periodically to eras of reconsideration and reconstruction of citizen participation in the United States. It is argued here that there have been three such periods in U.S. history: the first was precipitated by the demands by western settlers for greater access to government and coincided roughly with the Jacksonian era; the second was the result of reformist attacks on the control of politics by party machines and coincided with the Progressive Era; and the latest, and current, participation crisis was precipitated by significant changes in the social structure that have weakened mediating institutions such as the family and therefore focused new demands for service and access on the government. This crisis began in the sixties, and spurred by government mandates, has extended to the current decade.

FIRST PARTICIPATION CRISIS: PRESSURE FROM THE WEST

The first participation crisis occurred when demands arose to increase the numbers of citizens who could participate in government. The demands came from settlers who had moved westward beyond the Appalachians. Forced, as Boorstin points out, to form their own governments as they went, these new migrants still were controlled by a small group of political leaders in the established centers of power on the east coast. These new settlers demanded the right of political access despite the fact they were neither rich nor well-born. The changes that they demanded were the reduction of the legal barriers to voting and holding office. A major part of this participation crisis, then, concerned the first structural dilemma discussed above: Who will be given access to participate in politics?

The demands by the western settlers for political access were echoed by their less mobile eastern neighbors who were also disenfranchsed by the laws of the thirteen original states. In general, the initial change that occurred during this first participation crisis was a substitution of tax paying as opposed to property owning as a criterion for voting in the original states to bring them into conformity with the practice in the new western states. Although this change expanded the electorate, restrictions remained. (Perhaps the most notable one was the law that made voting strictly a male province.)

There were also changes in all stages of decision making that enabled more citizens to participate directly. At the predecision stage, citizens received greater control over the electoral agenda due to the creation of political parties. As participation in political parties increased, party members managed to broaden their control over selection of presidential and vice presidential candidates. The traditional method of selection was by caucus of only the party members in Congress. Eventually, however, the general party membership succeeded in substituting a national convention of party delegates for the more closed congressional caucus.

In addition, the public was given a greater role in choosing state and local officials. In 1822, both Boston and St. Louis specified that their mayors would henceforth be elected. This move toward choosing a local chief executive was part of a general trend in giving the public the opportunity to select an increasing number of public officials who previously had been chosen by appointment. This change was often referred to as the long ballot movement because of its obvious effect on the ballot with which voters were confronted.

In addition, some change was made in increasing the access of citizens to the decision stage of government. The eastern states for the most part required property ownership as a criterion for being elected to office in the government, a requirement slow to change. But the new western states had more liberal qualifications for office holding. Between 1816 and 1825, five states were admitted to the Union, which allowed all eligible voters to hold elective office.

Finally, there were also changes in the ability of citizens to participate in the implementation stage of decision. With the election of Jackson, the first westerner to become President, the practice of staffing government bureaucracy by appointment of the rich and well-born was eliminated. Jackson believed the government's business was simple enough that no special training was necessary.

The only qualification the spoils system demanded was loyalty to the party in office. While soundly denounced by reformers at the end of the century, at the time the Jacksonian period represented a significant democratization of a part of the government where participation had been previously restricted to an elite.

The result of the first participation crisis was a significant expansion in the number of citizens permitted to participate in politics and the ways in which they could participate. By the middle of the nineteenth century the first crisis was complete, its end no doubt hastened by the cataclysm of the Civil War. But the issue of participation was by no means resolved permanently. By the end of the nineteenth century, demands again began to arise that altered the structure of citizen participation. Ironically, many of the reforms of the first participation crisis became the focus of the reformers of the late nineteenth century. There was general dissatisfaction with the electoral system owing to the belief that it was not sufficient to keep elected officials responsible. Because of the large number of state and local officials who, as a result of the long ballot movement, were now elected, the ballot had grown to such proportions that it was impossible for the average citizen to vote intelligently or to keep straight, after the election, who as responsible for what.

Another source of dissatisfaction with electoral politics was the party system. Although parties were seen in the early nineteenth century as a way of broadening citizen participation, by the end of the century they actually had the effect of limiting popular control because they were dominated by local machines that grew in the vacuum of power created by fragmented city governments. These machines not only precluded control by the general party membership but also, in many instances, resulted in widespread corruption that was facilitated by the control that party machines had over appointments to the bureaucracy. The patronage appointment system was serving not to democratize the bureaucracy but to bring it more tightly under the domination of local cadres.

A number of precipitating events gave rise to the demands that lay at the base of the second participation crisis: First, the muckraking journalism of the period publicized to a mass audience the scandals that existed at all levels of government. Secondly, the assassination of President Garfield by a disappointed office seeker culminated the nation's disgust with the spoils system. Thirdly, and perhaps most importantly, the country suffered a series of economic declines at the end of the nineteenth century. Pain in the pocketbook is always an important precipitator of reform. Therefore, the stage was set for the second participation crisis.

SECOND PARTICIPATION CRISIS: THE ATTACK ON THE PARTY MACHINES

During the end of the nineteenth century and the beginning of the twentieth century, which is referred to as the Progressive era, demands escalated to eliminate the last significant barrier to voting participation. The end of this period was marked finally by the 19th Amendment, which extended suffrage to women. When considered with the Civil War amendments that extended suffrage to blacks, the effect was ostensibly to end the dilemma of who should participate. Legally, all adult citizens had been given access to vote and to hold office. In actuality, of course, this was not the case. During this period the Southern states were developing legal structures to eliminate participation by blacks. By the end of this period, blacks had been effectively disenfranchised in all Southern states by such techniques as the poll tax, literacy tests, and the white primary. The effect of the disenfranchisement was, of course, to sow the seeds that led, later in the twentieth century, to the emergence of demands by blacks for the right to participate. Despite the legal advances, this meant that the dilemma of who should be given access to participate remained.

With the exception of the demands for female suffrage, the major thrust of the second participation crisis was the demand for a more direct decision-making role for the general citizenry. The reformers believed that by giving the citizens more direct control over decision making the control of the party machines would be broken; thus, two major reforms were instituted.

First, to increase the control of citizens at the predecision stage, direct primaries were instituted at the state and local levels to replace caucuses or conventions as a means of selecting a party's nominees for office. By broadening control over candidate selection, reformers hoped machines would no longer be able to dominate the candidates once they were elected. Second, to increase the direct control of citizens at the decision state, many states delegated the legislative function of the state to the citizens. When the legislature failed to act, or acted contrary to the desires of citizens, the electorate could take matters into their own hands by initiative and referendum.

At the same time that moves were made to increase direct control by citizens through these methods, other reforms were instituted that actually had the effect of limiting the direct involvement of citizens both in elections and at the implementation stage of decision making. The short ballot movement resulted in reducing the number of city offices that would be contested in elections. The Pendleton Civil Service Act of 1883 represented the first step in replacing the patronage system of staffing the federal bureaucracy with a merit system. In many ways, of course, these two reforms appear not only contrary to the goal of increasing citizen control, but they also seem to contradict each other. The short ballot movement increased the use of appointment at the local level and the Pendleton Act decreased appointment at the federal level. Both, however, were aimed at the same two goals: to decrease the power of parties and to increase professionalism in government. At the local level, the idea was to remove offices from "politics" by staffing them by appointment rather than by election. Reformers believed that this would decrease the control of parties over office holders and permit a few top executives to appoint professionals to the bulk of city jobs. Responsibility for the city would then be centralized, making it easier for electors to reward and punish authorities. At the federal level, the goal was to choose federal bureaucrats on the basis of merit rather than party loyalty. Although in some ways these reforms limited citizen participation, it was believed that by weakening the machines, the reforms would give citizens both more control and good government at the same time.

In both instances, the reforms were a recognition of the nascent power that bureaucrats were developing in the U.S. system. The goal was to assure that the power would be used wisely by staffing the bureaucracy with professionals who could be insulated from political pressures. The corruption associated with the party machines had made "politics" an obscenity, and in the era of scientific management, the belief in professionalism was high. The effect of course was to insulate the bureaucracy and to decrease the impact of citizens on the implementation stage of decision making. This was one other seed that would bear fruit later in the twentieth century and, along with the blacks' struggle for political access, would be another major precipitator of the third participation crisis.

THIRD PARTICIPATION CRISIS: BREAKDOWN OF MEDIATING STRUCTURES

The world wars and the depression forestalled concern about participation in the first half of the twentieth century but, beginning in the forties and fifties, there were developments that would help touch off the third participation crisis. The first development that would help to bring about a new era of reconsideration of citizen participation in the United States was the perfecting of techniques of survey research. Equipped with these new techniques, political scientists, sociologists, and other pollsters set out to uncover what was in the hearts and minds of Americans. The results were unsettling to those who saw the individual rational-activist citizen as the prerequisite for the existence of democracy. What the researchers found was a populace with low levels of political activity, interest, and awareness. We called ourselves a democracy, and yet that which was believed to be the most basic prerequisite of a democracy—an informed and active citizenry—was found lacking.[8] Theory and empirical reality did not mesh.

This discovery set in motion a reanalysis of what role participation plays in a modern country such as the United States, which also happens to call itself a democracy. The result of this reanalysis was a set of beliefs that came to be known as revisionist democratic theory. They were based on the argument that participation was not an essential part of a functioning democracy. This was important in theory, but it also had significant practical implications because it helped to create a backlash in the sixties during which time both academics, and citizens in general, demanded that opportunities to participate be increased. It is therefore important to understand the basic characteristics of revisionist democratic theory.

Revisionist Democratic Theory

At the core of revisionist democratic theory is an attempt to explain the paradox that Bernard Berelson identified in one of the early empirical voting studies. That paradox, he writes, is that "*Individual voters* today seem unable to satisfy the requirements for a democratic system of government outlined by political theorists. But the *system of democracy* does meet certain requirements for a going political organization."[9] Having thus a priori *defined* the United States as a democracy, the problem was reduced to a simple requirement of describing the ongoing system—and that description then became democratic theory.

The description grew from a composite of various research. Voting studies provided information on the basically quiescent citizenry, but they also uncovered the existence of a minority of citizens who did conform to the tenets of the rational-activist citizen model. This attentive public would become part of the elite upon which revisionist theory would rely so heavily. Herbert McCloskey meanwhile was discovering that his elite—party activists and office holders—had a much greater comprehension of traditional democratic values (freedom and equality, for example) than did the common man.[10] As opposed to the common man, the elite was willing to express commitment to those values in the abstract and also able to see their relevance and to support their application in practical situations. In this way, the predominance of the elite was justified because of their greater commitment to the values of democracy.

Some recognition, of course, had to be given to the fact that democracy was, by definition, "rule by the people," but the revisionists narrowed the exercise of that rule to choice of which particular set of elites would actually be making the decisions in government. The focus then of citizen participation is on elections. As Robert Dahl wrote in a classic statement of revisionist theory ". . . the election is the critical technique for insuring that governmental leaders will be relatively responsive to non-leaders."[11] In this, Dahl is echoing Schumpeter's definition of democracy in purely structural terms: "That institutional arrangement for arriving at political decisions in which individuals acquire the power to decide by means of a competitive struggle for people's vote."[12] Thus, democracy entailed enabling the common man to choose which competing political elite would rule him for the next period of history.

And what if the common man did not partake of his opportunity to participate in elections? No matter, for as long as the opportunity existed, the requirements of democracy were met. Since the reforms of the first two participation crises had produced universal adult suffrage, the presumption was that the opportunity for participation was established. As Dahl wrote in obvious pride: "A central guiding thread of American Constitutional development has been the evolution of a political system in which all the active and legitimate groups in the population can make themselves heard at some crucial stage in the process of decision."[13] Of course, he had already established that elections were the most crucial stage of decision—thus democracy was ensured. Nonparticipation was explained by the simple argument that either the common man does not see his interests at stake, and therefore has no motivation to participate, or believes that the elite are doing an adequate job of protecting his interests. In this way, it becomes rational for him to abstain politically since the costs of participation are not outweighed by the perceived benefits.

Nonparticipation is not an indictment of the system but a testimony to its success in satisfying the interests of its polity. And far from being a threat to the system, it is a benefit since the lack of participation shields the political system from unreasonable or overwhelming demands and gives the political elite the necessary maneuvering room to govern effectively.

Like all political theories, this revisionist theory of democracy bears the strong imprint of the society and of the historical period in which it was conceived. The United States, in the late forties and fifties, did in fact have most of the social characteristics that Dahl had posited were essential for the existence of the ideal system he calls "polyarchy." Consensus was the kernel of these social prerequisites, and the United States—with some notable exceptions, of course—was relatively consensual during the mid-twentieth century. There were murmurings of discontent (the blacks in Little Rock, the fear of the communists both in and outside our borders) but for the most part, the United States during this period was involved in self-congratulation for having saved itself from the depression of the thirties and having saved the world from Hitler in the forties. It was primarily interested in getting back to normalcy. The complacency with which the political analysts viewed the functioning of the political system was but a reflection of the complacency with which the country viewed itself in general. The period of complacency was not to last, however, for the fifties gave way to the sixties and suddenly the analysts were confronted with conditions which were inexplicable from the perspective of revisionist theory. No longer was it possible to say that all was right with the world. Unrest and even violence were the order of the day, and political scientists were forced to reexamine the complacent doctrine of revisionist democratic theory.

As Bachrach would later complain, the problem was that revisionists failed to realize that democratic theory was never intended to be solely empirical.[14] Democracy had served for centuries as a normative goal as much as or more than an empirical explanation of reality. As Cobb and Elder argued, a "crisis of relevance" arose because the revisionist theory provided "... no guidelines for social change or direction for political action."[15] By focusing on what was empirical reality in the fifties and establishing stability, the predominant characteristic of that time, as the major goal, the theory "... forces major social conflicts and social movements to be viewed more as aberrations than a normal part of political life ..." and, therefore, "... provides neither the knowledge nor the perspective to implement remedial social action."[16] With stability sanctified as a prime value by academicians, the demands from groups seeking greater access to government then were "aberrations" to be ignored in the hope they would disappear. What happened instead was that the unwillingness of officials to respond only increased the citizens' frustration and thus contributed to the creation of the third participation crisis.

Other Sources of the Crisis

In addition, there were other social changes that contributed to the demand for increased political participation in the sixties. First, there were some significant societal changes occurring. For example, mobility had sliced the traditional ties that had bound Americans to their roots. Mobility, of course, had always been a factor of U.S. life, but with different results. As many historians have argued, mobility has generally meant a restless searching for goals and ideals not realizable in familiar places.[17] But, as those same historians pointed out, the mobility generally carried people into new and unchartered areas where realization of their ideals was at least possible. In the United States of the sixties, the frontier was gone and the mobile groups looking for the 'American dream' only could move from one closed society to the next. So, unlike prior periods of U.S. history, mobility did not serve as the safety valve. Rather, it was a source both of increasing frustration to those restlessly looking for their ideals and as a source for rootlessness for those in transit.[18] This was a classic source for the growth of anomie that could spawn demands for radical change in the system.

The questioning of traditional groups, especially the family, was another major change in this period. This was partially due, no doubt, to the increased mobility, but there were also other social changes, such as the sexual revolution and women's liberation. If the traditional family structure was questioned, it followed that there was reason to question the values that were taught in the family. Although the American family had never devoted much effort to direct political instruction, research on political socialization points to the importance of the indirect political learning that takes place in the family.[19] It was from the family that Americans had learned such values as trust of others and attitudes toward authority—values that have direct political implications. The fact that Americans had traditionally learned to be trusting of others and to have a benevolent view of authority was traced to family socialization and was used to explain the stability of the American political system. It follows, therefore, that merely questioning such basic values could undermine the stability of the system. In fact, the combination of increased mobility of Americans and the weakening of the traditional family structure served to increase the atomization of society—traditional sources of support and assistance were gone.[20] Perhaps the atomization was the source of another change in the sixties: the increased political awareness of Americans. Government was increasingly seen as the source for solving the problems of society as a whole, as well as those of the individuals in that society. Of course, the government itself encouraged the perception of itself as problem solver by creating the package of social welfare programs that comprised Johnson's Great Society.

The increased importance of government in our lives was accompanied by a new set of political issues: crime, drugs, poverty, and others. Presumably, it only seemed logical that if government were to assume greater responsibility for solving our problems, then we should carry increasing numbers of our problems to the government's doorstep. These new issues had some important characteristics in common. Although people were united in their opposition to such problems as crime, drugs, and poverty, there was no consensus on how to resolve these problems.[21] Since they touched people's lives in intimate ways, however, the issues were highly salient. The combination of potentially explosive issues and a lack of consensus on how to resolve them provided fertile ground for significant political conflict. By the end of the sixties, another issue arose that would produce even more political conflict—Vietnam.

Since government was seen as more crucial to people's lives, it should follow that people would have become more aware of it and of political issues. In the sixties and early seventies it seemed that that was exactly what was happening. The traditional voting studies had documented that Americans appeared to be abysmally unaware of issues or of party stands on those issues. Yet writing in 1976, Nie, Verba, and Petrocik argued that the importance of issues had increased. They conclude that ". . . the public has come to focus on a new set of issues; the new set covers a wider range and those that drew most attention are ones of particular intensity and divisiveness. More important, perhaps, is the fact that political issues have come to 'intrude' into the personal lives of citizens."[22]

In addition to these societal intrusions, changes in government were being recognized, most of which had been developing for years, but had only become dominant political concerns in the sixties. In the first place, there was a recognition of the extent to which governmental decision making was being centralized. Increasingly, "government" meant the national government rather than state and local governments. The reason for this centralization can be easily found. The mobility of Americans not only reduced their ties with family, but also reduced the importance of local politics. Mobility and a national mass media made the concerns national ones and they, therefore, looked to the national government for resolution. Perhaps most importantly, the national government simply had more resources than did state and local governments, and there was a belief that equality could only be achieved by using those national resources to subsidize the activities of the latter. Residing in a poor state, it was argued, should not permanently damn one to a life of inadequate services. Rather, the national government should provide the resources necessary to ensure services equal to those in wealthier states.

A second major change in government was the increased role of the bureaucracy. Again, this change could be easily explained. The bureaucracy, charged with the implementation of governmental policy, of necessity must increase with the increasing role of government in the lives of its citizens. The increase in the role of the bureaucracy had been occurring at least since Roosevelt's New Deal. But the increase of programs in the sixties was of such a degree it could not longer be ignored. As Richard Neustadt has argued, the social legislation of the sixties meant ". . . a quantum jump of Federal oversight and funding for public services that have the most direct effects on private lives."[23]

As Neustadt indicates, the growth in bureaucracy is important to us precisely because it tends to touch our lives in intimate and unavoidable ways. Any government policy, be it tax policy, welfare policy, foreign policy, or whatever, is a dry and uninteresting item until a bureaucrat brings it home to us by auditing our tax returns, refusing us food stamps or drafting us for military service. Because the areas in which the government was becoming involved were so complex and because there was no consensus among its public on how to resolve the problems, Congress facilitated the increased power of the bureaucracy by effectively delegating power to it. Congress did this simply by drafting legislation so broadly that bureaucrats in effect had to write the legislation themselves in the process of implementing it.

This delegation of power is not new, as Lowi would argue.[24] In fact, it is the broad acceptance of bureaucratic discretion that had increased bureaucratic power. The infamous phrase "maximum feasible participation" (included in the legislation creating the war on poverty) is a perfect example of a legislative guideline too vague to provide guidance. Such vague mandates in effect made the bureaucrats the legislators of policy.

Thus, it is the bureaucrat who forces us to see the implications of government policies in our lives. Bureaucrats influence our lives, and yet, as will be documented more fully in Chapter 5, it is not easy to succeed in influencing the bureaucracy in return. In fact, the structure of the bureaucracy is designed to insulate bureaucrats from outside influence. The Civil Service System, designed to lessen the control of "politics," places bureaucrats in office and maintains them there on the basis of merit, rather than on the basis of how well they have pleased the party or the electorate. Although some attempts are being made to change the value premises of bureaucrats, the traditional values include expertise and nonpolitical "administration" of policy.[25] Neither of those values permits much openness to outside control from citizens because they are seen as lacking in expertise—their appeals may be viewed solely as an application of "politics."

In conclusion, then, what are the impacts of the social and governmental changes in the sixties? The population was becoming more mobile and therefore less able to rely upon traditional sources for resolution of problems. This meant that people were more likely to look toward government to resolve the problems they perceived. Thus more was being demanded of government. At the same time, however, citizens were becoming less trusting of government. The level of trust is crucial because, as Gamson argues, citizen trust provides the government with leeway that is essential for action.[26] Despite this, throughout the period government did increase its impact on our lives. Yet, because of the increasing centralization of government and the increased role of the bureaucracy in policy making, the government was growing more distant and less amenable to citizen influence.

It was in this context that the third participation crisis emerged. It began with the "movement," an amorphous term that was used to refer to an equally amorphous set of concerns. In general, the goal of the movement was participatory democracy. Far from being satisfied with a theory of democracy based upon the opportunity to participate in periodic elections, those who advocated participatory democracy wanted to extend active citizenship into all areas of our lives. The participatory democrats were Aristotelian in their view of man as political man, only achieving self-fulfillment through active involvement in politics, with politics broadly defined to include all decisions that are relevant to an individual. They were Rousseauian in their desire to achieve self-mastery in organizations of which they necessarily were a part. They had a fundamental disdain for passivity, for being governed. As Kateb writes, they wished to be ". . . the source of benefits and not merely the passive recipient of them."[27]

The aims of the movement were revolutionary. This did not necessarily involve violence, although it certainly did accompany much of the political activity of the sixties. The revolutionary aspect of the sixties was the goal of totally restructuring American society. The American Revolution of the eighteenth century had not in any meaningful way restructured society. Many historians in fact question the extent to which the circumstances of American separation from England constituted a real revolution since those in power in America before the war were still in power after it. The only change was in the transfer of legitimacy—sovereignty, if you will, a transfer that had little to do with a meaningful redistribution of power. In the sixties, however, the goal was specifically the redistribution of power. To destroy the distinction between governed and governors, between us and them, was the ultimate goal of the movement and the slogan "Power to the people" symbolized this aim.

Not all Americans took part in the movement's search for redistribution of power. Yet many did in fact play a role in the participation crisis, often without even being aware of it. Three main changes in the participation of Americans in the sixties and seventies constitute the core of the third participation crisis.

Nature of the Crisis

First, there has been a decline in the role of parties in the political process and a decline in the number of Americans who identify with parties. U.S. parties have always existed to contest elections, and throughout most of U.S. history, the parties learned the lesson that elections were not won on the basis of precise issue appeals or ideology. Instead, the elections were geared to pragmatic politics that, in reality, meant pandering to the electorate's affinity for a party label and a candidate image. The parties were undercut in two ways.

First, reforms in delegate selection procedures limited the role of the party leadership in their ultimate concern: the choice of candidates for office. By in effect forcing an increase in the role of primaries as a means of choosing delegates to the national nominating conventions, and by binding the delegates to a given candidate, the influence of party leaders in selecting candidates and contesting elections was severely limited. In addition, the campaign finance reform provided funding for all those who could meet the minimal requirement of raising $5,000 in each of twenty states, in contributions of $250 or less. What, then, did a party have to offer a candidate? Delegates were won through personal appeals to citizens voting in primaries and campaign finance was assured (if one were a member of one of the two major parties) by meeting certain minimal requirements of individual fund raising. The party, then, provided a label, perhaps legitimacy, but little else. Small wonder, then, that the party ceased to be a major part of candidate considerations. The effective candidacy of Jimmy Carter served to give notice that the party barons were no longer essential for success. As Richard Neustadt observes, "we have left the age of barons and entered the age of candidates."[28]

The decline in party identification was no doubt a reflection of the decline of importance of parties in their ultimate function of contesting elections. If candidates did not need parties to run campaigns, why should we need parties to make our choices? But the decline in party identification can probably also be traced to other, perhaps more significant, roots. The parties have been afraid of issues. (The campaigns of 1964 and 1972 taught both parties that issues too clearly discussed could be deadly.) And yet, as has been argued before in this chapter, issues have held increasing importance in the decision rule of U.S. voters. Americans have been concerned about crime, drugs, poverty, Vietnam, and yet, the parties have so far been successful in avoiding precisely those issues that have preoccupied Americans.

Perhaps the best illustration of the unwillingness of both parties to confront issues was the 1968 Presidential election. There was no doubt that Americans differed on their attitudes toward the Vietnam war, so the conditions were present for an issue-based election. Yet, as Page and Brody illustrate, neither Humphrey nor Nixon delineated issue stands clearly enough to provide the basis for voting rationally on the basis of an issue relevant to most Americans.[29] It is probably no accident that the 1968 election marked the beginning of the rise in the number of party independents.[30] If the parties refuse to stake out issue positions, even if the voters themselves have strong issue stands, is there any wonder why the parties should be seen as irrelevant by the voters?

Not surprisingly, the decline of parties has been accompanied by an increase in the role of interest groups. Twenty years ago Schattschneider argued that parties were the natural antagonists of interest groups, for the latter differ from parties not only in terms of membership, but also in basic political strategy.[31] Parties, aimed toward successful competition of elections, deal in a world in which the goal is maximizing numbers of people. Interest groups, on the other hand, forever incapable of contesting effectively in the electoral arena because of fewer numbers, focus on limiting the numbers involved in decisions in order to maximize the resources that they dominate: expertise and information. As parties decline, the role of interest groups expands to fill the power vacuum.

This change simultaneously implies a change in the resources of politics from numbers to information and expertise. As the focus changes, so does the scope of conflict. Fewer people can compete effectively in a politics dominated by information and expertise than in politics based on numbers. In fact, Lowi has eloquently argued that the effect of delegation of power to interest groups is to create a politics of privilege in which resources are inequitably parceled out to those groups who can effectively compete in the battle among interests.[32] And William Dean Burnham, one of the first political scientists to explore the implications of declining party identification, argues that "political parties, with all of their well-known human and structural shortcomings, are the only devices thus far invented by the wit of western man which, with some effectiveness, can generate countervailing collective power on behalf of the many individually powerless against the relatively few who are individually—or organizationally—powerful."[33]

The effect of the increased importance of interest groups is not only to close out those who are not organized and who cannot command equal resources, but it is also to create an atomization of politics equal to the atomization of society. Single issues became the focus of political action and commanded levels of interest and intensity that are rarely seen in U.S. politics. The net result of this has been both to increase the number of interest groups active in politics and the intensity with which they pursued their political goals.[34]

Finally, there has been a decrease in concern with electoral politics and a concomitant increase in concern with the policy implementation agencies of government. This is, perhaps, only to be expected in an era when policy issues seem to be of crucial concern to Americans and when electoral politics provide no options or alternatives to U.S. voters. In addition, it is quite clear that the bureaucracy has been delegated increasing control over both policy implementation and formulation.

The force of all of these changes has been to thrust U.S. residents more directly into the processes of government without mediating structures. Parties had served to aggregate interests and to establish priorities among them. The decline of parties has meant an increase in the complexity of the electoral arena where parties no longer can be used to sort out the "buzzing, blooming confusion" of politics.

The second aspect of the participation crisis, the increase of interest groups, has served to decrease the buffer between the people and their government. Interest groups, as envisioned by many of the revisionist theorists, were to fulfill the function of mediation. They were to aggregate demands from citizens, thus buffering the government from the "noise" of the multiple interests of a vast and pluralistic people. Yet, as the numbers of groups increase, the specificity of their demands also increases. "Single-issue politics" has become the order of the day with the resulting increase in the responsibility of government itself to attempt to aggregate demands.

At the same time that buffering institutions have declined, citizens are becoming more intimately involved in bureaucratic decision making. By becoming involved in the bureaucracy, citizens are being given access to those institutions responsible for the day-to-day operations of government, which means an intimate involvement of citizens in government without the benefit of the traditional mediating institutions.

Of course, the government itself has participated in encouraging the participation crisis. It was the government that legislated campaign finance laws that accelerated the breakdown of parties. But more importantly, one reason for citizen involvement in bureaucracy was the mandates by the government itself. Perhaps the most infamous of the dictates was the "maximum feasible participation" mandate of the Economic Opportunity Act of 1964 mentioned above. Since that time, virtually every major federal legislation aimed at sharing resources with state and local areas has included some form of participation mandate. Why, in fact, has the national government cooperated in the breakdown of the traditional participation structures?

Part of the answer can be found in the description of the circumstances leading up to the crisis. The breakdown in trust of the system, the new demands on the government, and the realization that government was increasingly being seen as remote and inaccessible led naturally to a response by government to increase the number of people involved in government. Since the first participation crisis, the lesson that had been learned most effectively by political leaders was that when groups of people become powerful enough to threaten the system, the safest response is to try to incorporate those groups into the government. Selznick called it "cooptation."[35] The goal is to institutionalize the conflict created by protesting citizens by bringing them into the system.

The effects of this institutionalized conflict have in the past been twofold. On the one hand, coöptation has been a conservative force since bringing in protesting groups in effect assured the continuation of the existing system. On the other hand, however, the cooptation has provided for a constant democratization of a political system that, as noted above, was never designed to function as a democracy. In summary, then, the overall effect has been evolution rather than revolution.

In the past two participation crises the people were mainly brought in through the electoral arena. In the first participation crisis, an increased number of people were given the vote. In the second participation crisis, the goal was to make the ballot more meaningful by the processes of initiative and referendum. In the third participation crisis, the franchise again was extended. This time the beneficiaries were the 18- to 21-year-olds. But the real thrust of the third crisis was to transfer the focus of citizens from electoral politics to bureaucratic politics.

There is precedent for citizen involvement in the bureaucracy. Jacksonian democracy was based on the belief that the work of government was simple enough that any citizen could perform it; hence, ordinary citizens were appointed to the bureaucracy. This made the bureaucracy not only politically responsible, but also perhaps the most democratic part of national government. The Civil Service System, however, ended the reliance upon patronage as the primary means of staffing the bureaucracy. This change was in part due to the revolt against politics and parties during the Progressive era. But it was also due to a belief that the job of government had become too complex, in an era of technological sophistication, for it to be possible for anyone and everyone to be capable of performing effectively.

The Civil Service System signaled the start of an era when information and expertise were becoming resources of political power. There is no reason to believe that the era has come to an end. If anything, information and expertise are more important power resources than ever before. An important question concerns what can be accomplished by citizen participation in the bureaucracy? Before addressing that question, it is important to examine more fundamental dilemmas concerning citizen participation in the United States. As argued in the first chapter, a primary problem has been the plethora of conceptions about what citizen participation actually is in practice and what specific effects are expected to be produced by it. Therefore, before specifically considering participation in a bureaucratic context, we will turn to an examination of what effects participation is expected to produce and alternative means of structuring citizen participation.

NOTES

[1] Lucian Pye, *Aspects of Political Development* (Boston: Little, Brown, 1966), p. 65.

[2] Ibid.

[3] Daniel J. Boorstin, *The Americans: The Colonial Experience* (New York: Vintage Books, 1958), p. 145.

[4] Ibid., p. 66.

[5] Ibid., p. 67.

[6] James Madison, *Journal*, in *Records of the Federal Convention*, ed. Max Farrand, vol. I (New Haven: Yale University Press, 1921), p. 68.

[7] Alexander Hamilton, James Madison, and John Jay, *The Federalist Papers* (New York: The New American Library of World Literature, 1961), p. 81.

[8] Bernard R. Berelson, Paul F. Lazarsfeld, and William N. McPhee, *Voting: A Study of Opinion Formation in a Presidential Campaign* (Chicago: University of Chicago Press,

1954), p. 312; Angus Campbell, Philip E. Converse, Warren E. Miller, and Donald E. Stokes, *The American Voter* (Chicago: University of Chicago Press, 1960), chapter 10.

[9] Berelson, et al., *Voting*, p. 312.

[10] Herbert McCloskey, "Consensus and Idology in American Politics," *American Political Science Review* 58 (1964):361–383.

[11] Robert Dahl, *A Preface to Democratic Theory* (Chicago: University of Chicago Press, 1956), p. 125.

[12] Joseph A. Schumpeter, *Capitalism, Socialism and Democracy* (New York: Harper and Brothers, 1942, 1947, 1950), p. 269.

[13] Dahl, *A Preface to Democratic Theory*, p. 137.

[14] Peter Bachrach, *The Theory of Democratic Elitism: A Critique* (Boston: Little, Brown, 1967), p. 100.

[15] Roger Cobb and Charles D. Elder, *Participation in American Politics: The Dynamics of Agenda-Building* (Boston: Allyn and Bacon, 1972), p. 7.

[16] Ibid.

[17] See, for example, Boorstin, *The Americans.*

[18] Ibid.

[19] M. Kent Jennings and Richard G. Niemi, *The Political Character of Adolescence: The Influence of Families and Schools* (Princeton: Princeton University Press, 1974).

[20] Roger Kasperson and Myrna Breitbart, *Participation, Decentralization and Advocacy Planning,* Resource Paper #25 (Association of American Geographers, 1974), p. 57; Stuart Langton, "Citizen Participation in America: Curent Reflections on the State of the Art," in *Citizen Participation in America*, ed. Stuart Langton (Lexington, Mass.: Lexington Books, 1978), pp. 6–7.

[21] John Petrocik, Sidney Verba, and Norman Nie, *The Changing American Electorate* (Cambridge, Mass.: Harvard University Press, 1976), p. 105.

[22] Ibid., p. 109.

[23] Richard Neustadt, *Presidential Power* (New York: John Wiley & Sons, 1980), p. 177.

[24] Theodore Lowi, *The End of Liberalism: The Second Republic of the United States*, 2nd ed. (New York: W. W. Norton, 1979), p. 70.

[25] H. H. Gerth and C. Wright Mills, *From Max Weber: Essays in Sociology* (New York: Oxford University Press, 1946), pp. 196–198.

[26] William A. Gamson, *Power and Discontent* (Homewood, Ill.: The Dorsey Press, 1968), pp. 42–48.

[27] George Kateb, "Comments on David Braybrooke's "The Meaning of Participation and of Demands for It," in *Participation in Politics,* eds. J. Roland Pennock and John W. Chapman (New York: Lieber-Atherton, 1975), p. 92.

[28] Neustadt, *Presidential Power*, p. 176.

[29] Benjamin I. Page and Richard A. Brody, "Policy Voting and the Electoral Process: The Vietnam War Issue," *The American Political Science Review* 66 (September, 1972): 983–984.

[30] Nie, Verba, and Petrocik, *The Changing American Electorate*, p. 109.

[31] E. E. Schattschneider, *The Semi-Sovereign People* (New York: Holt, Rinehart and Winston, 1960). See especially chaps. 2 and 3.

[32] Lowi, *The End of Liberalism*, pp. 58–61.

[33] William Dean Burnham, "The End of Party Politics," *Transaction* (December, 1969):12–22.

[34] Norman J. Ornstein and Shirley Elder, *Interest Groups, Lobbying and Policymaking* (Washington, D.C.: Congressional Quarterly Press, 1978), p. 65.

[35] Philip Selznick, *TVA and the Grassroots: A Study of Politics and Organization* (Berkeley: University of California Press, 1949), pp. 259–261.

3

THE GOALS OF CITIZEN PARTICIPATION

There is little doubt that the vast majority of Americans strongly support the concept of citizen participation, at least in the abstract. As Weissberg argues in his study of political socialization, ". . . almost from the beginning of grade school the norm of political activity gains wide acceptance."[1] Yet to support the ideal and to understand exactly what that may mean in practice are two very different things. As Herbert McCloskey demonstrated in his classic article on the political ideology of Americans, there is widespread consensus on the desirability of democratic values and yet little understanding of or support for specific applications of those values in practice.[2] Terms such as freedom and equality have been transformed into symbols (analogous to the flag) that evoke responses that are at base affective rather than cognitive.

Like the concepts of freedom and equality, citizen participation raises issues that lie at the base of democratic theory. All governments depend ultimately on the acquiescence of the people for survival, yet if a government claims to be a democracy there are certain expectations of the relationship. In fact, for most conceptions of democracy there is a definitive connection between the idea of democracy and that of citizen participation in government. Therefore, it is incumbent on a government that invokes the mantle of democracy to find a means for citizens to have access to governmental activities.

There is a lack of clarity on what citizen participation actually is in practice, which is not due solely to the tendency of Americans to avoid thinking deeply about political ideologies. Theorists have provided little guidance in the search for a clearer understanding of either democracy or the role of citizen participation in democracies. Pennock in his examination of democratic theory claims that ". . . a democracy is rule by the people."[3] Yet, as he and others have amply demonstrated, no single, absolute democratic theory exists. In fact, the distinctions among the versions rest largely on the different conceptions of what "rule by the people" may be. Therefore, it is impossible to refer to a single democratic theory to resolve the dilemma of what role citizens should play in a democratic government.

The point is that there is no consensus on what citizen participation is. And yet, in recent years, citizen participation has become a particularly powerful symbol in the lexicon of U.S. politics. In the calls for "Power to the People" (ironically, issued in identical form by both conservatives and liberals in the United States), are implications of a return to some halcyon past where participation thrived, or at least to the final fulfillment of a democratic ideal with roots deep in U.S. history.

How citizens are to take part in the activities of government, and what will result from the participation remain debatable and often hotly contested questions. The basic problem is that citizen participation is a vague concept, and a vacuum has been created from the lack of clarity. To fill this vacuum, a horde of expectations has been released (as in the proverbial Pandora's box) concerning the use of citizen participation. Governments are expected to be transformed in accordance with Lincoln's rhetorical ideal of a government "of, by, and for the people." This combination (of high expectations that are simultaneously vague and conflicting) is the core of the current participation crisis in the United States. Therefore, to understand the crisis, it is important to examine the differing expectations of what citizen participation is expected to produce and the problems that result from these expectations.

Democratic theorists agree that citizen participation of some kind is a valued commodity; however, there is disagrement on the question of why it is valued. To some, participation is viewed as an intrinsic good and an essential component of an individual's humanness. For example, Peter Bachrach, referring to the beliefs of Rousseau, Kant, Mill, Lindsay, and others, argues that ". . . man's development as a human being is closely dependent upon his opportunity to contribute to the solution of problems relating to his own actions."[4] Kateb traces current demands for increased participation to the Movement, the amorphous core of social activism in the sixties.[5] The Movement, according to Kateb, originated in a search for public action and for self-mastery in organizational life. In the same vein, Robert Pranger has argued that our society must stop "socializing" chidren and begin to provide ". . . political education in the form of sufficient participatory experience . . ." to prepare people to become citizens.[6] This is necessary, according to Pranger, because "The adult citizen is almost dead, and with him will vanish the human being, autonomous and social . . ."[7] An interesting practical example of the same argument is Needleman and Needleman's study of community planners:

> In the view of most community planners, citizen participation represents not a means to an end but the end itself. Delivery of a tangible product, though important, is secondary. In fact . . . for many community planners the prime significance of product delivery is its key role in arousing community interest and confidence, and thus sustaining a high level of citizen participation.[8]

The core of each of the above arguments is that participation is an end in itself. Others, however, reject the notion that participation is intrinsically good,[9] and argue that it is philosophically impossible to establish the intrinsic goodness of participation. Therefore, they believe that arguments about the value of participation must rest on a determination of what empirical effects participation has on the political system and on the participants. Seen from this perspective, then, participation is a purposive activity.

In the minds of those who view participation as a purposive activity, arguing that participation is good because it is integral to human self-fulfillment is equivalent to arguing that it is good because it produces certain desired effects on the individual. From this perspective, it would seem that the distinction between the concept of participation as an intrinsic good, as opposed to its being a purpose activity, is purely one of semantics—and yet, this distinction can have significant practical implications.

To those who view participation purposively, the mere presence of participatory mechanisms is not per se satisfactory. To these people, participatory mechanisms, be they voting, public hearings, advisory boards, citizen surveys, and others, must operate in such a way that they produce desired impacts, in order to be evaluated as satisfactory. This explains why some may believe that the battle for participation has been won when a participatory mechanism is established, yet others may reject that same mechanism. What the rejection implies is that "real participation" to them is not merely the ability to take part in some aspect of government, but rather, real participation is an activity that produces the desired effect—that which motivated the participation in the first place. It thus becomes important to consider what effects people expect from citizen participation.[10]

THE DIVERSE GOALS OF CITIZEN PARTICIPATION

The goals posited for citizen participation may be differentiated by where the impacts of participation are aimed or, in other words, where changes resulting from participation are expected to occur: one level of change is societal. For some, the goal of participation is to achieve a radical restructuring of society. Participating in making decisions is a form of power.

Some believe that, by solely distributing this power in the form of citizen participation, the fundamental distinction between governors and governed will break down.[11] This should result in the creation of a society that embodies the democratic ideals of equality and freedom since all would be free to share equally in the decision making.

Restructuring society is a goal that is undoubtedly the most encompassing of the goals of citizen participation. What is the evidence that such a goal is empirically feasible? It is clear that a radical transformation of society has not occurred as a result of citizen participation up to this point. What is the possibility that such a restructuring would actually occur? It is possible to argue that such a transformation is a long-run impact and may yet happen. Empirical proof suggests otherwise: the government seems to give no evidence of withering and dying. In addition, utopian experiments throughout history have demonstrated little success in establishing societies, even on a small scale, in which a basic distinction between leaders and followers did not seem essential to ordered existence.[12]

Despite this empirical evidence, some participation advocates denounce participation programs because they do not produce what is considered to be meaningful citizen power. For example, many student radicals of the late 1960s and early 1970s denounced any participation that did not result in an instant capitulation to their demands. They were, in effect, demanding total decision-making power.

In many cases, the goal of societal transformation is not posited in such an extreme form. For example, Greenstone and Peterson identified the goal of participation in the community action program as the ending of "... the virtual exclusion of low-income groups from political life by distributing power."[13] In this conception, the goal is not the revolution of society, but rather the attempt to include all groups in it. Participation in this case is used as a compensatory strategy. Redistribution of power is aimed, not at destroying the distinction between governors and governed, but at assuring that all the governed possess equal power resources when interacting with the governed. As before, participation is aimed at increasing freedom and equality in society, but this conception recognizes, in the immortal words of George Orwell, that some will be more equal than others as long as governors continue to exist.[14]

There is evidence that the goal of using participation to equalize interactions with government officials may be empirically feasible. One result of the impacts of the community action programs mentioned above was the creation of indigenous political leadership in the poverty areas.[15] Fainstein and Fainstein have found that this leadership has been successful over time in bargaining for resources.[16] Their success, however, has been limited to the local level, which is a significant fact since the priorities of local government are often set at the level of the national government.

A second set of changes that are believed to result from participation are at the level of the individual. Perhaps the most encompassing individual impact posited for citizen participation has been previously mentioned: the fulfillment of one's self as a human. This notion springs from the Aristotelian concept of a political man who can only be fulfilled as a human by taking part in the actions of the polity. This idea derives from basic assumptions concerning the nature of man. It is obviously difficult to test for the "humanness" or "nonhumanness" of individuals. It may be possible, however, to test for improvement (in a generalized sense) of the well-being of participating citizens. Experiments on small group behavior appear to substantiate the contention that humans are generally more satisfied in democratically controlled groups.[17] It seems, however, that the "participation hypothesis" does not hold for all personality types; nor may it hold in all cultures.

Other, more specific, predictions concerning the impact of citizen participation on individuals exist and these hypotheses are more easily testable empirically than the hypothesis concerning self-fulfillment. One hypothesis predicts that participation will reduce the extent of citizen alienation from both the political system and those around them. It is argued that by taking part in the activities of government, citizens will identify more with the political system and, therefore, feel less the estrangement from politics that is so prevalent in the United States.[18]

As part of this argument, it is also believed that participation will educate citizens about the activities, problems, demands, and conflicts of government. This education could give citizens a better comprehension of the necessary compromises and "satisficing" that characterize government decisions. In other words, educating the citizens might make them more tolerant and trusting of government, and more likely to acquiesce to its decisions.[19]

It is also argued that participation in politics increases the citizen's sense of efficacy. If one feels that government is not some remote object, if through education one learns how government functions and thus begins to have trust, it seems logical that one's belief in his ability to affect the decisions of government should increase.[20]

It is believed that participation will decrease citizen alienation from the government, as well as from the community, and will make a citizen aware that his interests, at least in large part, are shared. Thus, individual goals become group goals and a sense of identification with others, or with a community, develops.[21] As Bachrach argues, participation provides ". . . a greater sense of purpose and pride and a greater awareness of community."[22] (This same logic has been used by proponents of participatory management, for it is believed that an employee's participation in decision making will increase his support for, and identification with, the goals of the organization.[23]) These changes in the individual brought about by citizen participation are also believed to reduce the incidence of such pathological behaviors as delinquency, drug addiction, and others.[24]

Many studies have been completed on the effects of citizen participation on attitudes. The evidence tends to be mixed. For example, Cole concluded that those who do participate have higher levels of trust in government than the general citizenry.[25] Others, however, have failed to find confirmation for Cole's conclusions.[26] There are many possible explanations for this disparity: methodological problems of the studies, differences in measures used, changes in the time frame, and differences in the type of participation being examined, to name only a few. A more thorough review of the literature and these factors will be included in Chapters 6 and 7.

Even though the major focus of the changes being discussed are at the individual level, such changes also have significance for society. If the changes did occur, society would become more stable through a reduction in pathological behavior, an increase in citizen trust, and sense of community. Society would also become more equitable since an increase in efficacy would make it more likely that all citizens could use government to attain their desired goals.

This search for desired goals is the third area in which changes are expected to occur through citizen participation. The administration of government is expected to be improved by citizen participation. It is believed that participation is a means that citizens can use to protect their self-interests and to achieve what they desire from government. Through it, citizens can communicate what they desire to the government. Because of the improved communication, government should find it easier to respond in a way that is satisfactory to citizens. Therefore, citizen participation should improve both the effectiveness and the efficiency of service delivery.[27] Some studies have in fact indicated that changes in service delivery do occur as a result of citizen participation.[28]

A composite list of what is expected of citizen participation is staggering, for participation appears to be akin to the snake oil of ancient venders. It is supposed to cure whatever is ailing the body politic at the moment. Unfortunately, it is doubtful that any single participatory process can be the palliative that citizen participation has been promised to be. If the case is that no single participatory process can achieve all of the goals posited for participation, this leads to some fundamental problems for those who are either implementing or evaluating citizen participation.

PROBLEMS CAUSED BY CITIZEN PARTICIPATION GOALS

The first problem raised by the "shopping list" of goals is how to determine which goal is most important to both the citizens and the officials with whom they will interact. Although there is considerable overlap in the lists from various sources, there is no single "official list" of goals. Because of the lack of consensus on goals it is difficult to determine whether a particular participatory experience is satisfactory or not: those expecting one outcome may not be satisfied if another result occurs. Here, as in most areas, beauty is in the eye of the beholder.

Accentuating the problem is the fact that the goals are largely undefined, which leaves each group devising its own set of goals to use as standards for evaluation. Since no one participatory mechanism is likely to achieve all the goals, it follows that there must be some dissatisfaction with all participatory mechanisms.

Apparently, this dissatisfaction often results in rejection of a particular participatory experience. Rather than be willing to compromise by saying "I got something, although not what I wanted," many participants denounce the whole experience by saying, "It's not real participation." One of the hallmarks of American policitics has traditionally been the willingness to compromise, so why is it that Americans frequently do not respond to the achievements of participation in the traditional manner? There are two explanations. On the one hand, the vagueness of the goals may be the source of the problem. If the participants fail to specify their own goals clearly, they may also be unaware of alternatives. If this is the case, they would certainly be unable to recognize the need for compromise among the alternatives. A second explanation, however, suggests that because the goals expected from participation are so important to the individual participants, they are unwilling to compromise.

An especially fertile ground for conflicts is in the fundamentally different perspectives of government officials and citizen participants. William Gamson has argued, in his analysis of *Power and Discontent*, that "potential partisans" (citizens) are interested in influence, while "authorities" (government officials) are interested in social control.[29] Although empirical reality may not be quite so neat as his theoretical conceptualization, there is ample evidence that citizens and officials frequently view participation from fundamentally differing perspectives. Evaluations of the community action agencies of the sixties have demonstrated that both citizens and officials saw that program through the rosy-colored lenses of their own viewpoints. It was frequently the case that citizens expected to achieve a redistribution of power. Officials on the other hand were searching for increased citizen trust and acquiescence as well as for improvements in the resources and knowledge necessary to deliver satisfactory services to the citizens.[30] It is not difficult to understand why the perspectives of the two groups would produce such conflicting goals and how these conflicting views could cause problems in evaluating participation.

The multiple goals might also cause problems because of conflicts between the goals themselves. It is not necessarily the case that the goals are mutually exclusive; however, in practical terms the fulfillment of one may complicate the attainment of another. For example, there is no logical reason why giving citizens increased power in governmental decision making (the societal goal of redistributing power) cannot also lead to increased effectiveness and efficiency of service delivery; yet, there have been instances in which increasing the role of citizens in government decision making has led to conflict and even deadlock, which results in worse service delivery.[31]

Another problem in implementing and evaluating citizen participation is whether these goals are empirical or normative. In other words, it is not clear whether participation can produce a particular goal, if it is executed correctly, or if these goals are the result of "wishful thinking." If there is no empirical evidence that citizen participation can produce a given goal, it is clearly unfair to denounce it for not achieving that goal.

This confusion on the distinction between empirical and normative analysis of participation is a serious flaw of much of the participation literature. As critics have pointed out, many empirical studies of participation have concluded that what is empirical reality must of necessity be good.[32] For example, the results of the initial voting studies indicated that few Americans were interested in or informed about politics.[33] This empirical picture conflicted with the image of the rational-activist citizen believed to be essential to democracy in classical theory. To eliminate the contradiction between theory and practice, the empirical researchers have constructed an alternative conceptualization of democracy, often called revisionist democratic theory.[34] In this revised conception, democracy does not depend on active participation by citizens (empirically shown to be minimal) but rather on four requisites:

> (1) Social pluralism; (2) diverse and competing elites that are circulating and accessible; (3) a basic consensus at least among the elites on the rules of democratic competition; and (4) elections that provide regular opportunities for citizens to participate in the selection of public officials.[35]

These researchers did not stop at revising the conception of democracy, for they also invested this conception with the normative mantle of desirability. In an early and classic example of such a normative conclusion, Bernard Berelson argued that:

> Extreme interest goes with extreme partisanship and might culminate in rigid fanaticism that could destroy the democratic process if generalized throughout the community. . . . Low interest provides maneuvering room for political shifts necessary for a complex society in a period of rapid change.[36]

What Berelson is doing is proclaiming the value of stability, which, paradoxically, may evolve from the lack of participation.

The problems with such a leap from empirical discovery to normative prescription are twofold. First, it is simply illogical. Second, critics of revisionist theory have argued that it is seriously lacking. For example. Bachrach argues that such a theory ignores the essential component of classical theory, as he writes:

> . . . the supposition that man's dignity, and indeed his growth and development as a functioning responsive individual in a free society, is dependent upon an opportunity to participate actively in decisions that significantly affect him.[37]

What critics like Bachrach are arguing is that, if the concept of mass participation is removed from democratic theory, although it may be justified on empirical grounds, the heart of the normative theory of democracy may also have been removed.

Ironically, however, such critics have created another serious error for, in many cases, they have thoroughly divorced empirical reality and normative prescription. For example, Bachrach provides an incisive and damning critique of revisionist theory. He clearly believes that a theory of democracy should be based on the normative goal of providing citizens the opportunity to participate equally in community decisions.[38] In fact, he argues that participation must be extended beyond solely government decision making and into "private governments," such as General Motors.[39] Nevertheless, he fails to provide any guidance on how this normative prescription can be achieved.

Of course, the problem of the appropriate melding of values and empiricism is a constant dilemma for social scientists. There is good reason why the problem is especially acute when discussing citizen participation, which is, itself, both an empirical reality and a value. What is desired may well outstrip what is empirically feasible. The fact, along with the vagueness of goals and the conflict among the goals of participation, complicates both the process of implementing citizen participation and of evaluating it.

COSTS AND BENEFITS OF PARTICIPATION

In addition to the problems caused by the goals of participation, another factor affects the evaluation of citizen participation: the necessity of balancing the expected benefits of participation with the inevitable costs. One form of cost is the time and effort involved in participation. Meetings are always time-consuming, but so are individualized efforts by citizens to contact and persuade officials. In addition, the timing of such meetings may be beyond an individual's control and, therefore, especially inconvenient. In addition to the time involved in the act of participation, there is also an investment of time in becoming informed prior to participating and information costs also involve effort.[40]

Effort is also expended in the inevitable confrontation and conflict that citizen participation creates, for citizens must sometimes attempt to force their will upon government officials. In addition, citizens often have to confront fellow citizens with vastly different desires in a zero-sum conflict over the scarce resources of government. While Verba and Nie have argued that some citizens have more tolerance of conflict than others,[41] Weissburg argues that the socialization process tends to lead to an avoidance of conflict:

> Despite the obvious necessity of some toleration of conflict in order for meaningful (rather than playacting) political participation to occur, most American children fail to develop this orientation. Little doubt exists that Americans are overwhelmingly trained to prefer harmony and consensus to conflict.[42]

Finally, in addition to the time and effort of participation, citizens must also bear the innumerable opportunity costs of profit or pleasure sacrificed for participation.

Just as the list of expected goals of participation is individualized (that is, that the ratio of expected benefits and obvious costs is unique to each individual) so is the list of costs. While no claim of pure human rationality is made here, it does seem reasonable to assume that there is some point at which many involved in participation–both citizens and officials–will ask themselves if it is worthwhile. Then, the individualized, and very probably unstructured and unformalized cost-benefit ratios, must play a significant role.

Another major problem is the fact that the benefits of participation may often be realized only in the long term. Restructuring of society or alteration of one's orientation to politics might accrue, but are not likely to be realized immediately. The costs, on the other hand, have to be borne immediately. This balancing of costs and benefits complicates the process of evaluating citizen participation. It may well be that citizen participation is rejected–not for its failure to produce the desired goal, but because the costs involved in attaining the goal were considered too high.

There are some who argue that there is no problem if the costs of participation are perceived as outweighing the benefits. In fact, a basic tenet of revisionist democratic theory is the argument that as long as the opportunities are present for citizens to participate, the requirements of democracy are met.[43] If citizens do not participate, it is because they are basically satisfied and the effort of participation would be greater than the marginal utility that they could expect to receive in return. Others, however, would argue that opportunities to participate are meaningless if the costs of participation are so high, and the benefits so low, that citizens abstain.[44] This is a real problem because the costs of participation seem to weigh most heavily on those who may need government services the most—the uneducated and the poor.

Many have proposed means by which the benefits of participation could be increased to outweigh the costs. Schattschneider, for example, argued that the party system had a responsibility to define issues that were relevant to the large numbers of nonparticipants. This, he expected, would increase their perception of the importance of party choice, which, in turn, would increase their participation in the electoral arena.[45] Bachrach has argued for an expansion of the concept of political to include private governments.[46] People, therefore, could participate in making decisions on "issues which directly affect them in their place of work, issues which are comparatively trivial, yet are overlaid with tensions and emotions that often infuriate and try men's souls."[47]

SUMMARY

However one feels about the importance of increasing the benefits of participation, the basic point is still that the expectations of what will be produced by participation complicate the processes of implementing and evaluating citizen participation. In many cases, too much is expected and no single participatory mechanism can fulfill the goals. In other cases, the expectations are so vague and unspecified that each individual forms his own goals, and again no single mechanism can be satisfactory. In still other circumstances, the expected goals of one group conflict with others, making it impossible for all expectations to be realized. What is obviously needed is a clearer specification of the goals posited for participation—with this should come a clearer understanding of what can be realistically expected from participation.

NOTES

[1] Robert Weissberg, *Political Learning, Political Choice and Democratic Citizenship* (Englewood Cliffs, N.J.: Prentice-Hall, 1974), p. 65.

[2] Herbert McCloskey, "Consensus and Ideology in American Politics," *American Political Science Review* 58 (1964):361–382.

[3] J. Roland Pennock, *Democratic Political Theory* (Princeton, N.J.: Princeton University Press, 1979), p. 7.

[4] Peter Bachrach, *The Theory of Democratic Elitism* (Boston: Little, Brown, 1967), p. 99.

[5] George Kateb, "Comments on David Braybrooke's 'The Meaning of Participation and Demands For It'" in *Participation in Politics*, eds. J. Roland Pennock and John W. Chapman (New York: Lieber-Atherton, 1975), p. 92.

[6] Robert J. Pranger, *The Eclipse of Citizenship: Power and Participation in Contemporary Politics* (New York: Holt, Rinehart and Winston, 1968), p. 102.

[7] Ibid.

[8] Martin L. Needleman and Carolyn Emerson Needleman, *Guerrillas in the Bureaucracy* (New York: John Wiley & Sons, 1974), p. 237.

[9] M. B. E. Smith, "The Value of Participation" in *Participation in Politics,* eds. Pennock and Chapman, pp. 126–136.

[10] Some discussion of the extent to which research indicates the goals are empirically feasible will be given in this chapter. A more thorough review of the literature concerning the impacts of participation can be found in Chapters 6 and 7.

[11] Kateb, "Comments" in *Participation in Politics*, eds. Pennock and Chapman, pp. 89–97.

[12] For an argument of the inevitability of oligarchy see Robert Michels, *Political Parties* (New York: Free Press, 1949), p. 32.

[13] J. David Greenstone and Paul E. Peterson, *Race and Authority in Urban Politics: Community Participation and the War on Poverty* (New York: Russell Sage Foundation, 1973), p. 154.

[14] George Orwell, *Animal Farm* (New York: Harcourt, Brace, 1946), p. 123.

[15] Daniel Patrick Moynihan, *Maximum Feasible Misunderstanding: Community Action in the War on Poverty* (New York: Free Press, 1969), p. 129.

[16] Norman Fainstein and Susan S. Fainstein, "The Future of Community Control," *American Political Science Review* 70 (1976):905–923.

[17] Kurt Lewin, Ronald Lippitt, and R. White, "Patterns of Aggressive Behavior in Experimentally Created Social Climates," *Journal of Social Psychology* 10 (1939):271–299; and Sidney Verba, *Small Groups and Political Behavior* (Princeton, N.J.: Princeton University Press, 1961), pp. 216–225.

[18] Roland L. Warren, Stephen M. Rose, and Ann F. Bergunder, *The Structure of Urban Reform: Community Decision Organizations in Stability and Change* (Lexington, Mass.: Lexington Books, 1974), p. 106.

[19] Carl W. Stenberg, "Citizens and the Administrative State: From Participation to Power," *Public Administration Review* 32 (May/June 1972):192.

[20] Ibid., pp. 191–192; and Bengt Abrahamsson, *Bureaucracy or Participation: The Logic of Organization* (Beverly Hills: Sage, 1977), p. 229.

[21] Lawrence A. Schaff, "Two Concepts of Political Participation," *Western Political Quarterly* 20 (September 1975), p. 449; Frederick C. Mosher, ed., *Governmental Reorganization: Cases and Commentary* (Indianapolis: Bobbs-Merrill, 1967), p. 518.

[22] Peter Bachrach, "Interest, Participation, and Democratic Theory" in *Participation in Politics*, eds. Pennock and Chapman, p. 50.

[23] Lester Coch and John R. French, Jr., "Overcoming Resistance to Change," *Human Relations* 1 (1948):512–532; Carole Pateman, *Participation and Democratic Theory* (Cambridge: Cambridge University Press, 1970); Peter F. Drucker, *The Practice of Management* (New York: Harper & Row, 1954), pp. 121–136, especially.

[24] Warren et al., *The Structure of Urban Reform*, p. 106.

[25] Richard L. Cole, *Citizen Participation and the Urban Policy Process* (Lexington, Mass.: Lexington Books, 1974), p. 113.

[26] Robert K. Yin et al., *Citizen Organizations: Increasing Client Control Over Services* (Santa Monica, Ca.: Rand, 1973), pp. 33–35.

[27] Advisory Commission on Intergovernmental Relations, *In Brief: Citizen Participation in the American Federal System* (Washington, D.C.: ACIR, 1979), p. 4.

[28] Robert K. Yin, "Goals for Citizen Involvement: Some Possibilities and Some Evidence," in *Citizen Participation Certification for Community Development: A Reader on*

the Citizen Participation Process, ed. Patricia Marshall (Washington, D.C.: National Association of Housing and Redevelopment Officials, 1977), p. 52.

[29] William A. Gamson, *Power and Discontent* (Homewood, Ill.: Dorsey Press, 1968), p. 18.

[30] Peter Morris and Martin Rein, *Dilemmas of Social Reform: Poverty and Community Action in the United States*, 2nd. ed. (Chicago: Aldine, 1973), p. 266.

[31] J. David Greenstone and Paul Peterson, "Reformers, Machines and the War on Poverty," in *The New Urban Poltics: Cities and the Federal Government* ed. Douglas M. Fox (Pacific Palisades, Ca.: Goodyear, 1972), p. 169.

[32] Carole Pateman, *Participation and Democratic Theory*, Chapter 1; Bachrach, *The Theory of Democratic Elitism*, pp. 32–35.

[33] Bernard R. Berelson, Paul F. Lazarsfeld, and William N. McPhee, *Voting: A Study of Opinion Formation in a Presidential Campaign* (Chicago: University of Chicago Press, 1954), p. 308; Angus Campbell et al., *The American Voter* (Chicago: University of Chicago Press, 1960), p. 542.

[34] Berelson, Lazarsfeld, and McPhee, *Voting*, chapter 14.

[35] Roger Cobb and Charles D. Elder, *Participation in America: The Dynamics of Agenda Building* (Boston: Allyn and Bacon, 1972), p. 3.

[36] Berelson, Lazarsfeld, and McPhee, *Voting*, p. 314.

[37] Bachrach, *The Theory of Democratic Elitism*, p. 101.

[38] Ibid.

[39] Ibid., p. 102.

[40] Anthony Downs, *An Economic Theory of Democracy* (New York: Harper & Row, 1957), Chapter 11.

[41] Sidney Verba and Norman H. Nie, *Participation in America: Political Democracy and Social Equality* (New York: Harper & Row, 1972), pp. 83–86.

[42] Robert Weissberg, *Political Learning, Political Choice and Democratic Citizenship*, p. 69.

[43] Robert A. Dahl, *A Preface to Democratic Theory* (Chicago: University of Chicago Press, 1956), chapter 5.

[44] Bachrach, *The Theory of Democratic Elitism*, p. 103.

[45] E. E. Schattschneider, *The Semi-Sovereign People* (New York: Holt, Rinehart and Winston, 1960), p. 141.

[46] Bachrach, *Theory of Democratic Elitism*, pp. 102–103.

[47] Ibid., p. 103.

4

THE STRUCTURE OF CITIZEN PARTICIPATION

The last chapter argued that vague and conflicting goals complicate the processes of implementing and evaluating citizen participation. In this chapter, it is argued that there are also problems caused by a lack of consensus on what citizen participation is in practice. As noted in Chapter 1, there has been an explosion in the types of activities being used by citizens to interact with government, and yet, there is no consensus on the "good" or even "acceptable" ways of structuring citizen participation. The problem is the lack of consensus on which criteria should be used for evaluating citizen participation structures.

It is argued here that there are fundamentally different criteria, which are ultimately derived from differing conceptions of the public interest. It is possible to delineate, in ideal form, two conceptions of the public interest, each of which has different implications for how citizen participation should be structured and that role it should play: these are labeled the collectivist and the individualist models. Since they are ideal types, no claim is made that they exist empirically as coherent sets of beliefs in such a pure form; however, it is believed that aspects of these models are used to evaluate citizen participation.

COLLECTIVIST VERSUS INDIVIDUALIST MODELS OF PUBLIC INTEREST

The collectivist model is based on the belief that the primary goal of government is to act fairly in achieving the common good for all citizens. It is also assumed that the public interest is separate from the aggregation of individual and group demands; that is, the whole is greater than the sum of its parts. Given this conception of the public interest, the collectivist model specifies that the role of government is to act for the aggregate good of the people. Since the collective goods of society may be threatened by the imposition of individual or group demands, the collectivist model requires that government have the authority to act contrary to such demands. The guideline for government action should be general rules and principles, not citizen demands.

Theodore Lowi is a primary spokesman for the belief that government should act according to general rules rather than in response to demands from groups. In his denunciation of the government's tendency to delegate decision making to interest groups, Lowi argues that:

> Considerations of the justice in or achieved by an action cannot be made unless a deliberate and conscious attempt was made by the actor to derive his action from a general rule or moral principle governing such a class of acts.[1]

To Lowi, failure to act according to general rules means that a government is unjust.

In the individualist conception of the public interest, however, the public interest results from the aggregation of individual or group interests: the whole is equal to the sum of its parts. In the individualist model, the government should respond to citizen demands. The guideline for its action should be the creation of decision-making processes that are broadly inclusive and provide citizens with the means to force government to respond to their demands.

Aaron Wildavsky is a major spokesman for the view that public interest results from aggregating demands from individuals and groups speaking for their own self-interest. He argues that:

> A partial adversary system in which the various interests compete for control of policy (under agreed-upon rules) seems more likely to result in reasonable decisions—that is, decisions that take account of the multiplicity of values involved—than one in which the best policy is assumed to be discoverable by a well-intentioned search for the public interest for all by everyone.[2]

In Chapter 2, it was argued that there are three basic dilemmas in structuring citizen participation: who should be included?; should participation be direct or indirect?; at what stage of decision making should citizens be included? The individualist and collectivist models each has different positions on these issues.

Since the individualist model posits that the public interest results from the aggregation of the separate interests that exist in society, it follows that attempts should be made to structure participation to be broadly inclusive of all interests. According to the model, government decisions should reflect those interests and citizens should be given direct access to all stages of the decision process—the ultimate ideal would be the inclusion of all through direct democracy. The result should be the allocation of government resources so that each interest receives its fair share.

According to the collectivist model, however, the public interest is separate from the aggregation of separate interests. Since the demands of separate interests may conflict with the general good, it follows that efforts should be made to limit the impact of citizens. This would be achieved by providing some form of indirect participation through representation. Since government should act authoritatively, on the basis of general rules, citizen demands should only be considered when these rules are first established. Therefore, citizen input should be limited to the predecisional and decisional stages of policy making. Input should be limited to bargaining on the general rules only and not include bargaining on the allocation of government resources to satisfy the specific interests of the citizens. Thus, the output of government should be to the aggregate not to separate groups or individuals.

PARTICIPATION IN THE COLLECTIVIST MODEL

As argued above, these models have been described as ideal types; yet, in the ways Americans have evaluated citizen participation there is ample evidence of these basic conceptions. The Founding Fathers were eloquent spokesmen for the collectivist model. As indicated in Chapter 2, Madison in *Federalist #10* made a damning evaluation of direct democracy. He argued, in part, that democracy ". . . can admit of no cure for the mischiefs of faction . . . ," provides ". . . nothing to check the inducements to sacrifice the weaker or obnoxious individual . . ." and that such governments ". . . have ever been spectacles of turbulence and contention."[3] This is a clear statement of the collectivist conception. The public good—personal security and the ever-important rights of property—would be endangered by providing all direct access to government decision making.

In place of direct democracy, Madison recommended a representative form of government, which he contended is superior for two reasons. First, the views of the public are refined and enlarged by being passed

> . . . through the medium of a chosen body of citizens, whose wisdom may best discern the true interest of their country and whose patriotism and love of justice will be least likely to sacrifice it to temporary or partial considerations.[4]

Secondly, since many people will participate in choosing the representative, ". . . it will be more difficult for unworthy candidates to practice with success the vicious arts by which elections are too often carried."[5]

What Madison is saying is that not only can people not be trusted to make the decisions of government, but they also cannot always be trusted to make the choice of those who will become decision makers. In other words, the impact of citizens should be carefully limited. Of course, this essay was written nearly two hundred years ago; yet the collectivist position has not disappeared from the thinking of those who analyze and evaluate American politics. Theodore Lowi has labeled the American government as unjust and illegitimate because it has delegated too much decision making to interest groups.[6] Bernard Berelson argues that the lack of political interest and involvement by U.S. residents was good because it provided the government with necessary "maneuvering room."[7] Other examples could be given. For example, Almond and Verba in their study of political culture make essentially the same argument:

> The maintenance of a proper balance between governmental power and governmental responsiveness represents one of the most important and difficult tasks of a democracy. Unless there is some control of governmental elites by nonelites, it is hard to consider a political system democratic. On the other hand, nonelites cannot themselves rule. If the political system is to be effective–if it is to be able to initiate and carry out policies, adjust to new situations, meet internal and external challenges–there must be mechanisms whereby governmental officials are endowed with the power to make authoritative decisions.[8]

And even the people themselves at times seem to agree that citizen input is not necessarily the best guideline for governmental action. Consider the praise often heaped on officials who take action that they know and proclaim to be "not politically popular."

Of course, even if there were consensus that government should be structured on the basis of representation, there would still be ample room for disagreement on how to structure that representation. The concept of representation is as complex as that of participation, as Hannah Pitkin has illustrated by delineating three different conceptions of representation. As with participation, the different conceptions also imply different standards of evaluation.[9]

The first conception is that of "formal representation," which refers to the formal arrangements by which some are chosen to hold public office. In this conception, the fact that citizens are given the right to elect someone to act for them constitutes representation; thus, the opportunity to vote is the only requirement in meeting the standards of formal representation.

In the second conception, however, an additional criterion is added, which Pitkin labeled "descriptive representation." The representatives must ". . . reflect accurately the social characteristics of those whom they formally represent."[10] Therefore, it is necessary for the representatives to share some characteristics with their constituents, although these are not specified. Representation will be evaluated not only on the basis of whether people can vote but also on whether those chosen have particular, relevant characteristics.

In the third conception, "substantive representation," the representative must act in the interests of his constituents and his actions must be influential. This is the most difficult conception to implement and to measure because of the problem in determining what the interests of the constituents are. Basic to the collectivist model is the belief that what constituents want may not be identical to what they need; that is, responding to separate demands may mean that the more fundamental interests of the collectivity are ignored. Madison hoped that elected representatives would be wise enough to filter and refine the public opinion to achieve substantive representation of interest of the people (defined in terms of their needs rather than their demands). It is not clear, however, how the representatives were to develop this wisdom, for well-meaning men can differ significantly on what they think is in the public interest. This is the basic thesis of this chapter.

Even if the problem of determining citizen needs is ignored and representatives focus solely on responding to explicit citizen demands, there are still operational problems. The fundamental question concerns to which citizens the official should listen. Of course, no aggregation of citizens is in total agreement and in the predominant case when the citizens disagree, the representatives must choose among the various positions.

An easy solution to the problem would be to listen to the majority. There are, however, multiple difficulties in attempting this. Typically, only small numbers of people ever contact their representatives. For example, Verba and Nie found that in their sample, only 20 percent have ever contacted a local official about an issue or a problem.[11] Given the low rates of citizen contact with representatives, the official often does not know what a majority wants, and the few who do communicate may have an atypical view.

An additional problem is that there may be no majority. As Arrow illustrated, in the presence of more than two alternatives, there may be no single one on which a majority agrees.[12] And, natural dualists to the contrary, most issues of public concern are complex enough to involve more than two alternatives. A final problem is the fact that, although Americans have reverence for majority rule, they also demand protection for minority rights. The resolution of this paradox is unclear, but the paradox does illustrate that Americans do not have a total and unquestioned commitment to majority rule.

Of course, rather than listening to a majority, a representative might choose simply to listen to those who contact him. This is obviously easier than searching for the majority, which in any event, might not exist or be right even if it does. Because it is easier to listen to those who do communicate, their opinions are undoubtedly used more commonly as a decision guideline, if only because of the ease of implementation. It can be argued, however, that those who make the effort to communicate feel more intensely about the issues and their preferences than do those who do not communicate. Since intensity is considered by some as a variable that should be taken into consideration when making a choice, then listening to those who communicate their preferences can be considered valid.[13]

Nevertheless, communication of preferences by some citizens cannot be interpreted as representation of all citizens. This intensity of concern is atypical, in fact, and may not give the formal representative an accurate picture of general public opinion. The formal representative may in effect be ignoring the preferences of the vast majority of the constituents. In this case, as in the case of conflict with minority rights, the basic dilemma is that of making decisions that preserve, or perhaps create, an equality of influence among those concerned.

There are, obviously, many problems with operationalizing indirect participation; yet, for some, these problems are irrelevant because they reject indirect participation and demand increased opportunities to participate directly in government. These demands can be traced to the individualist model of the public interest.

PARTICIPATION IN THE INDIVIDUALIST MODEL

If indirect participation has the force of the Founding Fathers behind it, then direct participation has the force of virtual religious zeal. Consider, for example, the argument of Emmett Redford that universal participation is a component of "democratic morality," on par with such ideals as "Man is, for man, the ultimate measure of all human values," and ". . . all men have worth deserving social recognition."[14] These tenets are akin to those of the Judeo-Christian faith and Redford's call for universl participation is analogous to Luther's demand that intermediaries be removed to enable men to communicate directly with whatever powers that be.

Redford is by no means alone in his participatory zeal. In many writings, Peter Bachrach has argued that men can only achieve self-esteem by participating in decisions that affect their lives. For example, in *The Theory of Democratic Elitism* he writes,

> . . . the issue is whether democracy can diffuse power sufficiently throughout society to inculcate among people of all walks of life a justifiable feeling that they have the power to participate in decisions which affect themselves and the common life of the community.[15]

Robert Pranger has argued that participation is essential not only for self-esteem but also for self-realization.[16] Numerous articles, government policies, and officials extol the virtues of participation.

The justification given for citizen participation ranges from the argument that participation is integral to the nature of man, to the more practical defense that policy can be more effective with citizen input. (No one knows where the shoe pinches but the wearer.) Regardless of the justification given, creating opportunities for direct participation is no easy task. There is still the basic government structure that was created two hundred years ago by a group of men vehemently opposed to the concept of direct participation—yet, the country now calls itself a democracy. With the realization that saying it does not necessarily make it so come demands to create forms of direct participation to realize the ideal. The fact remains that direct participation is an accretion to a republican government, although not particularly compatible with that structure. If citizens are to make decisions themselves through direct democracy, both the purpose and role of representatives become unclear.

Aside from the above dilemma, there is the fundamental problem of how to structure direct participation in a country of such vast size and with such a large population. Robert Sherrill has argued that technology does exist to permit instant referenda on issues.[17] Computer consoles put in each home could be used to transmit policy views of citizens to government officials. A cable TV company in Columbus, Ohio has established a process where citizens could communicate directly with government officials on a limited basis. In one nonpolitical experiment, viewers were allowed to select plays for one team in a high school football game. After an ignominious first half, the coach finally took over the play selection in the second half. This might indicate potential problems with direct interactive decision making. On the surface, it would appear that such a proposal could make universal direct democracy possible.

There are limits even with this radical proposal, for there would be significant questions concerning what issues would be on the agenda and how the issues and alternative resolutions would be defined. These are significant questions because, as Bachrach and Baratz have argued, the ability to determine what will, and therefore what will not, appear on the agenda is an important form of power.[18] There is no more effective political strategy than simply ignoring one's opponents. This process of forbidding access to the agenda is what Bachrach and Baratz call "non-decisionmaking."[19] Others, most notably E. E. Schattschneider, have argued that not only what is discussed, but how it is discussed, are crucial issues in political outcomes.[20] The way an issue is defined will determine who is likely to be involved in a conflict. The numbers, in turn, will affect the balance of power and, therefore, determine the winner and the loser.

It is often the case that citizens want to participate in government to avoid a situation where officials could monopolize control over the agenda. In effect, this is turning Schattschneider's argument around, for the numbers involved in a conflict will determine which issues must be considered and how these will be defined. By increasing the control citizens have over the agenda, citizen participation could also increase their sovereignty. On the other hand, if citizens were limited to responding to an agenda controlled by officials (through the use of consoles), no basic change in power would occur. It might be possible, however, to realize the individual and administrative goals of participation.

An alternative means for increasing direct participation would be a large scale decentralization of government decision making. This, of course, would be contrary to the pattern of centralization that has characterized American government for at least the last fifty years. This centralization has had the effect of making citizen participation more difficult because major decisions were moved beyond the local and state levels where citizens had greater access. Centralization, however, was deemed necessary to create a broad enough resource base that would enable the government to provide certain desirable services, and to ensure that those services would be distributed equally nationwide. In other words, there were public goods that could only be provided on an equal basis by a centralized government. Hence, there must be a trade-off of values: to decentralize for easier participation would threaten equitable access to certain government services.

The basic point is that to achieve an individualist goal of broad, inclusive direct participation involves a serious threat to equality, another basic value of the American political system. Ironically, this is the case despite the fact that demands for participation are often motivated by the belief that enabling all to participate will increase equality.

In practice, decision making by all presents another threat to equality, for everyone is not equally able to influence group decision making. Although demagoguery may not be inevitable in a system of universal direct participation, it is far from inconceivable—the result may well be a serious cementing of inequality.[21]

This raises another problem with universal direct participation: the question of how decisions would be reached. Some might feel that if all were involved some consensus might emerge but, as Madison observed, ". . . democracies have ever been spectacles of turbulence and contention."[22] For anyone who has sat through a meeting of any large group searching for a decision, Madison's critique should ring a familiar bell!

If consensus does not emerge, then in most cases the alternative decision rule becomes majority rule. Yet, as mentioned earlier, majority rule is no palliative, for in the case of more than two alternatives, no majority may exist. Majority rule may also create another threat to equality since minority rights might be threatened.

This analysis has focused on an extreme position and there are few who would argue that universal direct participation is feasible. There are, however, many participation advocates who would argue for increasing the numbers of citizens involved in government. Other major issues arise from this vague prescription. How many more citizens is enough? Which citizens should be included who are not now active? What structures should be provided? What should be done if, once the structures are provided, citizens still do not participate? If not all are involved, how does such a system differ from one based upon the republican principle of representative government?

OTHER IMPLICATIONS OF THE COLLECTIVIST AND INDIVIDUALIST MODELS

Neither the individualist nor the collectivist model offers adequate guidance for operationalizing citizen participation. These models do, however, affect the evaluation of citizen participation. Two other dilemmas concerning citizen participation evolve from these models: at which stage of decision making should citizens be involved and what type of output should result from that decision making. The collectivist model would seek to limit the impact of participation and restrict the stage at which it would occur. For example, Theodore Lowi argues for bargaining to be allowed only at ". . . those points in the system where decisions on rules can be made or reformed."[23] Once those general rules have been formed, presumably through Congressional law-making, he argues that a just government should apply them equitably and not allow citizens to have an impact on their implementation, since they would only use that access to obtain special benefits or privileges.[24] Lowi, then, would limit the role of citizens to the stage of general policy making and exclude citizens from the stage of policy implementation.

The individualist model, however, which evaluates government decisions on the basis of their inclusiveness, aims to increase the impact of citizens at all stages of the policy process. For instance, Emmett Redford, in direct contradiction to Lowi's position, argues that more efforts should be made to maximize citizen access to the administrative organizations responsible for the implementation of policy.[25]

Chapter 5 will examine why the demands have increased for participation in policy implementation and which dilemmas are involved in instituting such participation. This chapter will now address the final issue about which the collectivist and individualist models differ: the outputs of the policy process.

The collectivist model favors policy outputs that provide aggregate public goods rather than benefits that can be divided among separate individuals or groups. For two reasons, citizen participation can often impede efforts by government to provide aggregate public goods. In the first place, citizen demands are more likely to focus on the goods that will benefit them specifically, and therefore, citizen participation will provide no spokesman for the aggregate good. Secondly, citizen participation may create opposition to such goods because of the individualized costs that might be involved. For example, many have denounced citizen participation for interfering with efforts to achieve renewal of the nation's cities.[26] On the other hand, the individualist model contends that such complications are eminently desirable because, if any people oppose a policy, it would not be in the public interest to implement it.

Of course, buried in such discussions is a fundamental concern over whose "ox is being gored." Significantly, in the fifties it was the center city businessmen who supported public renewal efforts. Although they claimed that they would achieve a collective good by rebuilding the downtown—they definitely received an individualized benefit. It is clear that distinguishing individual from collective benefits is easier to do analytically than operationally. As Aaron Wildavsky persuasively argues,[27] it is unclear who can be trusted to speak for the public interest that is conceived as an aggregate whole. Nevertheless, some complain that special interests have been allowed to impede the public interest because of the creation of participatory mechanisms.

There is little doubt that trends in the last two decades have made the realization of individualist ideals more feasible, although perhaps it is now more difficult to attain collectivist ideals. Both the increase in the number of interest groups, and the increasing tendency for such groups to focus on single issues have created a political system in which it is easiest to divide up the spoils of government among the competing groups. The simultaneous decline in the role of political parties has removed one possible source of aggregating demands and therefore having adequate perspective to establish priorities among the interests. And, finally, the direct involvement of citizens in the bureaucracy, which thrusts citizens into the implementation stage of the policy process, also makes it virtually impossible to develop a broad enough perspective to consider priorities among various government activities. The focus of such participation is to determine how that small piece of the governmental pie will be divided among various competing interests. In each case, the concern has been with particular rather than universal interests.

In addition, due to the breakdown of party, the government has become more vulnerable to the demands of these interests. The parties might have served as buffers for the government by acting as channels through which demands would have been processed and their control over the electoral process might have been a resource to balance the power of the narrower interests. Instead, with the party breakdown and the direct involvement of citizens in the bureaucracy, the government must become more responsive to individual demands.

Establishing priorities is not so crucial in a period of affluence, when all are sure to receive a piece of the pie; however, conflict over priorities becomes inevitable as the country moves from the politics of affluence to the politics of scarcity. As the shift occurs and the government lacks aggregating and mediating structures, its ability to make the hard decisions about allocation of resources may be threatened.

TYPES OF CITIZEN PARTICIPATION

So far the discussion of structuring citizen participation has focused on general criteria and dilemmas. It is also important to examine the specific kinds of activities that are labeled citizen participation and to consider what each can accomplish. The problem in discussing types of citizen participation stems from the bewildering variety of procedures and structures that are referred to as citizen participation.

All seem to agree that no single procedure or structure can accomplish the multiple expectations connoted by citizen participation. Those who have considered the procedures and structures of citizen participation in depth agree that the various processes can be differentiated by considering which goals each process would be most likely to accomplish. This section will outline briefly some of the various procedures and structures of citizen participation, and then it will examine their potential to accomplish the goals discussed earlier in this chapter, and in Chapter 3.

Electoral participation is, perhaps, the most venerable form of citizen participation in this country. The simplest manifestation is, of course, to cast a ballot. As discussed in the second chapter, American electoral history has been characterized by a consistent decrease in the legal limitations on suffrage—universal adult suffrage is now a reality. In addition to the simple act of casting a ballot, Americans have also participated in elections through various party activities, such as voting in party primaries or attending caucuses and conventions. Also Americans have worked to aid the party or candidate of their choice by taking part in such campaign activities as stuffing envelopes, canvassing door-to-door, raising or contributing money.

A major change in the traditional electoral participation occurred during the Progressive Era when the enactment of statutes in various states permitted initiative and/or referendum elections. Under such statutes, citizens are given direct authority to make government decisions, instead of remaining limited to the indirect role of merely choosing decision makers. The power of these statutes has been recently rediscovered in some states and used with renewed vigor by such citizen activists as Howard Jarvis, who successfully spearheaded California's Proposition 13 initiative.

Another major area in electoral participation that has undergone some limited experimentation has been the use of coaxial cable TV. Citizens are presented with issues and alternatives and then permitted to respond immediately via an electronic system. As in a citizen referendum, this form of participation allows citizens to vote on issues and thus take part directly in making government decisions. The electronic participation has the advantage of immediacy and ease (because there is no need to leave home); however, unlike the initiative, citizens can only respond to issues and alternatives defined by others.

A second general type of citizen participation is group participation. One of the American characteristics that amazed de Tocqueville was their tendency to be joiners,[28] which still prevails. The number of Americans who belong to politically active groups is estimated to be only between a quarter to and a third of the population, yet any examination of registered lobbyists in Congress gives testimony to the group basis of American politics. As indicated before, the major changes in the area of group politics have been the increase in interest groups, and in their tendency to focus on a single issue.[29]

Another major change in group politics has been government involvement in creating citizen interest groups. Although the government had provided the impetus in the past, especially in the agricultural area, these activities increased significantly in the sixties, with the policies designed to combat poverty in the cities. In both cases, the goal was to organize target groups who were clients of government programs. Although most of the poverty programs have been dismantled, the organization of client groups is still evident at various levels of government; for example, advisory and review boards exist to involve citizens in the decision-making processes of various government agencies. The citizens on the boards are chosen in various ways, and are not necessarily representatives of a client group or some other specific interest. At the local government level, citizens are sometimes organized into groups that represent the interests of individual neighborhoods. Often, these city citizen groups are established to act as intermediary between officials and citizens: they may act as a channel for communicating citizen interests to officials and, simultaneously, be the overseers of government actions.

A third area of citizen participation is called citizen-government contacting. The ambiguity of the label is symbolic of the wide variety of procedures and structures that have been designed to facilitate the communication process between individual citizens and their government. The traditional forms of contact have been limited: writing, phoning, or personal meetings were the primary methods an individual used to establish government contact.

In the last two decades, perhaps, the major change in citizen participation has been the enormous increase in the new forms of citizen-government contacts. For example, there are a number of procedures that governments use to solicit citizen views on policy planning and implementation: there are meetings at both the neighborhood and city-wide level, workshops and conferences on specific problem areas, surveys of citizen opinions, and ombudsmen to channel citizen demands to proper authorities.

In addition there are various procedures that the government uses to make government information accessible to citizens. These include the creation of specific communication channels such as telephone hotlines, drop-in centers, or public information programs. At the legal level, the Freedom of Information and Sunshine laws were designed to help citizens obtain information about government. Taking these policies further, some governments have established an open door policy in which citizens are encouraged to walk into project offices at any time to obtain information.

A final type of citizen participation involves actual citizen participation in the government. Although this may sound like the most radical form of citizen participation, it is as time-honored as electoral participation. In actuality, the Founding Fathers envisioned that the legislative branch of government would provide an opportunity for citizens to participate periodically in the government. It was assumed that service in the legislature (especially at the national level) would be onerous. Because of the problems of travel, and the time it would take from a man's normal occupation, they expected constant rotation among office holders.

On the contrary, of course, the national legislature has virtually become a life-long profession and the idea of citizen legislator is no longer valid. Therefore, experiments are being made with other means of bringing citizens directly into government policy making: these include placing citizen representatives on policy making boards, or hiring clients of a program to administer the program. In addition, some of the other procedures discussed before, especially the creation of citizen groups, may actually bring citizens into government decision making, if they are given adequate authority.

In many cases, governments have facilitated citizen participation by providing opportunities for access and information and by stimulating the creation of citizen groups. They have also trained citizens to participate effectively by providing them with technical assistance to develop plans and alternatives. These proposals are often in opposition to those of government agencies.

Table 4.1 is a marketing list of citizen participation procedures and structures. It is not comprehensive, nor does any one government agency employ all of these techniques. This listing was designed solely as a sample of the vast number and types of techniques that are labeled as citizen participation. It should also give the impression of a government that generally is open to citizen participation and also active in soliciting such participation. How then can citizens complain about lack of access?

Their complaint is generally that merely providing opportunities may not be adequate for the satisfactory implementation of citizen participation. Firstly, both citizens and government officials who are involved must be motivated in order to assure successful participation and that motivation may not always be present (as will be discussed later).

John Staley, City Forester of Grand Forks, North Dakota, has suggested the following general rules for the administrator attempting to foster citizen participation:

1. Administrators should believe in and mean what they are doing. Their attitude should be positive and receptive to input.
2. Administrator's role should be to lead, facilitate ideas, and supply objective information, not to manipulate.
3. All alternatives presented should be viable and possible, if selected.
4. Participants should be given adequate information beforehand.
5. Only those issues that solely affect the target population should be presented for decision making (for example, neighborhood concerns at neighborhood meetings, city-wide concerns at city-wide meetings, and so on).
6. Tailor the citizen participation structure to the target population (that is, group size, location, and so on) and to the issue to be addressed.[30]

Secondly, efforts at implementing citizen participation may still not be judged successful, if those involved bring to the participatory situation differing expectations. Thus far, this study has examined two sets of expectations that are important for evaluating citizen participation: those concerning the goals of participation and those concerning how it should be structured. The choice of technique will determine which of these expectations can be realized.

For example, bringing citizens into the policy process by placing them on official boards will allow them greater authority, which could change the policy and, possibly, their attitudes. To a certain extent a more equitable distribution of power may also be achieved, depending on which citizens are included. As indicated in the discussion of direct participation, however, there are limits to how many people can be hired or put on a policy board, so such techniques cannot be considered inclusive.

Meetings, hot-lines, drop-in centers, and similar techniques could conceivably provide inclusive participation, but the contact between officials and citizens would be transitory and focused on single issues. Thus, these techniques might help to resolve some particulars of controversy. They may not be adequate, however, for long-term change in policy or in the attitudes of citizens, and they certainly do not involve any redistribution of power.

As the government found (with some dismay) in the sixties, government-initiated citizen groups can be effective in forcing it to take particular actions. Nevertheless, no one group can be inclusive, although it is conceivable to repre-

TABLE 4.1

Participatory Mechanisms

TECHNIQUE	FUNCTION													
	Identify Attitudes and Opinions	Identify Impacted Groups	Solicit Impacted Groups	Facilitate Participation	Clarify Planning Process	Answer Citizen Questions	Disseminate Information	Generate New Ideas & Alternatives	Facilitate Advocacy	Promote Interaction Between Interest Grps.	Resolve Conflict	Plan Program and Policy Review	Change Attitudes Toward Government	Develop Support/ Minimize Opposition
Arbitration and Mediation planning	X							X		X	X			
Charrette	X			X	X	X		X		X	X	X	X	X
Citizen's Advisory Committee	X			X	X	X	X	X			X	X	X	X
Citizen Employment	X		X	X	X	X	X	X					X	X
Citizen Honoraria			X	X	X							X	X	X
Citizen Referendum	X			X							X	X	X	
Citizen Representatives on Policy-Making Bodies	X			X	X			X					X	X
Citizen Review Board				X								X		X
Citizen Surveys	X		X											
Citizen Training				X	X				X				X	
Community Technical Assistance	X			X	X			X	X					
Computer-based Techniques	Depends on specific technique chosen													
Coordinator or Coordinator-Catalyst				X	X	X				X	X		X	X
Design-In	X	X		X	X	X		X				X		X
Drop-In Centers		X		X	X	X						X	X	X
Fishbowl Planning				X	X	X	X	X			X	X	X	X

Focused Group Interview	X		X	X		X				X				
Game Simulations					X					X		X		X
Group Dynamics										X	X		X	
Hotline		X		X		X								
Interactive Cable TV	X	X	X	X			X	X				X		
Media-based Issue Balloting	X			X		X	X					X		
Meetings–Community-Sponsored	X		X	X	X	X	X	X				X		X
Meetings–Neighborhood	X		X	X	X	X	X	X				X		X
Meetings–Open Informational			X		X	X	X					X		
Neighborhood Planning Council	X			X				X	X			X		
Ombudsman		X			X	X	X					X	X	
Open Door Policy		X		X	X	X	X					X	X	
Planning Balance Sheet	X											X		
Policy Capturing	X													X
Policy Delphi	X							X						
Priority-Setting Committee	X			X								X	X	
Public Hearing		X	X	X		X	X					X		
Public Information Programs					X		X					X	X	
Random Selected Participation Groups	X		X	X				X	X			X		
Short Conference	X			X	X	X	X	X		X	X	X		X
Task Forces			X					X				X	X	X
Value Analysis	X			X								X		X
Workshops	X		X	X	X			X		X	X	X	X	X

Source: Judy B. Rosener, "A Cafeteria of Techniques and Critiques," p. 17. Reprinted from Public Management Magazine, December 1975, by special permission, © 1975, of the City Management Association.

sent all sectors of the population by groups. In this way, particular interests in society would not be systematically excluded, yet the structure of group power would most likely divide government resources among those groups rather than allocating them to a more universal public good.

Elections have not figured prominently in the recent thinking of practitioners and theorists of citizen participation, even though they can be broadly inclusive. In addition, elections put final decision-making responsibility in the hands of citizens. By expanding the use of modern technology, the role of elections could be enlarged, which might result in an increase of the direct control citizens have over government decisions. But, as indicated above, if the definition of issues remains with officials, no significant restructuring of power will result.

All of the techniques can be used to facilitate communication between the citizen and his government. If information were transmitted more clearly at the administrative level, it could result in making policy more compatible with citizen demands. If this happened at the individual level, citizens might become educated about government, which could conceivably result in a decrease of citizen alienation. These techniques may also help to assure that particular groups are not consistently excluded from contact with government. In the absence of a direct transfer of authority to citizens, for these impacts to be realized government officials must heed the information from citizens.

Essentially, the goals and techniques of participation are interrelated. Ideally, the goals should be clearly specified so that a technique can be chosen that might conceivably achieve those goals. This, of course, is rarely done. Much of the current participation is only in response to mandates from the federal government, and these do not specify the goals that participation is to achieve or the techniques to be employed. Therefore, techniques are often chosen to implement participation without clarifying what the ultimate purpose of the techniques is. This has led to a situation where goals are often implied, although, as the study has argued, the goals are no less important for not being explicit.

It appears that if participants expect broadly inclusive participation and a meaningful redistribution of power in society, they will likely be dissatisfied. The techniques that provide opportunities for large numbers of people to participate do not, at the same time, involve any transfer of decision-making authority. Going to a meeting or calling in a gripe on a hotline may be techniques accessible to all, but it should be clear that no great change may result.

SUMMARY

Chapters 3 and 4 have attempted to clarify some of the disagreements and conflicts that surround citizen participation. Not only do people have unrealistic expectations of participation, but they also have conflicting and vague notions of how it should be structured. A more explicit recognition of realistic expectations and goals is needed. The next chapter will examine the special problems involved in implementing citizen participation in the bureaucracy.

NOTES

[1] Theodore J. Lowi, *The End of Liberalism: Ideology, Policy, and the Crisis of Public Authority*, 1st ed. (New York: W. W. Norton, 1969), p. 290.

[2] Aaron Wildavsky, *The Politics of the Budgetary Process*, 2nd ed. (Boston: Little, Brown, 1974), p. 167.

[3] James Madison, "Federalist #10," in *The Federalist Papers* (New York: The New American Library, 1961), p. 81.

[4] Ibid., p. 82.

[5] Ibid.

[6] Lowi, *The End of Liberalism*, p. 289.

[7] Bernard R. Berelson, Paul F. Lazarsfeld, and William N. McPhee, *Voting* (Chicago: University of Chicago Press, 1954), p. 314.

[8] Gabriel Almond and Sidney Verba, *The Civic Culture* (Boston: Little, Brown, 1965), p. 341.

[9] Hannah Pitkin, *The Concept of Representation* (Berkeley: University of California Press, 1967), chapter 4.

[10] J. David Greenstone and Paul E. Peterson, *Race and Authority in Urban Politics: Community Participation and the War on Poverty* (New York: Russell Sage Foundation, 1973), p. 167.

[11] Sidney Verba and Norman H. Nie, *Participation in America: Political Democracy and Social Equality* (New York: Harper & Row, 1972), p. 31.

[12] Kenneth J. Arrow, *Social Choice and Individual Values* (New York: John Wiley & Sons, 1951).

[13] Robert Dahl, *A Preface to Democratic Theory* (Chicago: University of Chicago Press, 1956), chapter 4.

[14] Emmett S. Redford, *Democracy in the Administrative State* (New York: Oxford University Press, 1969), p. 6.

[15] Peter Bachrach, *The Theory of Democratic Elitism: A Critique* (Boston: Little, Brown, 1967), p. 92.

[16] Robert J. Pranger, *The Eclipse of Citizenship: Power and Participation in Contemporary Politics* (New York: Holt, Rinehart and Winston, 1968), p. 45.

[17] Robert Sherrill, "Instant Electorate," *Playboy*, November, 1968, pp. 155+; Lawrence Mosher, "Cable Television–It Can Work Two Ways," *National Journal*, February 23, 1980, p. 310.

[18] Peter Bachrach and Morton Baratz, *Power and Poverty* (New York: Oxford University Press, 1970).

[19] Ibid.

[20] E. E. Schattschneider, *The Semi-Sovereign People* (New York: Holt, Rinehart and Winston, 1960), chapter 4.

[21] Jane J. Mansbridge, "The Limits of Friendship," in *Participation in Politics*, eds. J. Roland Pennock and John W. Chapman (New York: Lieber-Atherton, 1975), pp. 246–275.

[22] Madison, "Federalist #10," p. 82.

[23] Lowi, *The End of Liberalism*, p. 155.

[24] Ibid.

[25] Redford, *Democracy in the Administrative State*, p. 30.

[26] James Q. Wilson, "Planning and Politics: Citizen Participation in Urban Renewal," in *Urban Renewal: People, Politics and Planning*, eds. Jewel Bellush and Murray Hausknecht (Garden City, N.Y.: Doubleday, 1967), pp. 287–301.

[27] Wildavsky, *The Politics of the Budgetary Process*, p. 167.

[28] Alexis deTocqueville, *Democracy in America*, ed. and abr. by Richard D. Heffner (New York: New American Library of World Literature, 1956), pp. 198–202.

[29] Norman J. Ornstein and Shirley Elder, *Interest Groups, Lobbying and Policy-making* (Washington, D.C.: Congressional Quarterly Press, 1978), p. 65.

[30] John Staley, "Bureaucratic Politics and Citizen Participation," Presentation to Political Science Colloquium, University of North Dakota, March 27, 1981.

5

CITIZEN PARTICIPATION IN THE BUREAUCRACY

It should be clear to everyone that bureaucracies are becoming increasingly important parts of our lives. What transpires in our passage from the cradle (which is constructed according to safety regulations) to the grave (whose location and standards are determined by health regulations) is increasingly regulated by universal standards that are established by large, impersonal organizations. The increasing predominance of bureaucracies is a result of the growth and concomitant complexity of society. It seems safe to assume that neither characteristic of society will be greatly reduced in the near future, so bureaucratic control will remain a ubiquitous and inevitable part of our lives.

A major problem associated with bureaucracies is our belief that we are unable to control them, even though they control us. The organizations are complex and distant, and citizens feel powerless in the face of regulations that are ordained by the bureaucracy in a modern version of the tablets being brought down from on high. The frustration resulting from not being able to control bureaucracies is compounded by the fact that more and more of them are public, rather than private. Since the United States designates itself a democracy, the implication is that citizens and their elected representatives should in some way control the bureaucracy. This chapter will discuss the growth of the bureaucracy, the problems resulting from this growth and, finally, how citizen participation can be a means of gaining democratic accountability of the bureaucracy.

GROWTH OF PUBLIC BUREAUCRACY

According to Max Weber, "The decisive reason for the advance of bureaucratic organization has always been its purely technical superiority over any other form of organization"[1] The ideal bureaucracy has five basic characteristics which create efficiency and rationality in the modern world. Unfortunately, as will be noted below, these characteristics also contain the seeds of the "bureaucracy problem" that plagues modern society. The characteristics of the ideal bureaucracy are: division of labor, hierarchy, formal rules and procedures, personal objectivity, and full time, merit employment.[2] The first characteristic, division of labor, allows bureaucrats to specialize and develop expertise. Hierarchy enables the organization to establish clear lines of authority and to fix responsibility. The development of formal rules and procedures facilitates stability and provides uniformity and regularity in interpersonal relations. Objectivity, the fourth "ideal" characteristic, results in detached, rational, impersonal decisions: favoritism is thereby eliminated. Finally, full time, merit employment provides a basis for the development of loyalty and professionalism.

The need for rational bureaucracy increased as the nation grew and became more complex in reaction to changes in the economic, social and political fabric. The size and shape of the public bureaucracy has paralleled the development of the United States from a relatively homogeneous, independent nation of farmers to a heterogeneous, interdependent industrial and organizational society. In the days of the Republic, the function of the central government was limited. The major functions of the federal government were to provide a stable monetary system (Treasury Department) and foreign and domestic tranquility (State, War, Navy, and Attorney General). The limited administrative system accords with Hamilton's conception of the executive branch set forth in *Federalist #72*, which was to perform the "details" of administration.[3] The original bureaucracy was staffed by a relatively apolitical group of the rich, well-born, and able. The staffing system was changed from neutral competence to political allegiance with Jackson's institution of the "spoils system," but the tasks of the bureaucracy remained limited. The politicization of the bureaucracy led to favoritism and a great deal of corruption, which was most rampant at the local level. These urban bureaucracies grew, not only because of the need for services, but also because of the desire of machine bosses to provide patronage jobs. Growth at the federal level was restrained until the last part of the nineteenth century. After the Civil War, with rapid industrialization and the concentration of capital, the growth of the public bureaucracy was part of a societal change. As Presthus has noted:

> Beginning about 1875, social, economic, and political trends in the United States prepared the way for the "organizational society," characterized by large-scale bureaucratic institutions in virtually

> every social area. The master trends included the separation of ownership from management; increasing size and concentration in business, industry, and eleemosynary fields; the decline of competition as the financial resources required for entry in almost every sector became prohibitive; the development of a political economy; and the emergence of an employee society.[4]

The growth of government in the "organizational society" has been attributed to many forces. Galbraith views the growth as part of a need for balance or equilibrium for society. As industry concentrated and grew, government also had to grow to act as a "countervailing power."[5] Lowi also traces the role of government in the emerging political economy of the late nineteenth century and argues that changes in society created disequilibrium and a breakdown of self-regulation and social control. "*Rationality applied to social control is administration.* Administration may indeed be the *sine qua non* of modernity."[6] This in turn results in a change from laissez faire government to positive government. In addition, it led to institutionalized pluralism, whereby the heterogeneous society could be assured "legitimate" access to the minions of power.[7]

Weber sums up the inevitable growth of the administrative state as follows:

> . . . [b]ureaucratization is a function of increasing possession of goods used for consumption, and of an increasingly sophisticated technique of fashioning exernal life—a technique which corresponds to the opportunities provided by such wealth. This reacts upon the standard of living and makes for an increasing indispensibility of organized, collective, inter-local, and thus bureaucratic, provision for the most varied wants, which previously were either unknown, or were satisfied locally or by a private economy.[8]

The growth of the federal bureaucracy after 1880 is characterized by two factors: neutral competence and clientelism. Since the initial growth of the bureaucracy occurred during the reformist Progressive Era, the effect of the Progressive Movement was to emphasize neutral competence in the bureaucracy, which resulted, for example, in the establishment of a civil service system by the Pendleton Act of 1883. The size of the bureaucracy was not necessarily affected but the desire to depoliticize it was affirmed, as was the desire to create an effective and efficient structure to deal with the increasingly complex nature of society.

In another effort to establish an apolitical bureaucracy that would simultaneously maximize neutral competence and deal with economic and social problems, the federal government established the first of many independent regulatory agencies, the Interstate Commerce Commission (ICC) in 1887. Commissioners, chosen by the President with the advice and consent of the Senate, were to represent both political parties and remain insulated from political pressures by being given fixed terms. Expertise was necessary because of the technical issues involved, so these complex issues were insulated from the influence of politicians. "Social, economic, and political control could be firmly established only by the routinized and authoritative administration of public policy that his [Weber's] model of the bureaucracy described."[9] The bureaucrats, who were now sheltered from political pressures, would be vested with power to control the development of transportation in America (ICC); the business practices (The Federal Trade Commission) and other private activities.

The second characteristic of bureaucratic expansion in the second half of the nineteenth century was the growth of clientelism.[10] The establishment of the Department of Agriculture in 1862 marked the beginning of an era of rapid bureaucratic growth and a shift in bureaucratic organization from one of purpose, for example, War, State, Treasury, and so forth, to one of clientele recognition. This trend was to continue with the establishment of the Department of Labor in 1888, and a separate Department of Commerce in 1913.

The bureaucracy expanded slowly at the beginning of the twentieth century and it was not until the great depression and the New Deal that there was another surge in the growth of the bureaucracy.[11] As industrialization had forced government into a major role in economic development, so the great depression led to an increase in government activity in the economic sphere and in the social area. People who had always provided for themselves and their families were no longer able to do so, and private relief agencies were swamped—the government was the only feasible solution. The New Deal created a precedent for social intervention and the expectations of the proper role of government have changed as a result of this. Once the government had created programs, and beneficiaries, it was difficult to cease this activity, although the move toward deregulation of business in the late 1970s and early 1980s is a notable exception. What has occurred during this time, however, is that there has been a shift in government activities, which accounts for the stability in the size of the federal government workforce. Meanwhile, the state and local governments have grown in size by 117 percent in the last 20 years.[12] Government bureaucracies remain involved in all aspects of our lives and there is little reason to expect any significant change.

It is unlikely that the bureaucracy had significant power prior to the end of the nineteenth century. While some bureaucrats may have had a disproportionate amount of power, the role of the bureaucracy itself was limited. The growth of bureaucratic power was an unanticipated consequence of the growth in size, for the underlying premise of the initial growth phase at the end of the nineteenth century was still that bureaucrats were to function as apolitical actors. Woodrow Wilson clearly distinguished the role of the bureaucracy in the political system: "Public Administration is the detailed and systematic execution of the public law."[13] He also establishes a political-administrative dichotomy. "The field of administration is the field of business. It is removed from the hurry and strife of politics."[14] The Civil Service and Independent Regulatory agencies may have insulated bureaucrats from direct political pressures, but they were making political decisions. The polite fiction (that the bureaucrat was involved only in questions of means and not ends) provided a source of power for the bureaucracy. The reformist aphorism, "There is no Republican or Democratic way to pave a street" belies a more basic question: "whose street will be paved?"

> Through the conversion of practical questions turning around social norms into technical questions, purportedly solvable only by experts, bureaucracy takes on an apolitical appearance. This hides the fact that it continues to make political decisions, though these are now handily removed from public participation.[15]

This is not to argue that power will necessarily be abused, but the assumption that bureaucracy is neutral does not make it so. The technical superiority of the bureaucracy, as well as its goals of rationality, efficiency, and stability, place the bureaucracy in a strategic position in modern society.

The American political system, which is based on separate powers, creates a power vacuum that the bureaucracy could fill. The American political system is designed to prevent any one branch of government from obtaining too much power. Considering the American political culture at the time the Constitution was written, it is not surprising that the Constitution created a government that is cumbersome and slow to act. Because the Founding Fathers feared centralized power, they built a system of checks and balances that required multiple consensus by different constituencies. The result was deliberate, incremental policy making. Ironically, the checks and balances system is one of the major reasons for the growth of bureaucratic power.

The absence of strong, centralized parties also slows down the process. If there were a disciplined party structure, it might serve to bridge the gap between institutions. A "responsible party system" could present coherent policies that would be passed and implemented virtually automatically; however, given our fragmented party system, policy making becomes slow and arduous.

Society requires faster action at the end of the twentieth century than it did in the eighteenth century. The day-to-day work of government must continue, even while major policy pronouncements are being deliberated. In order for the political branches to reach compromise positions, it often means that policies will have only general statements of purpose, which are likely to be vague compromises with many specifics to be worked out at a later time, when policy is implemented. It is the bureaucracy that does the implementing, and political power shifts from the political to the bureaucratic arena.[16]

The checks and balances system also devolves power to the bureaucracy for another reason. Since politicians are involved in all areas of policy making, they must often depend on others for the information necessary to make informed choices. To a large extent, it is the bureaucracy that monopolizes that information.

> This is not to suggest that once elected, chief executives and legislators lack power and influence. Rather, their capacity to alter policy outcomes is mitigated by the scarcity of their attentiveness to any given policy issue and by the necessarily serial nature of their consideration. They are further hampered in their capacity to make decisions by a set of factors inherent to professionalized bureaucracy. The factors center around the complex division of specialized knowledge into enduring patterns of bureaucratic institutionalization.[17]

The bureaucracy, then, emerges as the major force in governmental policy making and implementation in the 1980s.

PROBLEMS OF BUREAUCRACY

The growth of the bureaucracy has been a mixed blessing. We have traded "technical superiority" and "neutral competence" for decreased democratic accountability and increased distrust and alienation. It appears that we cannot live with or without bureaucracy. Some argue that there is a paradox inherent in the characteristics of the ideal bureaucracy: while it creates order and stability in our complex society, these same characteristics create an uncontrollable monster which dehumanizes all who come in contact with it. There appears to be a general feeling in America that somehow we must regain control of our lives through control over the bureaucracy. In a prescient observation made many years ago, Max Weber warned that:

> Under normal conditions the power position of a fully developed bureaucracy is always overtowering. The 'political master' finds himself in the position of the 'dilettante' who stands opposite the 'expert,' facing the official who stands within the management of administration.[18]

Many times the political master attempts to keep the bureaucracy in its place by creating a smokescreen to hide the real problems. Much of the discontent with the bureaucracy is little more than political rhetoric aimed at an amorphous entity. One seldom hears of successful programs that were designed and implemented by bureaucrats–successful programs seem to be designed by politicians. On the other hand, when programs fail or scandals occur, it is rarely because of elected officials. Program failure is generally blamed on an inept bureaucratic administration and the faceless bureaucrat becomes the whipping boy for politicians and the polity. People complain about the growth of government and the proliferation of programs that breed bureaucratic expansion and continue to intrude on our lives. They advocate a reduced bureaucracy and the end of needless programs, which, unfortunately, help others. Programs that are essential for the growth, stability, and well-being of society (that is, those that benefit us) must continue, and a sufficient bureaucracy is needed to administer them. In order to monitor programs for fraud and waste, however, bureaucrats should not ask us embarrassing and time-consuming questions. The point is that the bureaucracy is often placed in a compromising situation, and much of the current malaise and distrust is unfair. We often blame controversial political problems on bureaucrats: for example, educational bureaucracies face impossible situations when dealing with problems of busing and sex education, and police bureaucracies are criticized for enforcing anti-marijuana, vice, and gambling laws rather than catching crooks.

There are also very real problems to be faced in maintaining democratic control while coping with vast bureaucratic structures. The myth of an apolitical, professional bureaucracy is a weapon that is used to free bureaucracy from democratic control. In a classic study of government in New York City, Sayre and Kaufman argue that the most important strategy a bureaucracy can use to gain autonomy is to abhor "political" or "special interest" interference. "Once armed with this status, the organized bureaucracy can assert boldly, . . . a claim to freedom from supervision."[19] Since bureaucrats are political and do make policy, accountability is a problem: ". . . [Each] agency shapes important public policies, yet the leadership of each is relatively self-perpetuating and not readily subject to controls of any higher authority."[20] And, if bureaucracies affect policy making, they have an even greater influence on policy implementation.

> It is in the execution that the bureaucrats have their most nearly complete monopoly and their greatest autonomy in affecting policy. They give shape and meaning to the official decisions and they do so under conditions favorable to them. Here the initiative and discretion lie in their hands; others must influence them.[21]

Access to the bureaucracy is generally limited to those who possess an expertise. In addition, the maze-like hierarchy and structure frighten the uninitiated, which means that the special interests often have preferred access. "The flaw in the pluralist heaven is that the heavenly chorus has an upper-class accent."[22]

Among others, Freeman, Rourke and Lowi argue that bureaucrats and interest groups often ally themselves with one another because of common interests.[23] Special interests come to Congressional committees and subcommittees to press their demands. Dodd and Schott note that Congress is becoming increasingly specialized due to the transfer of power to subcommittees whose raison d'etre is to oversee a bureaucratic agency. Bureaucrats are enlisted to expand and enhance the committee's power by eliciting support from interest groups in front of a Congressional subcommittee, which is generally predisposed to aid these groups and expand programs.[24] This tripartite relationship is often known as the "iron triangle," and public interest is lost to the special interests.[25] Although the bureaucracy might be expected to cooperate with powerful interests in order to maintain and enhance itself, there is the danger that some of its other clients might lose in the process. The support of the powerful interests is essential, however, and the result is unequal accessibility and, perhaps, service.

Accountability is not only a problem for the general public and the clients, but also for the head of the executive branch, the president. It can be argued that some of the excesses of the Nixon Presidency were caused by his frustration at being unable to control the bureaucracy.[26] Heclo and Seidman both document the difficulty that faces political appointees who try to control the career civil service.[27] In one study of high level bureaucrats, Aberbach and Rochman find bureaucratic attitudes to be out of step with a conservative presidency.[28] They conclude that in a government with multiple lines of authority one might expect ". . . administrators to safeguard the interests of their particular agencies and to promote their own conceptions of proper public policy. . . ."[29]

The so-called "neutral principles" may not be neutral at all, for the titular head of the bureaucracy and his political appointees may be little more than boxes at the top of an organization chart. Many years ago, James Burnham wrote of the danger of a new managerial class that would use its knowledge and position for its own purposes.[30] The general maze-like organization of our government, and the bureaucracy, in particular, make fixing responsibility all but impossible. Does the bureaucracy respond to the President, Congress, special interests, or the general public? And should it? There could be a danger of the bureaucracy playing each monitor off against another, until a situation is created where no one is responsible–no one decides anything–things just happen.

Those characteristics of bureaucracy that facilitate its dominant position simultaneously create difficulty in a democratic society. Participation in government and in control over one's life are deemed essential to self-fulfillment, yet the ideal bureaucracy stresses rationality and impersonality, which results in dehumanizing both bureaucrat and citizen. Hummel argues that a gap develops between the bureaucracy and the rest of society on five bases: power-politically; culturally; psychologically; socially; and linguistically.[31] In other words, inherent in the nature of the bureaucratic organization is the powerlessness of the individual—bureaucracy controls the public, it does not serve it. The individual is apt to feel alienated in a society dominated by large bureaucracies, unless mediating structures exist or are developed.[32] Hummel argues that, culturally, a new set of norms develops which estrange the bureaucracy from the citizenry. Efficiency and control become preeminent and compassion ceases to exist. Psychologically, the bureaucrat is divorced from society and structures interactions, internally and externally, on the basis of hierarchy, which creates dependency-dominance relationships. Socially the bureaucrat depersonalizes his contacts to facilitate rational efficient behavior. Linguistically, also, the bureaucratic process separates bureaucrat and citizen by talking about "cases" not people. While this negative picture may be extreme, it is clear that the bureaucracy can, in many ways, be dysfunctional.

Rules, which are actually designed to facilitate efficiency and equity, all too often become ends in themselves through the process of goal displacement. In a mechanical environment, it becomes easy to see oneself as a cog in a machine, and human reason can give way to automatic responses that dehumanize both bureaucrats and their clients. Rules and routines may produce another unfortunate consequence. The "neutral procedures" may result in unintended inequities in the administration of various programs. Levy et al. note that, ". . . benevolent norms . . . , which ought to help everyone, end up helping some more than others. . . . [Many] 'neutral' decision rules are not neutral. They have a class bias."[33] In his general review of the service delivery literature, however, Jones concludes that by and large bureaucracies do not consciously discriminate against poor and minority neighborhoods.[34] However, he found that there is systematic bias in some agencies. This is the result of rules that require, for example, equal garbage collection in all neighborhoods. There is a weight rule, though, which benefits the wealthier neighborhoods, and an extra effort rule, which benefits center city neighborhoods.

> Both the weight rule and the extra effort rule were formulated according to and justified in terms of technical criteria for effective and efficient delivery of public services. . . . The model of a goal-oriented bureaucracy with technical and goal-related implementing rules producing distributional effects that for the most part, are unintended, unanticipated, and often unrecognized is . . . appropriate. . . . If you are a beneficiary, that's your good luck. If you are hurt, that's too bad. The rules are rational.[35]

Jones makes one additional point, which is especially relevant to this study. He notes that many agencies have a demand rule that establishes a criterion for service distribution based on citizen initiated contacts. The standard model of participation indicates that higher socioeconomic people are more likely to participate than those with low socioeconomic status. While this model seems to hold for most types of participation because of increased skills possessed by the higher socioeconomic status (SES) group, there seems to be little impact of SES in contacting government officials. Verba and Nie note only a .07 Pearson's correlation.[36] Jones notes a slight tendency of poor neighborhoods to make less contacts; however, he argues that the magnitude of the problems also has a significant impact on citizen initiated contacts.[37]

The fact is that citizens have, at the very least, a high degree of ambivalence toward the bureaucracy. With the demand for services, it would appear that there is more need for an organizational society, not less. If growth of the federal bureaucracy and its programs were reversed, we could only expect greater growth at the state and local level. At the same time, as we become more dependent on government bureaucracy, we feel a growing need to increase its democratic accountability. Citizens feel that power in society is being dominated illegitimately by politically irresponsible organizations. They also feel that policies produced by bureaucracies are not responsive to their needs, and, they feel alienated from a political system they neither understand nor trust. Citizen participation is expected to resolve these problems. As other democratic controls falter, it is inevitable that demands should be made for increased opportunity to participate.

REASONS FOR PARTICIPATION IN THE BUREAUCRACY[38]

Although not always made explicit, justifications for increasing citizen participation in the bureaucracy may be inferred. (1) Citizens know as well, or perhaps better, than bureaucrats what constitutes desirable policy. This is usually defended by arguing that bureaucrats lose touch with reality. The people on the other hand are close to the problems, and are better able to evaluate solutions. (2) Because the government is increasingly large and complex, due primarily to the growth of bureaucracy, citizens must be encouraged and aided in establishing contacts to counter the otherwise inevitable citizen alienation. The argument here is that growth of government has made it difficult for the citizen to know how to impact on decision-making. If the citizen is not encouraged to participate, and if provisions are not made to facilitate that participation, the citizenry will become increasingly alienated and may become a destabilizing or destructive force. It is significant that underlying both of these premises is a certain distrust of the bureaucracy, and a belief that participation should be an important component of bureaucratic decision making. Stated in the extreme, bureaucrats are believed to be incapable of making good decisions, at the same time they are believed to impede those who should be involved in the decision-making process. The resolution appears to be in forcing bureaucrats to yield some power to citizens; thus citizen participation would be an ultimate means to assure bureaucratic responsibility. This represents the pure democratic ideal of having those affected by decisions take part in the formulation of those decisions.

ASSUMPTIONS

There are several assumptions that underlie the analysis of the feasibility of citizen participation in bureaucracies. The first assumption is that both the bureaucrats and the citizen participants are self-interested. A corollary of this assumption is that the interests differ at times and conflict can be expected. This does not, however, rule out the possibility of altruism on the part of either citizen or bureaucrat. In fact, the "New Public Administration" makes an explicit appeal for bureaucratic behavior to become more clearly aligned with citizen interests.[39] If these appeals were heeded, the degree of conflict between the citizenry and the bureaucracy could become low or nonexistent. However, there is a need to encourage greater coordination of the bureaucrats' and citizens' values, which implicitly acknowledges that such value congruence does not yet exist.

A second assumption is that the degree to which there is conflict between bureaucrats and citizens is important. Bureaucrats have access to resources that they could manipulate to control the impact of citizen participation on bureaucratic decision making. Of course, citizen participation in bureaucracy is mandated by legislation; however, bureaucrats can often establish the structures for channeling citizen participation by writing rules to govern it. For example, by creating boards composed of disinterested citizens, or by specifying that participation is to be "advisory" only, bureaucrats can significantly decrease the potential for citizen impact. It is for this reason that the orientation of the bureaucrat is considered such an important factor in achieving effective citizen participation. Therefore this section focuses primarily on the bureaucratic perspective on citizen participation.

A third assumption is that bureaucrats make their decisions based on certain basic premises of decision making. Herbert Simon has developed that concept of decision premise in *Administrative Behavior.*[40] (The usage here differs somewhat from his.) He argues that, to any decision situation, bureaucrats bring multiple decision premises. The argument here is that there are fundamental premises that are components of virtually all decision situations in bureaucracies. Simon's argument, in fact, lends support to this latter conceptualization by specifying efficiency and identification as ". . . the two most important special classes of decision premises."[41] Because some premises are significant only for specific decisions, they are transitory, while others are more fundamental and, hence, enduring, ubiquitous components of bureaucratic decision making. It is this level of decision premise that is most important. As noted by observers of bureaucratic behavior, four premises have been inferred from regularities in bureaucratic decision making: expertise, routinization and regularity, efficiency, and self-maintenance. Further substantiation for the importance of premises will be given later in a more extensive discussion of each premise.

PREMISES OF BUREAUCRATIC DECISION MAKING

To begin an examination of the viability of citizen participation in bureaucratic operations, it is important to understand the basic premises of bureaucratic decision making and the implications of these premises for viable citizen participation. An initial premise of bureaucratic decision making is the belief in the importance of expertise. Weber argued that one primary advantage of bureaucratic organization was its provision for specialization: "The more complicated and specialized modern culture becomes, the more its external supporting apparatus demands the personally detached the strictly 'objective' expert. . . ."[42] Hiring is supposedly governed by a concern for skills and ability, rather than the more irrational concerns such as religion, status, family, and others. The search for expertise governs, in part, the organizational structure of the bureau. As Simon writes:

> To gain the advantages of specialized skill in a large organization, the work of the organization is subdivided, so far as possible, in such a way that all processes requiring a particular skill can be performed by persons possessing that skill. Likewise, to gain the advantages of expertise in decision making, the responsibility for decisions is allocated, so far as possible, in such a way that decisions requiring particular knowledge or skill will rest with individuals possessing that knowledge or skill. This involves a subdivision of the decisions governing the organization into numerous component decisions, and a restriction of the activities of each member of the organization to a very few of these components.[43]

Thus, jobs are factored into specific functions to enable—indeed to force—one to become intimately and completely informed on specialized aspects of a task. In sum, the bureaucrat is expected to be an expert. As both quotes illustrate, expertise is expected to be the basis from which decisions are made.

In many circumstances, the belief in the importance of bureaucratic expertise conflicts with the functioning of citizen participation in bureaucracy. It was argued before that citizens are often close to problems and, therefore, may have more information and expertise than do bureaucrats. The bureaucrats, however, often do not perceive citizens as experts, and are unwilling to be tolerant of citizen participation. In actuality, the bureaucrats may sometimes be right, for citizens may be guided by uninformed opinions, or may not know all aspects of a problem. They may not have the depth and breadth of understanding that the bureaucrats can accrue by working with a problem over time. Bureaucratic experts can become quite suspicious of citizens who are lacking in expert knowledge.

> The beneficiaries have no importance. They probably do not understand the complexities of the problem, their technical awareness is minimal, and who has the time to worry about them? To consult them is to subject oneself to the indignities of political pressure. It is not atypical for experts to avoid any contact with the ultimate beneficiaries of their plans. . . . Ultimately, the revolt of beneficiaries who do not seem to understand the subtleties of the economic or social situations in which they find themselves, leads the expert to believe that planning has to be imposed from the top because the beneficiaries at the bottom cannot perceive the outcome of their own actions. He becomes increasingly impatient with democratic politics and insists that in time of crisis leadership has to be reaffirmed.[44]

Further problems are caused by the fact that the bureaucrat often establishes his worth in an organization by being an expert.[45] If he were to accept guidance from a citizen (qualified or not), then his status would be endangered. In addition, the citizens' views could conflict with those of the bureaucrat and, as counter experts they would be seen as a threat to the status quo. Nevertheless, if a citizen does have recognized expertise, bureaucrats will more likely be tolerant of his input, for two reasons: the shared expertise would create a common bond between bureaucrat and citizen, and therefore the gulf noted above would no longer be present; and citizens would have viable resources that could be used to do battle with the bureaucrats.

A second basic premise of bureaucratic decision making is regularity and routinization. Many of the components of Weber's ideal bureaucracy are designed to provide regular and routine procedures, for instance he argues for ". . . the principle of fixed and official jurisdictional areas, which are generally ordered by rules . . . , a firmly ordered system of super- and subordination . . . , written documents ('the files') which are preserved in their original or draught form."[46] Hierarchical structures, clear lines of authority, regular rules and procedures, and organized record-keeping provide stability. For instance, the hierarchical structures and lines of command are established to clarify where legitimate authority lies. Rules and regulations are established to limit ad hoc decision making and assure regularity in decisions. In addition, bureaucratic organizations establish extensive record keeping facilities to provide continuity. The very fact that these organizations establish standard operating procedures indicates the degree to which continuity and regularity are valued. One of the primary values of such organizations is that they provide a set of regularized expectations in a complex and everchanging environment. For the most part, individual bureaucrats value the routinization and regularity of organizations since they are characteristics that facilitate doing one's job well by stabilizing procedures and expectations. As Simon argues, organizational routine, like habit on the individual level, ". . . permits similar stimuli or situations to be met with similar responses or reactions, without the need for a conscious re-thinking of the decision to bring about the proper action."[47]

The effect of routinization may of course be a certain rididity in the functioning of a bureau, for once established, routines are difficult to change.[48] On the one hand, routinization may facilitate citizen impact, since knowing the hierarchy would make it easier for citizens to pinpoint who is responsible for various actions or programs. Regular rules and procedures would make it easier for citizens to learn the rules of the game, which would increase their potential for becoming effective players. On the other hand, the rigidity and inflexibility help to maintain the status quo. Because citizen participation is often ad hoc, it may be difficult to approach an organization committed to regularized procedures. In a study of the Community Action Program, Greenstone and Peterson found that bureaucratic routine was antithetical to the goal of fostering citizen participation:

> Bureaucratic requirements are not always consistent with organizational missions, particularly when the purpose of an organization is to foster democratic participation. A bureaucracy whose very structure requires rationalization runs contrary to the requirements of participation. . . . In particular bureaucratic routinization depends on well defined programs, specific prior training, and well delineated administrative activities. . . . Rationality and spontaneity in fact are inherently in tension with each other.[49]

Such inflexibility of procedure may also imply an unwillingness to alter programs. Graham Allison notes that if external forces demand a change in goals, the goal attainment process, itself, may rely on former procedures, which are antithetical to the new goals.[50] Usually, citizens are not motivated to political action by a desire to support the routine actions, but rather by a desire to complain about past actions or to demand new programs. In both these cases, citizen participation would be aimed toward creating change in programs or procedures, which could conflict with the goals of the bureau.

A third premise of bureaucratic decision making is efficiency. This is, in fact, the ultimate goal toward which both expertise and routinization are aimed. The argument is that hiring the best person and establishing the best procedures will assure the most efficient operation. Weber argued that "The decisive reason for the advance of bureaucratic organization . . ." was its superior efficiency.[51]

And Simon argues that, ". . . in the factual aspects of decision making, the administrator must be guided by the criterion of efficiency.[52] Citizen participation may prevent maximum efficiency by impeding the "best way" of doing things. Any requirement that forces consultation with additional people may slow the decision-making process, especially if the additional people have no special skills or knowledge, which could lead to better decisions. As indicated before, however, citizens are not normally experts, or, at least, not perceived as such by bureaucrats. Consulting with citizens in decision making is costly in both time and manpower because they must be instructed about problems, alternative solutions, and possible consequences. In addition, at least in the short run, citizens are probably unfamiliar with established procedures and may alter the routine, which itself slows decision making. As Greenstone and Peterson argue, citizen participation, ". . . insofar as it broadens influence over policy formation and invokes the amateur's enthusiasm, inevitably leads to confusion, delay, inefficiency, and, perhaps, even to outright corruption."[53]

A final premise of bureaucratic decision making is self-maintenance. This is perhaps most clearly stated by James Q. Wilson in *Political Organizations*:

> . . . the behavior of persons who lead or speak for an organization can best be understood in terms of their efforts to maintain and enhance the organization and their position in it. . . . Whatever else organizations seek, they seek to survive.[54]

It is significant to note that Wilson couples the goals of maintenance and enhancement, even though, in many ways, they conflict because maintenance implies stability and enhancement implies change. The latter goal also conflicts with the premise of routinization and regularity, as discussed before, since routinization is intended to create stability. The conflict may be best understood by realizing that bureaucracies do not exist in a vacuum. It was argued above that bureaus prefer to function with routinized and regularized procedures, for the regularity makes it easier for an individual to perform his job. In fact, Thompson has characterized attempts to regularize intra-bureaucratic operations as a "search for certainty."[55] As he notes, achieving certainty necessitates that the bureau be closed to inputs from the environment, and if not, that the inputs be predictable. To assure regularity and routinization, bureaus would attempt to "privatize" their operations and thus seal off all environmental inputs that are not predictable.[56]

Bureaucracies, however, cannot be totally closed to environmental influences. Relevant components of the bureaucratic environment may be conceptualized as superiors (executive and legislature), clientele, and the general public. Crises, changing technologies, and political developments, for example, affect those who are significant components of the bureaucratic environment and they, in turn, will manifest those changes in their dealings with the bureau. For example, changes in the economy of the country may affect the level of funds appropriated by the legislature for the functioning of the bureau. Succession in the executive may affect the level of support expected from the executive and may even mean a change in the leadership of the bureau itself. Technological changes or economic changes may affect the level and type of demands expected from the bureau's clients. Crises or publicity campaigns may affect the levels of awareness and satisfaction among the general public. In the first of these cases, there is little the bureau could do to isolate itself from environmental influences. The bureau has no control to stop legislative or executive actions relevant to the bureau. Only by increasing its interaction with the superiors by bargaining or compromising, for example, can the bureau hope to affect legislative or executive decisions. The bureau may in fact try to isolate itself from the demands and concern of the clientele and the general public, but such an attempt may be potentially dangerous. If sufficiently aroused, either of these groups may impress their displeasure on the executive and legislature, on whom, as noted, the bureau is dependent for support.

This discussion illustrates that it is not only impossible for the bureau to isolate itself totally from the environment, but it may be very unwise for a bureau to attempt it because isolation may conflict with the premise of bureaucratic self-maintenance. Therefore, to maintain itself, the bureau must interact with the environment. In sum, as Thompson writes, "Paradoxically, the administrative process must reduce uncertainty but at the same time search for flexibility."[57] In other words, as argued before, bureaus want to establish standard routines, but have to be flexible enough to adapt to the environment in order to maintain themselves.

It can be assumed that organizations, like the individuals of which they are composed, when forced to change, will try to structure that change to be as favorable to themselves as possible. The changes may be either programmatic or structural. Programmatic changes can include new programs and/or alteration of existing programs. Programs may be narrowed to increase particularized support or, alternatively, broadened to create generalized support. In extremes, programs that are no longer popularly supported may even be eliminated. Seidman argues that organizations will also undergo structural reorganization, if they believe such a change will put them in a better bargaining position vis-a-vis their environment.[58] The basic point is, however, that such changes are stimulated by environmental change and the strategy of adaptation is dictated by the goal of increasing political support to assure persistence and expansion in the future.

This strategy has significant implications for citizen participation. On the one hand, citizen participants may be seen as a destabilizing force and, thus, bureaucrats seeking to maintain stability and the status quo may attempt to insulate themselves against its effects. On the other hand, bureaucrats may in fact see citizens as useful resources in battles with other elements of the environment. In that case, bureaucrats may foster participation to recruit citizens' support.

In general, it appears that in attempting to conform to the predominant dictates of decision making in his profession, the bureaucrat must of necessity see citizen participation as an anomaly. And yet, for the last two decades, government mandates have required increasing involvement by citizens in the functioning of bureaucracies, especially at the local level. The next chapter will examine the extent to which this participation has overcome the barriers discussed here and has achieved the goals of participation.

SUMMARY

Political, social, economic and technological change in the last one hundred years has led the United States into an organizational society. Bureaucracies, because of their technical superiority, have grown in size and power. In the public sector, especially, this has not been an unmixed blessing. Many argue that bureaucracies are not accountable to the public. The result of this is increasing dissatisfaction with the services the bureaucracy provides and increasing alienation. Further, some argue that the nature of bureaucracy favors the status quo, which perpetuates the distinctions between the haves and the have-nots in our society.

Citizen participation in the bureaucracy is seen by many as the single most important remedy to the bureaucracy problem. Premises of bureaucratic decision making may limit the impacts of citizen participation in a bureaucratic context. The next two chapters examine some of the impacts of citizen participation.

NOTES

[1] H. H. Gerth and C. Wright Mills, eds. and trans., *From Max Weber: Essays in Sociology* (New York: Oxford University Press, 1946), p. 214.

[2] Ibid., pp. 196-198.

[3] Peter Woll, *American Bureaucracy*, 2nd. ed. (New York: W. W. Norton, 1977), p. 62.

[4] Robert Presthus, *The Organizational Society*, revised ed. (New York: St. Martin's Press, 1978), p. 84.

[5] John Kenneth Galbraith, *American Capitalism* (Boston: Houghton Mifflin, 1952), p. 118.

[6] Theodore J. Lowi, *The End of Liberalism: The Second Republic of the United States*, 2nd. ed. (New York: W. W. Norton, 1979), p. 21.

[7] Ibid., p. 22 and passim.

[8] Gerth and Mills, *From Max Weber*, pp. 212–213.

[9] Eugene Lewis, *American Politics in a Bureaucratic Age: Citizens, Constituents, Clients and Victims* (Cambridge, Mass.: Winthrop, 1977), p. 46.

[10] James Q. Wilson, "The Rise of the Bureaucratic State," in *Current Issues in Public Administration*, ed. Frederick Lane (New York: St. Martin's Press, 1978), p. 38.

[11] Woll, *American Bureaucracy*, p. 37.

[12] *Historical Statistics of the United States, Colonial Times to 1970*, pt. 2, U.S. Department of Commerce, Bureau of the Census (Washington, D.C.: Government Printing Office, 1975), pp. 1102, 1104; and *Statistical Abstract of the United States*, 100th ed., U.S. Department of Commerce, Bureau of the Census (Washington, D.C.: Government Printing Office, 1979), p. 412.

[13] Woodrow Wilson, "The Study of Administration," *Political Science Quarterly*, 1887, repr. in 56 (1941):496.

[14] Ibid., p. 493.

[15] Ralph P. Hummel, *The Bureaucratic Experience* (New York: St. Martin's Press, 1977), p. 166.

[16] Francis E. Rourke, *Bureaucracy, Politics, and Public Policy*, 2nd. ed. (Boston: Little, Brown, 1976), p. 38.

[17] Lewis, *American Politics*, p. 163.

[18] Gerth and Mills, *From Max Weber*, p. 232.

[19] Wallace S. Sayre and Herbert Kaufman, *Governing New York City: Politics in the Metropolis* (New York: W. W. Norton, 1965), p. 406.

[20] Theodore J. Lowi, "Machine Politics–Old and New," *Public Interest* 4 (Fall, 1967): 86.

[21] Sayre and Kaufman, *Governing New York City*, p. 21.

[22] E. E. Schattschneider, *The Semi-Sovereign People* (New York: Holt, Rinehart and Winston, 1960), p. 35.

[23] J. Leiper Freeman, *The Political Process: Executive Bureau-Legislative Committee Relations*, rev. ed. (New York: Random House, 1965); Rourke, *Bureaucracy, Politics, and Public Policy*; and Lowi, *The End of Liberalism.*

[24] Lawrence C. Dodd and Richard L. Schott, *Congress and the Administrative State* (New York: Wiley, 1979), pp. 170–184.

[25] Lowi, *The End of Liberalism*, passim.

[26] Richard P. Nathan, *The Plot That Failed: Nixon and the Administrative Presidency* (New York: John Wiley & Sons, 1975).

[27] Hugh Heclo, *A Government of Strangers: Executive Politics in Washington* (Washington: Brookings Institution, 1977), p. 172; and Harold Seidman, *Politics, Position and Power* (New York: Oxford University Press, 1975), pp. 121–122.

[28] Joel D. Aberbach and Bert A. Rockman, "Clashing Beliefs Within the Executive Branch," *American Political Science Review* 70 (June 1976): 456–468.

[29] Ibid., p. 468.

[30] James Burnham, *The Managerial Revolution: What is Happening in the World* (New York: John Day, 1941).

[31] Hummel, *The Bureaucratic Experience*, pp. 13–15 and passim.

[32] William Kornhauser, *The Politics of Mass Society* (New York: Free Press, 1959).

[33] Frank S. Levy, Arnold J. Meltsner, and Aaron Wildavsky, *Urban Outcomes: Schools, Streets, and Libraries* (Berkeley: University of California Press, 1974), p. 232.

[34] Bryan D. Jones, with Saadia Greenberg and Joseph Drew, *Service Delivery in the City: Citizen Demand and Bureaucratic Rules* (New York: Longman, 1980), Ch. 1.

[35] Ibid., p. 133.

[36] Sidney Verba and Norman Nie, *Participation in America: Political Democracy and Social Equity* (New York: Harper & Row, 1972), p. 132.

[37] Jones, *Service Delivery*, p. 77.

[38] The remainder of the chapter is adapted from Robert W. Kweit and Mary Grisez Kweit, "Bureaucratic Decision-Making: Impediments to Citizen Participation," *Polity* 12 (Summer, 1980):649–656, with permission.

[39] Frank Marini, ed., *Toward a New Public Administration: The Minnow-Brook Perspective* (New York: Chandler, 1971); see especially H. George Frederickson, "Toward a New Public Administration," pp. 310–316.

[40] Herbert A. Simon, *Administrative Behavior: A Study of Decision-Making Process in Administrative Organization*, 3rd ed. (New York: Free Press, 1976), p. xii.

[41] Ibid.

[42] H. H. Gerth and C. Wright Mills, *From Max Weber*, p. 216.

[43] Simon, *Administrative Behavior*, p. 137.

[44] Guy Benveniste, *The Politics of Expertise* (Berkeley, Ca.: Glendessary Press, 1972), pp. 13, 15.

[45] Robert Presthus, *The Organizational Society*, p. 55.

[46] Gerth and Mills, *From Max Weber*, pp. 196–197.

[47] Simon, *Administrative Behavior*, p. 88.

[48] Anthony Downs, *Inside Bureaucracy* (Boston: Little, Brown, 1967), p. 160.

[49] J. David Greenstone and Paul E. Peterson, *Race and Authority in Urban Politics: Communitive Participation and the War on Poverty* (New York: Russell Sage Foundation, 1973), pp. 220, 225.

[50] Graham T. Allison, *Essence of Decision* (Boston: Little, Brown, 1971), pp. 81–83.

[51] Gerth and Mills, *From Max Weber*, p. 214.

[52] Simon, *Administrative Behavior*, p. 197.

[53] Greenstone and Peterson, *Race and Authority*, p. 220.

[54] James Q. Wilson, *Political Organizations* (New York: Basic Books, 1973), pp. 9–10.

[55] James D. Thompson, *Organizations in Action: Social Science Bases of Administrative Theory* (New York: McGraw-Hill, 1967), p. 4.

[56] E. E. Schattschneider, *The Semi-Sovereign People*, p. 7.

[57] Thompson, *Organizations in Action*, p. 158.

[58] Harold Seidman, *Politics, Position, and Power*, pp. 24–28 and passim.

6

THE IMPACTS OF PARTICIPATION

Considering the confusion about what participation looks like in practice and what participation is expected to accomplish, it should not be surprising that there is no clear picture of what impact participation has had. This unclear understanding is not due to a lack of research. In fact, since the advent of the participation programs in the sixties, a prodigious amount of literature has accumulated that attempts to evaluate citizen participation. The confusion surrounding citizen participation has, however, been mirrored in the research findings, making these findings incomparable and/or contradictory. It is, therefore, impossible to draw definitive conclusions about the impact of participation.

The incomparability of the research arises from several causes. In the first place, the studies have focused on various types of participation structures. It could be hypothesized that holding a public hearing to achieve citizen acceptance of a proposed policy would have entirely different effects than would establishing a citizens' board to involve them in planning policy. In any event, assuming such different structures are comparable, without evidence to that effect, is questionable. Some researchers have made systematic attempts to assess the different impacts of various structures, but not enough of such research has been done. In many cases, researchers have made conclusions after viewing only one type of structure, which means that those who examine the literature often face a problem of comparing apples and oranges.

Another basic problem is the fact that there is no agreement among researchers on what is successful, as opposed to unsuccessful participation. This problem has two aspects. The first is the fact that, as discussed before, the impacts of participation may presumably be felt at three different levels: societal, individual, and administrative. These multiple and conflicting expectations of citizen participation complicate evaluation because participation may have an impact on one level, but not on another. "Success" then is dependent on what level the researcher focused and research should clearly specify at what level or levels attention has been focused—this is not always done.

A second aspect of the problem in determining success is establishing the criteria for success. If researchers draw conclusions concerning the success of participation, the criteria used should be clearly specified. Again, this is not always done, which serious endangers the comparability of the research findings. Although the same impacts may have been observed by two researchers, they may draw opposite conclusions about the success of a program because of their different standards.

Another problem that complicates the process of determining the impact of participation is the fact that, in many cases, the setting of the participation is not adequately considered—where participation occurs, for example, in a small town or a metropolis, may be a significant factor in determining its impact. Or, whether the target of participation is a legislature or a bureaucracy also may be important. Studies should clearly specify the context of the participation being researched.

This problem is related to another fundamental flaw of the participation literature: the paucity of attention given to relational studies. For research to be useful to those interested in understanding the participation process, it must go beyond categorizing programs according to various criteria, and must also attempt to discover how and why participation produces the impacts it does. One assumption made here is that participation is conditional; that is, participation does not always produce all of the expected impacts. This means that attempts must be made to uncover those factors that actually affect participation, and to relate these variables in systematic ways to the various impacts that participation is hypothesized to produce.

For the most part, the problems discussed above could be avoided, if researchers would recognize the complexity of citizen participation, and then specify clearly what that research was based on. There is, however, one other serious problem of the participation literature that cannot be so easily resolved: the lack of experimental research, which is probably the most fundamental flaw of the literature. Experimentation is the ultimate way to gather data on the impacts of any policy because it permits control of several factors that could threaten the internal validity of the research. Despite the desirability of experimentation, there is no real experimental research on participation and little that could be classified as quasi-experimental. This is partially due to the fact that there are several obstacles that prevent experiments which could determine the impacts of participation.

A first obstacle to conducting experimental research is the lack of clear goals. Although much of the participation of the last twenty years is the product of legislative mandates, these, unfortunately, do not include guidance about what the participation is expected to accomplish. This lack of clear goals makes it impossible to design measures to test for goal achievement. Another obstacle to experimentation is the fact that participation programs were instituted before there was an effort to measure precisely the existing state of either the participants or of government policy. This means that research on participation lacks a clear baseline to use for comparison.

This is further complicated by the fact that it may be impossible to find comparable control groups to use for comparison, which is often the case when doing experiments in the social sciences. In dealing with government agencies, cities, states, or policies, etc. as units of analysis, it is often difficult or even impossible to randomize assignment of subjects to the experimental and control groups. If the experimental and control groups are not randomized, it is technically invalid to conclude that differences observed between them are due to the experimental variable rather than to some other systematic difference in the composition of the groups or to other stimuli.

Some social research can be conducted by attempting to match the experimental and control groups on variables considered to be important; however, this may be impossible when investigating the impacts of participation mandated by the government. Because participation is mandated, it might be impossible to find a comparable agency that lacks it to use as a control. In other words, the mandate makes participation a constant rather than a variable. The lack of experimental studies and the resulting problems of validity must be kept in mind in the following review of the literature concerning the impacts of citizen participation.

IMAPCT OF PARTICIPATION: ADMINISTRATIVE LEVEL

Perhaps the most positive set of findings concerning the expected impact of participation are those that result from research on the effect of participation on service delivery. Although the literature is in agreement, and although the problems of comparability arise, there is indication that participation can indeed alter and improve the patterns of service delivery. Researchers, however, do not agree on what criteria should be used to measure effectiveness of service delivery. In some cases, achieving more equitable allocation of services is considered increased effectiveness and in others, making the policy accord more closely with citizen demands is used as the criterion. Sometimes, the criterion is to make the policy more sensitive to human needs. And, finally, in some cases the criteria are not clearly specified.

Cole in his examination of community action programs, motivated by the War on Poverty and Model Cities legislation of the sixties, concluded that the programs were somewhat successful in achieving a more favorable allocation of goods and services.[1] This finding was substantiated by Strange,[2] Sutton,[3] Rossi,[4] and Zurcher.[5] In fact, even Marris and Rein, in their generally negative evaluation of these same programs of the sixties, concluded that they did ". . . establish, especially with its legal programme, new services which substantially benefited poor people."[6]

In a more general study, Yin and Yates examined 215 case studies of the effect of decentralization. They found that 66 percent of all the studies reported an improvement in services was a benefit of decentralization, which was instituted to facilitate citizen access.[7] They conclude, "In summary, the two dominant outcomes for all 215 case studies were improved services and increased flow of information."[8] An increased flow of information, of course, could also be related to improvement in service delivery. The same conclusion was reached by Washnis in his in-depth case studies of the effect of municipal decentralization in twelve cities. He argued that "the decentralization of city operations can both strengthen the democratic process and improve government services."[9]

Not all evaluations on the impact of citizen participation on service delivery are so positive. Many studies have concluded that change has been slight, or restricted to certain types of benefits, actions, or certain functional service areas. For example, in a study of program officials conducted by Community Change Inc., 27 percent of the officials reported that the scope and type of services were improved as a result of participation.[10] In a study of 100 Community Action Agencies, Emily Starr found that 23 percent of the directors of the agencies reported changes in services as a result of the agencies' activity.[11] Whether these percentages are adequate to constitute the success of participation is dependent on which criteria of success are used.

Other studies have concluded that change will only occur in the provision of immediate and limited benefits. For example, Warren et al. concluded that participation could produce some slight substantive change, but that there was no meaningful institutional change.[12] In a similar vein, Pivan and Cloward argued that participation can create temporary and immediate benefits, but that permanent or institutional change is unlikely.[13] Strange has noted that citizen participation can be effective in altering the provision of such inexpensive services as streetlights and playgrounds, for example.[14] Similarly, Cole and Caputo found that those holding public hearings on spending revenue sharing money were more likely to spend the money on ". . . street and road repair, parks and recreation, social services, and health programs . . ." than were those cities with no hearings.[15] A partial explanation of these findings can be found in the research of Friedan and Kaplan. They discovered that "the citizens, usually without adequate staff for a close review, focused their attention on a few issues of immediate interest to them: jobs, service eligibility, and control."[16] Citizens may lack, or be perceived as lacking, adequate expertise to guide general or collectivist policy, but they may well be the best source of guidance on individualist policy, which affects them intimately.

The same effect of expertise may also explain the finding that participation may have more effect on service delivery in certain functional areas than in others. The Technical Assistance Research Program (TARP), under a grant from the National Science Foundation, examined research findings on the effect of citizen participation in eight municipal service areas: community action/model cities, urban renewal, health, education, welfare, legal system, environmental planning, and transportation planning. The study concluded that services were improved as a result of participation in four of the eight areas: community action/model cities, health, welfare, and legal systems.[17] These are areas in which the government deals with significant and intimate aspects of individuals' lives and it may be that officials believe that the input of citizens should be used to guide service delivery. They may see the other areas, such as environmental planning for example, as too technical for citizen involvement.

It has also been argued that citizen participation tends to have particular kinds of effects on service delivery. In a study of the Army Corps of Engineers, Mazmanian and Nienaber document the fact that citizen participation is more frequently effective in blocking government action rather than in creating initiatives for action.[18] Three of the projects they examined were not undertaken because the citizens could not agree—this pleased some citizens, but others failed to get what they wanted.

In another finding, the Advisory Commission on Intergovernmental Relations (ACIR), in a survey of city and county officials, has found that citizen participation tends to ". . . have a stimulative effect on localities' expenditures."[19] They found that the general thrust of participation was toward expanding the services provided, especially by means of obtaining federal grant money. In addition, they found that when grants ran out, participation was an important force in continuing the service because it forced the city to assume the costs.[20] Very few of the officials surveyed reported that participation had resulted in a program or service being discontinued.

On the surface, the Mazmanian and Neinaber and the ACIR findings appear contradictory, for one concludes that participation is most effective in blocking action, while the other finds that it is stimulative. The explanation for the contradiction may lie with the different kinds of services involved and the amount of conflict that they may create. The Corps of Engineers are involved with bricks and mortar projects, such as bridges and dams. Projects like this tend to have generalized or collective benefits, so it may be hard to mobilize specific and strong support. Often there are identifiable losers, such as the owners of land to be flooded or neighborhoods to be disrupted by increased traffic flows. Thus, they may fight hard to prevent the project or to support an alternative one which might burden someone else instead. In this case, stalemate would not be unexpected. The stimulative effect, however, found in the ACIR study, may be the result of a specific constituency that was developed as a result of federal grants. This constituency may press to continue their program. Since costs will be generalized and spread out, and since each group expects its fair share, instead of conflict, "logrolling" may result.

The whole review of the literature concerning the effect of citizen participation on service delivery raises again the fundamental problems of evaluating citizen participation because of conflicting and inconsistent standards and expectations. In a gross oversimplification, this literature can be summarized by saying that, in some circumstances, it is clear that citizen participation can alter service delivery patterns. It may have an effect only in a certain percentage of cases; only in the provision of short term benefits; only in certain functional areas; or only in certain ways, either as a blocking or stimulating agent. Whether these limits are tolerable is subject to individual discretion. In addition, whether the changes in service delivery are considered to produce increased effectiveness is also subject to shifting and often unclear criteria. These same problems plague the literature that focuses on the effect of citizen participation on the redistribution of power in society.

IMPACT OF CITIZEN PARTICIPATION: SOCIETAL LEVEL

It is clear that a fundamental restructuring of society has not occurred as a result of the expansion of citizen participation in the last twenty years. The distribution between the governors and the governed has not been eliminated. In fact, from one perspective the emphasis on participation in the bureaucracy may be seen as an acceptance of the status quo; that is, it is a recognition that the bureaucracy exists and has power. The demand is not for an elimination of that power, but rather for access to it.

Even if total restructuring does not occur, there are still ways by which power can be redistributed. Providing greater access to the existing centers of power is an attempt to ensure that the decisions made will reflect the interests of a broader number of people. For this to be successful, large numbers of people who are broadly representative of the public at large should be given access and take advantage of it. Thus, one way to determine if power redistribution has occurred, is to discover how many and what kinds of people have participated in various institutional settings.

Numbers alone, however, do not tell the whole story. Giving access to citizens may be no more than a symbolic act. For there to be an actual redistribution of power, citizens must in some way actually influence the decisions made in those institutions. To determine if power has been redistributed, it is also necessary to look at the impact citizens have on decision making.

It has been well documented that those citizens who tend to participate in any kind of political activity are likely to be from the middle and upper socioeconomic status. Verba and Nie have argued that the best predictor of citizen participation is what they call the "standard socioeconomic model."[21]

> According to this model, the social status of an individual—his job, education, and income—determines to a large extent how much he participates. It does this through the intervening effects of a variety of "civic attitudes" conducive to participation: attitudes such as a sense of efficacy, of psychological involvement in politics, and a feeling of obligation to participate.[22]

This bias in the scope of participation is significant. If policy makers do respond to citizen demands, then the demands they will bear will be those from an unrepresentative sample of the public. This would not be a problem if the interests of the lower socioeconomic status group were identical to the interests of the middle and upper socioeconomic citizens who do participate. But Verba and Nie again provide evidence that this is not so.

> Thus the relationship of social status to participation push in the same direction: the creation of a participant population different from the population as a whole. Our data show that participants are less aware of serious welfare problems than the population as a whole, less concerned about the income gap between rich and poor, less interested in government support for welfare programs, and less concerned with equal opportunities for black Americans.[23]

The intention of the participation programs in the early sixties was to provide mechanisms to mobilize participation among the lower status population and thus to eliminate the bias in the interests communicated to officials from citizen participants. It was believed, although rarely clearly specified, that poverty could be eliminated by providing the poor with the tools necessary for them to participate in politics. Once they were active, their interests would no longer be ignored by decision makers. Participation thus would be the means by which the poor could effectively demand the resources to pull themselves up the economic ladder.

There is evidence that this happened to only a minimal degree. Some evaluations tend to be almost totally negative. Austin, for example, wrote:

> While the federal program provided some sanctions that could be used to enforce a minimum level of compliance with the structural requirements for participation, it provided few rewards for develop-

> ing an active pattern of participation. . . . Where local interests were not mobilized, the existence of the federal regulations did not prevent a very limited development of participation.[24]

It might be added that not only were there few rewards offered to officials to mobilize the poverty population, there were some definite costs involved in doing so. Officials were not eager to be bombarded with a new set of citizens making new demands for government services. In addition, since the demands were very likely to differ from the demands of the middle and upper SES participants, the level of conflict could be expected to rise, causing further problems for officials.

With few incentives and obvious lack of incentives, it should not be surprising that officials did little to encourage anything but a "very limited development of participation." But, even a very limited development indicates some increase in participation occurred. The problem was, however, that studies have indicated that those among the target poverty groups who did participate were atypical of the poor in that they were more highly motivated and tended to be upwardly mobile.[25] These characteristics might be associated with interests and demands that are also atypical of the poverty population as a whole.

Atypical or not, these participants did in many cases continue to be politically active even after the federal programs withered and died. This meant that the poverty groups now could be represented by an indigenous leadership. As Moynihan argued:

> Very possibly, the most important long run impact of the community action programs of the 1960s will prove to have been the formation of an urban Negro leadership echelon at just the time when the Negro masses and other minorities were verging towards extensive commitments to urban politics. Tammany at its best (or worst) would have envied the political apprenticeship provided the neighborhood coordinators of the antipoverty program.[26]

Fainstein and Fainstein, writing four years after Moynihan, documented the continued existence of the indigenous leadership created in the sixties.[27] They found that deprived minorities could now participate in the pluralist bargaining system. The result, they argue, is that their interests must be reconciled with others and this means that policy is made by compromise, including occasional gain for the minorities. They conclude, however, that there has not been any major redistribution of power. This is especially the case since the impact of the groups has been limited to the local level, where increasingly policies are determined by the national government.[28]

If the participation programs of the sixties did not greatly increase participation among the target population, they did provide increased access to those who were already organized. Vanecko argued that effective community action programs could be found in cities with high levels of political activity among the poor.[29] In those cities, the program extended and complemented the activity of the poor. This increased access, however, was often accompanied by significant conflict. As Sundquist found:

> Where the neighborhood was strongly organized under militant leadership–perhaps 20 to 30 percent of the cities might be put in that class–the struggle for control of model cities took on many of the attributes of labor-management relations, but with more attendant animosity.[30]

To a large extent, this conflict led to the demise of the federal programs of the sixties that were aimed specifically at mobilizing the poor. Yet, these programs were followed by a myriad of other programs that included requirements that citizen participation be part of the process of implementation. It is important to consider the evidence concerning how successful these more recent programs have been in stimulating representative citizen participation.

The ACIR conducted case studies of five policy areas in which participation is mandated: community health centers, Title XX of the Social Security Act, the Coastal Zone Management Program, Community Development Block Grants, and General Revenue Sharing. The ACIR found substantial levels of citizen participation in the community health centers, but attributed the participation to factors besides the legislation itself.[31] Substantial levels of participation in community health centers existed prior to the legislation due to the neighborhood health centers established by the Community Action Program in the sixties.[32] To investigate the Coastal Zone Management Program, the ACIR focused on California and Oregon. The levels of participation in both states exceeded federal requirements. The ACIR attributes this to the importance that the coast has for both states rather than to the requirements themselves.[33]

In three areas, however, the ACIR did argue that some stimulation of participation had occurred, yet they qualified this finding. In the Title XX program of Social Security, evidence indicates that more participation exists now than before the participation requirements were legislated. In an evaluation of this participation, Rose, Zorn and Radin point out that 20 of the 24 states they investigated exceeded minimum participation standards.[34] However, in a study of the same program by the Urban Institute in five states, the Institute concluded that the general public was not nearly as active as the providers of funds and the organized groups who wanted the funds.[35]

Outside evaluation of the CDBG, by the Brookings Institution, led to a conclusion that ". . . citizen participation, contrary to what some observers anticipated, has been a very significant feature of the program's implementation in the first year. . . ."[36] Yet the in-house evaluation of the program by the Department of Housing and Urban Development found that complaints on citizen participation were the most frequent ones on the program. They centered on the representativeness of the participants as well as on the amount and impact of participation. In Congressional testimony at renewal hearings, it was also the case that there were many complaints about the level and impact of participation.[37]

Both HUD and Brookings concluded that the local communities were meeting the standards of the law, whether or not citizens were satisfied with the representatives of the participants and level of participation.[38] A survey of local officials by the ACIR and the International City Managers Association, however, indicated that the required level of participation was not being reached in many localities. Up to 13 percent of the counties and 7 percent of the cities surveyed, reported not even holding two public hearings, despite the fact that such hearings are clearly required by the law.[39] There is no evidence in the ACIR report on the actual representativeness of those who participated in the CDBG process.

The final area studied by the ACIR was General Revenue Sharing. They cite various studies that indicate that the original General Revenue Sharing Act did have some stimulative impact on participation, despite the fact that the participation requirements were limited basically to publicizing the budget.[40] Once again, however, there was evidence that those who were active had been politically active before the act was passed. In other words, few new participants were brought into politics due to the General Revenue Sharing Act.

In the reenactment of the program, the participation requirements were extended to include two public hearings, with adequate notice and publicity given before the hearings. To determine the impact of the extended requirements, the ACIR and the ICMA conducted a mail survey of budget officials in cities with a population of more than 10,000 and counties with a population greater than 25,000. As a result of that survey, the ACIR concluded that "The effect of GRS citizen participation requirements on participation in local and possibly state budget processes has been modest."[41] They found that 34 percent of the city and 41 percent of the county officials reported that citizen participation had increased in the last few years. When asked if the increase was due to the general revenue sharing requirements, 44 percent of the city and 49 percent of the county officials responded that it was.[42] However, there is no evidence to determine if this increase was due to new participants being brought into the system, or if it was simply due to those who had been previously active being given new access to the budgetary process.

One other study that has considered the types of citizens that become active under the new participation requirements was conducted by TARP Institute and the School of Public Health of the University of Michigan. As noted before, the study focused on eight functional areas. Widespread citizen participation was found only in neighborhood health centers and, occasionally, in civilian police review boards. In the area of community action/model cities, the study reported that most participants were middle class or had been previous citizen leaders.[43] In urban renewal, business interests predominated; in both health planning and education, the experts were the dominant influences.

It appears that the participation requirements, included in federal legislation for the past two decades, have not been completely successful in mobilizing participation by those segments of society who have not previously been politically active. In fact, even in those cases in which the legislation specifically targeted the poor and unorganized as groups to be involved, they were rarely as active as had been expected. The early programs may have created a leadership core—no mean achievement—but attempts at widespread participation of the poor failed. This lack of expansion of participation has been noted in more recent programs such as Title XX and the CDBG program. The ACIR concluded that one reason for the unsuccessful CDBG program was that mayors attempted to use the program and funds solely to create a broad-based constituency for themselves. Regardless of why efforts to involve the uninvolved were unsuccessful, the findings indicate that the extent to which the participation requirements could be effective in redistributing power must also be limited. As indicated above, however, there is a second aspect to the question of whether the requirements have had an impact on power redistribution. This concerns the extent to which citizens, once given access to the decision-making process, actually have an impact on the decision made.

The extent to which citizens influenced decision making is closely related to the issue discussed above of whether participation has improved service delivery. As in that issue, the evidence of influence by citizens on decision making is mixed. Evaluations of the early participation programs of the sixties tended to be highly critical of the extent to which citizens were given influence. Austin found that, in general, the target area residents had little impact on the programs and the priorities of the community action agencies.[44] Strange argued that "In some cases the number of groups participating in the pluralistic contest for power and influence had been expanded, but no radical changes in the distribution of influence, power, services, rewards, or other benefits had occurred."[45] And, in a bitter denunciation of one of the early programs, Arnstein wrote "Our experiences with unsympathetic and antagonistic officials . . . have convinced us that Model Cities is designed to deceive the community by pacifying our minds, our spirit, and our ambitions."[46]

Yet evaluations of the more recent programs have tended to be somewhat more positive, although many have qualified their conclusions. For example, evaluations of the CDBG program were conducted by both its parent agency, HUD, and the Brookings Institution. Both concluded that citizen participation had had an impact on setting priorities in the spending of the block grant funds.[47] Nevertheless, citizens testifying at hearings on the renewal of the program were critical of the citizen participation aspects of the CDBG. They frequently charged that the governments were unresponsive to citizen demands.[48] The inconsistency may well be due to the differing expectations of citizens, officials, and evaluators. Many of the officials who responded to the ACIR-ICMA survey thought citizens had had an influence on budgetary priorities, mainly by stimulating local spending.[49] The ACIR case study of the coastal zone program also indicated a high level of citizen influence.[50]

Other studies, however, have qualified the conclusion of citizen impact by arguing that influence can be felt only in certain areas, or only if the participation is structured in particular ways. For example, the TARP study of eight functional areas found widespread citizen influence only in the areas of neighborhood health centers.[51] A study of citizen participation in the Department of Health, Education and Welfare conducted by Yin and others of the Rand Corporation concluded that ". . . the organizational forms of citizen participation can and do have an impact on the conduct of local public activities and services."[52] Yin argued that some form of citizen organization was an essential precursor to citizen influence and that these organizations are more effective if they are given staff assistance and the power of investigation and if they are chosen by election.[53]

Some positive evidence concerning the impact of citizen participation on service delivery and power redistribution has been discussed, although the record is by no means unanimous. The lack of clear evidence concerning the impact of citizen participation is also evident in the research that focuses on changes in citizen attitudes.

IMPACT OF PARTICIPATION: INDIVIDUAL LEVEL

Citizen participation is expected by many to reduce the alienation of citizens from their government. Alienation is a vague concept and a variety of meanings have been attributed to it. Ada Finifter, examining solely the concept of political alienation, has concluded that there are two basic independent dimensions of alienation from the political system: trust and efficacy.[54]

The evidence of the impact of participation on trust has produced totally contradictory findings. Examining the community action programs of the sixties, Cole discovered that 64 percent of the participants reported that participation in the program had increased their trust and confidence in the government.[55] In addition, 60 percent of the respondents believed that their participation had increased the trust and confidence of the neighborhood as a whole.[56] Cole compared these levels of trust to responses given to trust questions included in surveys done by the Survey Research Center. He found that the participants had higher trust scores,[57] and concluded that:

> Since previous survey research has questioned the independent effect of trust attitudes on participation, it is reasonable to conclude that the difference in trust scores reported above are due, in part at least, to the act of participation.[58]

This conclusion was qualified by one other finding. Cole ranked the programs he studied on a one to five scale, based on the scope of participation and the influence exercised by the participants. Contrary to his hypothesis, Cole found a curvilinear relationship between the extensiveness of participation and the respondents' satisfaction with the program.[59] Programs that were the most, and the least, extensive were considered the least successful by the respondents. This finding is similar to that presented in research by Peterson,[60] Greenstone and Peterson,[61] and Sundquist.[62] Cole concluded that the important factors leading to satisfaction were cooperation and moderation. He argued that the most extensive programs involved the citizen participants in confrontation with both government officials and fellow citizens. This confrontation created stress, which reduced the citizens' satisfaction with the program.[63]

On the other hand, on the basis of a national study, Ada Finifter concluded that neither general participation nor organizational membership had any effect on citizen trust.[64] A 1970 national survey by the Institute for Social Research found no difference in trust when comparing nonvoters, voters, and active participants.[65] Finally, in ten cities, the Urban Observatory compared levels of trust in those who belonged to local organizations and those who did not. The results indicated that organizational participation had no influence on levels of political trust.[66] In reviewing these studies, Yin et al. concluded that ". . . regardless of the organizational form, *participation is unlikely to increase generalized trust in government*."[67]

The Yin study did find, however, some evidence that participation can affect citizen efficacy. The authors pointed to a survey conducted by the Institute for Social Research comparing the responses of nonvoters, voters, and active participants to a question measuring their belief in their ability to have a say about what government does. The conclusion was that ". . . a higher level of political participation is consistently related with an increased sense of efficacy."[68]

However, one study indicated that specific types of local participation may actually be related to a lowered sense of efficacy. In a study of 100 community action agencies, Bruce Jacobs found that leaders identified by a reputational methodology actually had a lower sense of efficacy than a comparable control group chosen from the ISR survey.[69] This finding was contradicted by a

TARP study of participants in citizen groups at four schools in the Boston area. This latter study concluded that participation had little effect on efficacy toward the city or national government. It did find, however, some evidence that participation was related to a sense of efficacy with regard to the particular school's affairs.[70] In conclusion, the Yin study argued that ". . . *political participation generally is related to a general sense of political efficacy, but participation in local organizations may be related only to a sense of efficacy in regard to the specific program or activity*."[71] The authors noted, however, that there were problems in determining the direction of causation because those who are more efficacious may also be more likely to participate.

The TARP study of eight municipal service areas reached a more negative conclusion concerning the impact of participation on general citizen attitudes. Since the study was based on a general review of literature, it did not focus solely on measures of trust and efficacy. Thus, the findings are not directly comparable to the prior conclusions. The study concluded, however, that "Evidence that citizen participation impacts upon citizen attitudes is the weakest area of findings."[72] In many of the areas studied, the study did find evidence that citizen attitudes had become less negative due to participation. These areas were legal system, health centers, urban renewal, community action, education, and welfare programs.[73] The authors point out that improvements among the welfare program participants may be due to the fact that "future-oriented" people are more likely to participate in the programs. In the area of education, the authors found that an improvement in the attitudes of citizens was due to their belief that they had influence over the program.[74] This belief the authors termed "false consciousness." They point out that ". . . certain participation activities are effective in raising hopes falsely and offering citizens an apparent sense of potency in municipal affairs which, in fact, is not really present."[75]

In the long run, such "false consciousness" may actually lead to an increased negativism toward government, if citizens become aware that they actually lack influence. Zurcher also found that participation could, in some circumstances, have negative impacts on citizen attitudes. Examining the poverty programs, Zurcher found that the participants developed an increased achievement orientation and activism, and a decreased normlessness, alienation, and particularism. Those in the target areas who were not active, however, experienced decreased activism and increased isolation, powerlessness and alienation.[76] Although these findings are weakened by the lack of statistical significance, they do point to the fact that participation can, in some cases, have effects that are the opposite of what is expected.[77]

In general, the research findings on the impact of citizen participation on citizen attitudes present a contradictory picture. Cole found a positive impact on trust, and there is some evidence that improvement in efficacy can result. Other studies have found no effect on trust and indicate that specific local participation may only produce increased efficacy with regard to specific local programs. In addition, there is some evidence that the impact may actually be negative in some circumstances. This points to another facet of participation impacts that should be discussed: the problems that result from citizen participation.

PROBLEMS OF CITIZEN PARTICIPATION

The problems that can result from citizen participation fall into three main categories: increased conflict in the political system, increased problems of government policy making, and ironically enough, decreased equality in society. Reference has already been made to the problems of increased conflict resulting from citizen participation, of which there are two sources: citizen-government and citizen-citizen.

In our political system, government officials are vested with legal authority which is derived from two sources. One is election by the citizenry as a whole. For such elected officials, responding to citizen demands is the means by which future success at the polls can be sought. Yet if officials delegate total power to citizens, by only responding to demands, they in essence divest themselves of their legal authority. Some analysts, such as Lowi, would argue that a government that makes decisions solely on the basis of citizen demands is illegitimate.[78] Although officials may not go so far to agree that responding to citizen demands is illegitimate, most are unwilling to act solely as ratifiers of demands transmitted to them by citizens, unless they happen to agree with those demands. In other words, officials tend to be jealous of their legal authority and are loathe to share it with citizens, which means, of course, that when the two have differing perspectives, conflicts can be expected. As Miles argued, where one stands is dependent on where he sits, so there is good reason to expect that citizens and officials will frequently have differing perspectives.[79] Of course, neither group is so monolithic that there is a simple battle between the good guys and the bad guys.

The second source of authority of officials is appointment on the basis of merit and expertise. As Chapter 5 argued, there is every reason to expect conflict between the citizens and the bureaucrats, who hold office on the basis of expertise. Bureaucrats frequently believe that expertise should be the basis of decisions and because citizens lack it, the bureaucrats feel that their influence on decisions should be minimized, Nevertheless, citizens are becoming increasingly aware of the power that the bureaucracy exercises over their lives and are demanding access to bureaucratic decision making.

Analyses of the early participation programs of the sixties documented the conflict that arose when citizens, intent on wresting power from government, came face-to-face with government officials intent on maintaining the status quo.[80] There were few satisfactory options to resolve the conflict. Government officials could have been forced to change (in contradiction to basic organizational motivations to maintain the status quo). In addition, acquiescing to citizen demands might have been dangerous, since citizens do in fact lack the expertise and skills necessary to participate effectively in decision making.[81] On the other hand, citizens could be ignored, at the risk of creating significant citizen frustration, which might have increased the urban unrest that was already so prevalent.[82]

Many of the evaluations of the community action programs have conveyed some of the bitterness that resulted from the confrontation between citizens and city officials. Moynihan concluded that

> At the risk of oversimplification, it might be said that the CAP's most closely controlled by City Hall were disappointing, and that the ones most antagonistic were destroyed.[83]

Pranger, examining the program from the perspective of the citizen, concluded that frustration was all but inevitable. Using an analogy of a football fan going professional for the day, Pranger argued that:

> The occasional player gathers little experience, never gains the team's confidence, contributes nothing to the joint enterprise, and because of his inexperience runs the risk of serious injury.[84]

In addition to conflict between the government and the citizens, there are also frequent conflicts among the citizens, for they are, by no means, united in their opposition to the government. Citizens have self-interests that conflict with each other and participation may at times become a free-for-all struggle in which, in Darwinian fashion, the fittest emerge as winners.[85] It has been documented that many Americans have a low tolerance of conflict, so that it may be assumed that there are many Americans who would be ineffective in such a free-for-all and would in essence be closed out. Needleman and Needleman quoted a community planner who was concerned about the problem:

> Without structural changes in United States society, we can only heighten participatory democracy and add to the number of self-seeking groups. This organizes the debate, not the results. It's a policy of "Screw thy neighbor."[86]

The problems of increased conflict in the system are related to the increased problems of policy making. As the community planner quoted above indicated, an increase in citizen participation will increase demands on the system, which will very likely make policy making more difficult. Norman Nie has argued that participation, in the absence of aggregating structures, will simply increase the "noise" in the system, therefore making it more difficult for policy makers to respond.[87] At the very least, such increased noise increases the time necessary for officials to listen and to reach decisions.

Others have argued that participation simply diverts such resources of time from other more constructive purposes.[88] For example, Kalodner has argued that the main purpose of participation is to remove alienation and powerlessness, yet, he believes the best way to eliminate these problems is to eliminate poverty. He therefore sees participation as counter-productive, since it diverts political energies from the main problem.[89]

Another problem identified by researchers has been the conflict between participation and rational policy-making. Increasing the numbers involved in decision making makes it difficult, if not impossible, to achieve consensus on one best policy. James Q. Wilson has argued that ". . . effective local planning requires *less*, not more citizen participation."[90] Since participation may make it difficult for consensus to form, it may be the case the policy making is effectively delegated to the separate interests. Numerous analysts have argued that such delegation may result in policy that benefits individualistic interests at the expense of the collectivistic good.[91] As Abrahamsen has pointed out ". . . the defense of one's own interests . . . cannot easily be reconciled with the development of 'public spirit.'"[92] It is also the case that participation per se may not always be a progressive force. For example, citizen movements can as easily be used to oppose the granting of civil rights to others, as they can to force the legal recognition of those rights. The history of the struggle of blacks to achieve recognition for their rights in this country illustrates both the power of citizen groups to demand progress, as well as the power of citizens to oppose such progress, even long after a majority recognized it as desirable.

A final problem with citizen participation is that, in direct contradiction to the expectations, it may actually operate to increase the concentration of power. Evidence for this has already been discussed. For example, Verba and Nie have documented that in the existing structures of participation, people of higher socioeconomic status predominate.[93] Thus, citizen demands tend to reflect the interests of those people rather than of the citizenry as a whole. Examination of the participation mandated under recent federal legislation has also indicated that, with few exceptions, the participants tend to be atypical of the population as a whole.[94] In fact, even with the Community Action Program that was targeted at low income people who do not normally participate, the participants tended to be more upwardly mobile than the target population as a whole.[95] If that is the case, then increased opportunities for participation may simply increase the access that an unrepresentative group of people has to the political system, without having any impact on the majority.

There are good reasons why increasing opportunities for participation may not increase the representativeness of participants, for participation requires resources and skills that are not evenly divided among the population. As mentioned before, at least some forms of participation demand tolerance of conflict.[96] In addition, the ability to communicate is an important prerequisite, as is the sense of confidence to use that ability. Those without some of these resources cannot effectively compete with others to achieve desired goals via political participation. In fact, as Mansbridge has argued:

> Face-to-face participation in political decisions, rather than creating community, may frighten away the very people it is supposed to bring into more active participation.[97]

It is also the case that participation can be used to manipulate the participants. Many analysts have criticized various participation programs for doing just that.[98] There are many ways by which the participation process can be structured to limit the actual impact of participants, for example, in examining efforts to institute worker participation in organizations, Mosher has pointed out that:

> Participation may be only an instrument of persuasion for what superiors have already decided upon (and this has been a fairly frequent charge). It may be restricted only to the consideration of means whereby management decisions should be implemented; in fact, this type of participative decision appears to be most frequent.[99]

Perhaps the major point was made by Mansbridge: ". . . replacing representative with direct democracy does not eliminate differences in power."[100] Nor does participation necessarily improve service delivery or the attitudes of citizens.

SUMMARY

Some evidence indicates that citizen participation can improve service delivery, but this improvement may only occur some percentage of the time, in some kinds of services, or on a short-term basis. There is also evidence that citizen participation can achieve some redistribution of power, although this evidence is mixed. Some mobilization of new participants has occurred, although this has been limited. Some have argued that participation has had an impact on government programs, yet many others, especially citizens, have not been satisfied with the extent of the impact. Finally, it appears that citizen participation has had minimal or no impact on the attitudes of the citizens. At the same time, there is also evidence of the negative impacts of participation: increasing conflict, complicating policy making, and inequality.

The main conclusion of this review of the literature is that the effectiveness of citizen participation is conditional—it does not always create the same impacts or the impacts expected. It is important, therefore, to examine which factors have been identified as determining effective citizen participation. These will be examined in the following chapter.

NOTES

[1] Richard L. Cole, *Citizen Participation and the Urban Policy Process* (Lexington, Mass.: Lexington Books, 1974), pp. 103–104.

[2] John H. Strange, "The Impact of Citizen Participation on Public Administration," *Public Administration Review* 32 (September 1972):457–470.

[3] Willis A. Sutton, "Differential Perceptions of Impact of a Rural Anti-Poverty Campaign," *Social Science Quarterly* 50 (December 1969):662.

[4] Peter H. Rossi, "No Good Idea Goes Unpunished: Moynihan's Misunderstandings and the Proper Role of Social Science in Policy Making," *Social Science Quarterly* 50 (December 1969):469–479.

[5] Louis A. Zurcher, Jr., "The Poverty Board: Some Consequences of 'Maximum Feasible Participation,'" *Journal of Social Issues* 26 (Summer 1970):85–107.

[6] Peter Marris and Martin Rein, *Dilemmas of Social Reform: Poverty and Community Action in the United States,* 2nd. ed. (Chicago: Aldine, 1973), p. 272.

[7] Robert K. Yin and Douglas Yales, *Street-Level Governments: Assessing Decentralization and Urban Services* (Lexington, Mass.: Lexington Books, 1975), p. 56.

[8] Ibid.

[9] George J. Washnis, *Municipal Decentralization and Neighborhood Resources: Case Studies of Twelve Cities* (New York: Praeger, 1972), p. 371.

[10] Community Change, Inc., and Public Sector, Inc., "A Study of Consumer Participation in the Administrative Process in Various Levels of HSMHA's Service Projects," Sausalito, Ca., June 20, 1972 (mimeographed), cited in Robert K. Tin et al., *Citizen Organizations: Increasing Client Control Over Services* (Santa Monica, Ca.: Rand, 1973), p. 42.

[11] Emily S. Starr, "How Much and What Kinds of Change Has There Been?" *Reports From the 100-City CAP Evaluation*, The National Opinion Research Center, University of Chicago; and Barss, Reitzel & Associates, Inc., Cambridge, Mass., May 1970, cited in Yin et al., *Citizen Organizations*, p. 30.

[12] Robert Alford and Roger Friedland, "Political Participation and Public Policy," *Annual Review of Sociology* 1 (1975): 460.

[13] Frances Fox Piven and Richard A. Cloward, *Regulating the Poor: The Function of Public Welfare* (New York: Pantheon, 1971), p. 331.

[14] John H. Strange, "Citizen Participation in Community Action and Model Cities Programs," *Public Administration Review* 32 (October 1972):660.

[15] Richard L. Cole and David A. Caputo, *Urban Politics and Decentralization: The Case of General Revenue Sharing* (Lexington, Mass.: Lexington Books, 1974), p. 115.

[16] Bernard J. Friedan and Marshall Kaplan, *The Politics of Neglect: Urban Aid from Model Cities to Revenue Sharing* (Cambridge, Mass.: The MIT Press, 1975), p. 96.

[17] Joseph Falkson, *An Evaluation of Policy Related Research on Citizen Participation in Municipal Service Systems: Overview and Summary* (Washington, D.C.: TARP Institute, 1974), pp. 27–29.

[18] Daniel A. Mazmanian and Jeanne Nienaber, *Can Organizations Change?* (Washington, D.C.: The Brookings Institution, 1979).

[19] Advisory Commission on Intergovernmental Relations, *Citizen Participation in the American Federal System* (Washington, D.C.: U.S. Government Printing Office, 1979), p. 5.

[20] Ibid., p. 174.

[21] Sidney Verba and Norman H. Nie, *Participation in America: Political Democracy and Social Equality* (New York: Harper & Row, 1972), p. 13.

[22] Ibid.

[23] Ibid., p. 298.

[24] David M. Austin, "Resident Participation: Political Mobilization or Organizational Co-Optation?" *Public Administration Review* 32 (September 1972):418.

[25] Ralph M. Kramer, *Participation of the Poor: Community Case Studies in the War on Poverty* (Englewood Cliffs, N.J.: Prentice-Hall, 1969), p. 200.

[26] Daniel P. Moynihan, "Community Action Loses," in *The New Urban Politics: Cities and the Federal Government*, ed. Douglas M. Fox (Pacific Palisades, Ca.: Goodyear, 1972), p. 173.

[27] Norman Fainstein and Susan S. Fainstein, "The Future of Community Control," *The American Political Science Review* 70 (September 1976):921.

[28] Ibid., p. 922.

[29] James J. Vanecko, "Community Mobilization and Institutional Change: The Influence of the Community Action Program in Large Cities," *Social Science Quarterly* 50 (December 1969):609–630.

[30] James L. Sundquist, "Model Cities as a Coordinating Structure," in *The New Urban Politics: Cities and the Federal Government*, ed. Douglas M. Fox (Pacific Palisades, Ca.: Goodyear, 1972), pp. 202–203.

[31] ACIR, *Citizen Participation in the American Federal System*, p. 135.

[32] Ibid., p. 132.

[33] Ibid., p. 142.

[34] Francis Zorn, Leilani Rose, and Beryle Radion, "Title XX and Public Participation: An Initial Assessment," *Public Welfare*, Washington, D.C., American Public Welfare Association, Fall 1976, in ACIR, *Citizen Participation in the Federal System*, p. 136.

[35] Jerry Turem et al., *The Implementation of Title XX: The First Years Experience*, Washington, D.C., The Urban Institute, under Contract 500-75-0010 with the Social and Rehabilitation Service, Department of HEW, working paper, November 1976, p. 4.

[36] U.S. House of Representatives, Committee on Banking, Finance and Urban Affairs, Subcommittee on Housing and Community Development, *Housing and Community Development Act of 1977: Hearings* (Washington, D.C.: U.S. Government Printing Office), p. 585.

[37] ACIR, *Citizen Participation in the American Federal System*, p. 145.

[38] Ibid., pp. 143–145.

[39] Ibid., p. 147.

[40] Ibid., pp. 151–153.

[41] Ibid., p. 163.

[42] Ibid.

[43] Joseph L. Falkson, *An Evaluation of Policy Related Research on Citizen Participation in Municipal Service Systems*, pp. 23–27.

[44] Austin, "Resident Participation," p. 412.

[45] John H. Strange, "The Impact of Citizen Participation on Public Administration," *Public Administration Review* 32 (September 1972):468.

[46] Sherry Arnstein, "Maximum Feasible Manipulation," *Public Administration Review* 32 (September 1972):389.

[47] ACIR, *Citizen Participation in the American Federal System*, p. 146.

[48] Ibid., p. 145.

[49] Ibid., p. 172.

[50] Ibid., p. 142.

[51] Falkson, *An Evaluation of Policy Related Research on Citizen Participation in Municipal Service Systems*, p. 24.

[52] Yin et al., *Citizen Organizations*, p. 31.

[53] Ibid.

[54] Ibid., p. 32.

[55] Richard J. Cole, "Citizen Participation in Municipal Politics," *American Journal of Political Science* 19 (November 1975):771.

[56] Ibid.

[57] Ibid., p. 774.

[58] Cole, *Citizen Participation and the Urban Policy Process*, p. 113.

[59] Ibid., p. 106.

[60] Paul E. Peterson, "Forms of Representation: Participation of the Poor in the Community Action Program," *American Political Science Review* 64 (June 1970):491–507.

[61] J. David Greenstone and Paul E. Peterson, *Race and Authority in Urban Politics* (New York: Russell Sage Foundation, 1973).

[62] James L. Sundquist and David W. Davis, *Making Federalism Work* (Washington, D.C.: The Brookings Institution, 1969).

[63] Cole, "Citizen Participation in Municipal Politics," p. 778.

[64] Ada Finifter, "Dimensions of Political Alienation," *The American Political Science Review* 64 (June 1970): 403.

[65] Reported in Yin, *Citizen Organizations*, pp. 33–34.

[66] Frank X. Steggart and the Secretariat of the National League of Cities, reported in Yin et al., *Citizen Organizations*, p. 34.

[67] Yin et al., *Citizen Organizations*, p. 35.

[68] Ibid., p. 63.

[69] Bruce Jacobs, "How Do Spokesmen for the Poor View Community Response?" *Reports From the 100-City CAP Evaluation*, The National Opinion Research Center, University of Chicago and Barss, Reitzel & Associates, Cambridge, Massachusetts, May, 1970.

[70] Ibid.

[71] Yin et al., *Citizen Organizations*, p. 39.

[72] Falkson, "An Evaluation of Policy Related Research on Citizen Participation in Municipal Service Systems," p. 33.

[73] Ibid., pp. 29–31.

[74] Ibid., p. 34.

[75] Ibid.

[76] Louis A. Zurcher, Jr., "The Poverty Board: Some Consequences of 'Maximum Feasible Participation,'" *Journal of Social Issues* 26 (Summer 1970):85–187.

[77] Ibid., p. 101.

[78] Theodore J. Lowi, *The End of Liberalism: Ideology, Policy, and the Crisis of Public Authority* (New York: W. W. Norton, 1969), Part 4.

[79] William Gamson, *Power and Discontent* (Homewood, Ill.: Dorsey Press, 1968), 2–19.

[80] James A. Riedel, "Citizen Participation: Myths and Realities," *Public Administration Review* 32 (May/June 1972):211–220.

[81] Roger E. Kasperson and Myrna Breitbart, *Participation, Decentralization, and Advocacy Planning* (Association of American Geographers, 1974), p. 2.

[82] Robert J. Pranger, *The Eclipse of Citizenship: Power and Participation in Contemporary Politics* (New York: Holt, Rinehart and Winston, 1968), p. 27; Daniel P. Moynihan, "Community Action Loses," p. 176.

[83] Moynihan, "Community Action Loses," p. 174.

[84] Pranger, *The Eclipse of Citizenship*, p. 27.

[85] Martin L. Needleman and Carolyn Emerson Needleman, *Guerillas in the Bureaucracy: The Community Planning Experiment in the United States* (New York: John Wiley & Sons, 1974), p. 340.

[86] Ibid., p. 341.

[87] Norman Nie, address on panel, "Critical and Unresolved Questions About Citizen Participation," in Stuart Langton, *Citizen Participation Perspectives: Proceedings of the National Conference on Citizen Participation* (Medford, Mass.: Lincoln Filene Center for Citizenship and Public Affairs, 1978), p. 61.

[88] John H. Strange, "Citizen Participation in Community Action and Model Cities Programs," *Public Administration Review* 32 (October 1972):660.

[89] Howard I. Kalodner, "Citizen Participation in Social Institutions," in *Participation in Politics*, eds. J. Roland Pennock and John W. Chapman (New York: Lieber-Atherton, 1975), pp. 182–183.

[90] James Q. Wilson, "The War on Cities," *The Public Interest* 3 (1966):29.

[91] Kalodner, "Citizen Participation in Social Institutions," p. 184; Lowi, *The End of Liberalism*, p. 104.

[92] Bengt Abrahamson, *Bureaucracy or Participation: The Logic of Organization*, vol. 51, Sage Library of Social Research (Beverly Hills, Ca.: Sage Publications, 1977), p. 223.

[93] Verba and Nie, *Participation in America.*

[94] ACIR, *Citizen Participation in the American Federal System*, Chapter 4.

[95] Don R. Bowen and Louis H. Masotti, "Spokesmen for the Poor: An Analysis of Cleveland's Poverty Board Candidates," *Urban Affairs Quarterly* 5 (1968).

[96] Verba and Nie, *Participation in America*, pp. 50–53.

[97] Jane J. Mansbridge, "The Limits of Friendship," in *Participation in Politics*, eds. Pennock and Chapman, p. 261.

[98] Sherry Arnstein, "Maximum Feasible Manipulation," *City* (1970):30–38; Judith V. May, *Citizen Participation: A Review of the Literature* (Council of Planning Libraries, 1971).

[99] Frederick C. Mosher, ed. *Governmental Reorganizations: Cases and Commentary* (Indianapolis: Bobbs-Merrill, 1967), p. 519.

[100] Jane J. Mansbridge, "The Limits of Friendship," in *Participation in Politics*, eds. Pennock and Chapman, p. 261.

7

DETERMINANTS OF SUCCESS

There appear to be three categories of factors that affect what the impact of citizen participation will be. One category includes characteristics of the structure of the participation that is established. The second category includes characteristics of the targets at which the participation is aimed, and the third category of factors includes characteristics of the environment in which the participation occurs. Before reviewing the evidence concerning the effect of each of these categories, it is important to point out that the literature does not always specify the type of citizen participation impact that is being discussed. This, once again, causes problems of comparability. In this review, when the impact has been specified, it will be identified.

CHARACTERISTICS OF THE STRUCTURES OF PARTICIPATION

The first category is the structural characteristics of the participation mechanism. There are many ways to structure participation, as was discussed in Chapter 4. In a Rand Corporation Study commissioned by the Department of Health, Education, and Welfare, Yin et al. concluded that ". . . citizen organizations have been successful in devolving power and are readily implemented, but that most other forms of participation, *as they have been approached in the past*, either have not been successful or would be difficult to implement."[1] It is clear from this that the Yin study was focused primarily on the redistribution of power, although consideration was also given to the effect on the attitudes of the citizens and the effectiveness of service delivery.

There were other forms of participation that Yin et al. specifically rejected as being unable to devolve power. Two of these were means of involving citizens in service delivery: volunteering and employing paraprofessionals. These forms had been used in the past and volunteering, they concluded, does not give real power to the volunteers. In addition, it is limited because the volunteers are usually of upper socioeconomic status. Volunteering might, however, affect the attitudes of those involved and may increase the effectiveness of service delivery.[2] A second form of participation that they judge to be ineffective in redistributing power is the employment of paraprofessionals. While the individuals hired may of course be given greater responsibility as a result of employment, this responsibility does not necessarily—or usually—involve control over the setting of policy that would indicate a change in the distribution of power.[3] This conclusion is supported by Austin on the basis of his study of the employment of nonprofessionals by community action agencies.[4] Once again, however, Yin et al. conclude that hiring paraprofessionals might help the attitudes of those employed and improve service delivery.[5]

Three other forms of participation that Yin et al. conclude are not effective means to redistribute power involve procedures to increase communication between the citizens and the department: grievance procedures, citizen polls, and citizen evaluations.[6] In the case of grievance procedures, they conclude that direct contact with the agency may not produce a response, if the grievance concerns basic policy directives. In fact, it may backfire and result in punitive action. Contact with other parts of government, such as the legislature or the courts, may be effective but, the effectiveness of the legislative route is dependent upon the willingness of legislators to act as intermediaries. The effectiveness of the court is limited by the time involved in the judicial process and the fact that many people may lack the financial resources, as well as knowledge, to use the court system.[7]

They acknowledge that an ombudsman may also be effective, but that grievance system, by definition, must be located outside the department itself, and, therefore, it is basically beyond the scope of their study. They argue, however, that an ombudsman would not really distribute greater power to the citizens, since the citizens would have no greater control over policy making.[8]

This same basic limit plagues the effectiveness of the two other forms of communication. Both polls and citizen evaluations can increase the government's awareness of citizen attitudes, but neither assures that the government will then take the citizens' views into consideration when making policy. With these procedures, the citizens certainly have no means to force the government to respond, and thus no change in the power distribution may occur.[9] Polls, in addition, suffer from other problems which concern the representativeness of the sample, the selection of the questions, and the wording of those questions. Evaluations also suffer from problems, including the unwillingness of program officials either to cooperate in the gathering of information, or to use the evaluation once it is completed because of concern over the implications for their jobs. Yin et al. conclude that, even if they do not devolve power, polls and grievance procedures may possibly affect the attitudes of the communicators and all of these forms of communication may improve service delivery. Both impacts are, however, dependent to a large degree on the willingness of officials to respond to the views communicated.[10]

The same type of conclusions could be drawn about another type of communication process that Yin et al. did not discuss: public hearings. The ACIR-ICMA survey documented the extent to which public hearings are used by local governments to apply for or administer federal grant programs. Out of nine categories of programs–community development block grant, law enforcement, water and sewer, housing, transportation, manpower planning, 701 planning, health, and other–only in the area of law enforcement did less than half the communities report using public hearings.[11] Hearings, however, can communicate information on citizen attitudes, but cannot assure government response, therefore no power redistribution occurs. The ability to vent one's spleen may, nevertheless, positively affect citizen attitudes and, if the government does respond, some improvement in services may occur. Cole and Caputo, for example, did find that there were differences in the way revenue sharing funds were spent between those cities that held public hearings and those that did not.[12]

On the basis of the analysis above, Yin et al. have concluded that citizen organizations of some kind are necessary to achieve a redistribution of power.[13] In their study, they examined organizations established by the Department of Health, Education, and Welfare and focused on two basic structures: Boards (that is, citizens are given legal authority), and Committees (that is, citizen advisory groups). It was recognized, however, that other ways of structuring citizen participation, such as neighborhood governments and community development corporations, may also have the potential of redistributing power, but that establishing such citizen groups outside of the Department is beyond the purview of its authority.

Others have agreed with the conclusion of the Yin study, that the creation of citizen organizations was the most effective way to structure citizen participation. Johnson, for example, argued that one key element determining the effectiveness of participation was the existence of citizen structures.[14] And Vanecko, in his study of community action agencies, concluded that institutional change occurred when the agencies emphasized community organization, and not when they emphasized education and social service.[15] It is important to point out that, although citizen organizations may be effective, they cannot be inclusive forms of participation. The numbers who can participate on a board are less than the numbers who can attend a public hearing. (This conflict between power and inclusiveness was alluded to at the end of Chapter 4.)

If the evidence seems to indicate that citizen organizations are the most effective way to structure citizen participation, it also seems clear that not all organizations are equally effective. The question then becomes what factors determine the effectiveness of those organizations. Research has identified several factors that increase the effectiveness of citizen organizations—one of the most important of these is the legal authority given to the organization. Yin et al. distinguish between citizen boards, which have legal authority to determine policy, and citizen committees, which have only advisory functions. Not surprisingly, they found that the citizen boards tended to have greater impact than did the committees.[16]

Many citizen organizations, of course, may be categorized between these two extremes. The Yin study identified several specific forms of legal authority that increased the effectiveness of citizen organizations. For example, control of the budget is identified as one of the most important types of authority.[17] This makes sense since, as many have indicated before, the budget effectively sets the parameters within which policy is made.[18] In addition, Yin et al. found that the authority to investigate the grievances communicated by other citizens was also a factor that increased the influence of citizen organizations.[19]

Other research has pointed to the importance of that stage of the decision process at which the organization's authority can be exercised. The TARP study cited previously reported that, not surprisingly, citizen participation was more effective in the early stages of decision making. By the later stages, ". . . professional and administrative dominance has had the opportunity firmly to orient policy and program directions."[20]

It is also important that this legal authority be clearly specified and understood by all involved. A variety of studies have pointed to the importance in specifying the roles of citizens' organizations.[21] The reason, obviously, is to try to avoid the development of expectations which cannot, or will not, be fulfilled, since such unfulfilled expectations may lead to frustration among all involved.

In addition to legal authority, evidence also suggests that an organization is more effective if it has an independent power base. Such a power base comes from support from the community, as a whole, as well as from the commitment and dedication of the membership. Support from the community may come because of the prestige of the members of the organization,[22] or because the goals of the organization rank high in the value structure of the community. Both of these goals may contradict the goal of inclusion of those parts of society that have not previously been politically active.

Bennett-Sandler has given a checklist of means that can be used to increase the support both of the membership and of the community as a whole: the organization needs causes; if the membership is poor, the causes should involve specific services rather than long-run issues; the organizational structure should be simple; the organization should be concerned with broad-based programs that are also specific and feasible; the clients should be the public as a whole; the staff's ideas should be used as a basis for discussion, not as a master plan; and there must be two-way communication.[23]

In addition to a power base, there are other resources that organizations need to be effective. Numerous studies have documented the importance of information and expertise. For example, in their study of organizational change, Mazmanian and Neinaber found two cases when even public hearings had an impact on policy, at least in terms of delaying or stopping action. This occurred when those with expertise appeared to contradict the government's proposals.[24] Two ways to help develop informational sources and expertise are by providing the citizen organizations with staff support and by training the citizens. The importance of staff support was underlined by the Yin et al. study: ". . . the most important way of giving participants the capacity to exercise power is to provide them staff over which they have control."[25]

Another potential determinant of the effectiveness of organizations is their structure. The Bennett-Sadler checklist had recommended that the organizational structure should be kept simple and to some degree, the Yin et al. study concurs. They found that simple organizations, which have a single purpose, have a greater impact on services than do umbrella organizations, which bring together representatives of several other organizations.[26] They also found, however, that the umbrella organizations had a greater effect on creating cooperation among the groups in the community. On the other hand, when considering the impact of staff on both types of structures, they discover that umbrella organizations with staff, not only have an impact on the community by helping to create cooperation, but that they also have as much impact on service delivery as do the single-purpose organizations. If it is provided with staff support, the umbrella organization would, therefore, seem to be the most effective organizational structure.[27]

Another important facet of the organizational aspect is the method of selecting the members for the organization. The Yin study found that appointed organizations tended to have the least effectiveness. They attribute this to the fact that there is a tendency for officials to pick those who are already, or who can easily be made, supportive of the existing agency. Thus, such organizations tend to be passive.[28] There are also problems with self-selection as a means of staffing. Evidence presented before indicates that those who would become involved most likely would be from the upper socioeconomic status. In addition, the Yin study argues that self-selection may result in participation that is "ephemeral and/or rancorous."[29] They conclude, as do others, that the best method of recruitment is election.[30]

Peterson, however, has qualified this by arguing that direct elections usually have low turn-out rates that threaten the legitimacy of those chosen. In addition, he argues that direct elections do not ensure continuing relationships with the constituents. Therefore, he recommends that elections should take place within constituent organizations,[31] which would further buttress the argument for the use of umbrella structures.

A final organizational factor concerns the goals and strategies of the organization. Several researchers have argued for the importance of specifying clear goals.[32] In addition, several have argued that it is important that the goals be realistic to avoid the frustration of unfulfilled expectations.[33] Others have argued that, as well as clear goals, the organization should use a strategy that takes a middle position between cooperation with and antagonism of political officials.[34] Cooperation could probably result in little impact, and antagonism may create so much conflict, that nothing would be accomplished. This would support Moynihan's conclusion that the Community Action Agencies that cooperated with City Hall were ineffective, and those who opposed it were destroyed.[35] As noted above, Cole found that those CAAs that were in the middle range of scope and influence resulted in the greatest amount of citizen satisfaction.[36] It appears that here—as elsewhere—moderation is the key. Yet, if this is the case, it is highly doubtful that any significant change in the structure of society will occur—at least not in the short run.

CHARACTERISTICS OF THE TARGET ORGANIZATION

In addition to the characteristics of the organization itself, the characteristics of the organization at which the participation is targeted are also important in determining the success of citizen participation. There are three that can be identified here, although all are closely interrelated. In the first place, the resource base of the target organizations is important, for if the target groups' resource base is lacking, it may be that citizen participation could act to fill that resource void.[37] This would then make the target groups dependent, at least in part, on the citizen organizations. And, as May has argued:

> . . . as organizations become more dependent on other organizations or social groups and classes in their environment, they will become more responsive to their needs.[38]

Of course, participation is usually aimed at government officials. Therefore, the question becomes the extent to which such officials could lack adequate resources, and the extent to which participation could potentially supply them. (It is often the case that officials lack adequate resources.) In a system of government that is as fragmented as the U.S. system, each branch must compete with the others to achieve desired goals. Since so many of the officials in government are elected, citizen participation could be an especially important resource. Such officials rely ultimately on those citizens, in their role of voters, for continuance in office. Therefore, it may well be that they would be supportive of citizen participation to fill a void in their resource base.

A second characteristic of the target organization, which may affect the amount of impact citizen participation will have, is the organizational structure of the target. Organizational theorists have identified two basic types of organizational structure: mechanistic and organic.[39] The mechanistic organization has a large degree of sub-unit specialization, multiple levels of authority, a large ratio of managers and supervisors to total personnel and a large amount of program specification.[40] The basic idea of a mechanistic structure is that it deals with relatively static problems, which permit a high degree of division of labor, specialization, and routine. The organic organization, on the other hand, is the polar opposite of the mechanistic model. It is characterized by less technical specificity, broader distribution of power, fewer specialized subunits and less program specification than the mechanistic model.

Harvey has argued that organic organizations ". . . tend to exhibit flexibilities of organization and general readiness for change which facilitated innovation when the need for it arose."[41] He also argued that the increase in innovation tends to lead to a need for greater resources. As Aiken and Hage argue, and as May argued above, the need for more resources may in turn lead to an increased tolerance for cooperative joint projects with other organizations.[42] It might be hypothesized, therefore, that organic organizations would tend to be more tolerant of citizen participation.

The question then is: under what circumstances may organizations be expected to assume organic rather than mechanistic structures? Burns and Stalker have identified the rate of technical and market change as an important determinant of the choice of an organic or mechanistic model.[43] The greater the change in the environment, the less it is possible to establish a strict division of labor and established routine, both of which are prerequisites for the mechanistic model. It may, therefore, be the case that those organizations dealing with a rapidly changing environment, and with functions that cannot be easily routinized, will be more likely to have organic structures. In other words, both the functions with which the organization deals and the environment of the organization are important determinants of its structure.

Needleman and Needleman have examined one type of government organization that tends to verify the hypothesis concerning the impact of both function and environment on organizational structure. They claim that in most cities the planning department is not a traditional, mechanistic organization.[44] This is so, they argue, because the department must adapt itself to the fragmented decision making of the political system—the effect of the environment.[45] Another factor, they believe, is the fact that community planning tends to be characterized by many fit and start programs.[46] This means, of course, that functions of the department are difficult, or impossible, to routinize or divide into areas of technical specialization. Significantly, Needleman and Needleman use this to explain why planning departments may be more willing to encourage citizen participation.[47] The environment and functions of most elected officials tend to encourage an organic structure and most are expected to be generalists, and deal with a varied and changing environment. This is, of course, not true of all bureaucratic agencies, for some agencies may feel they operate best in a traditional bureaucratic structure. Those agencies that deal with relatively technical and stable functions such as paving highways or treating sewage may be examples. Other agencies, however, may prefer (or be forced to use) a more flexible organic structure. The planning department example is a case in point.

The third major characteristic of the target organization is closely related to the other factors. This characteristic is the attitude of the target organization members.[48] Both of the previous two factors very probably have an impact on the effectiveness of citizen participation by affecting the attitudes of those to whom participation is focused. If the target organizations feel that citizen participation can reinforce their limited resources, or if the organization finds itself in a technically complex and changing environment in which constant information and flexibility is important, then the members of such organizations will be more likely to be tolerant, and possibly even supportive, of citizen organizations. It should be obvious that the tolerance or support of the target group could greatly increase the impact of the citizen organization.

CHARACTERISTICS OF THE ENVIRONMENT

The final set of characteristics that affect the impact of participation are the environmental characteristics, some of which have already been mentioned. For example, it was just pointed out that change in the environment of the target group tends to make that group flexible and willing to search for means to adapt to change—one such means of adaptation is the use of citizen participation. It was also mentioned previously that the degree to which the participation organization ranks high in the value structure of society—either because of the nature of the membership or because of the goals of the organization—will determine the degree of impact the organization can be expected to have.

In addition, there are other important characteristics of the environment that analysts have identified. In the first place, structural characteristics may have an effect, being the extent to which a local government is reformed. Traditional forms of city government are based on an analogy with the national government: the policy-making powers are basically divided between the mayor as executive, the council as the legislature, and with a separate judiciary to adjudicate policy disputes. At various times in the history of urban politics, this traditional structure has come under attack by reformers. Herbert Kaufman argues that there has been a cyclical pattern of values at the level of local government, with the predominant pattern being alternatively representativeness, executive leadership, and nonpartisan competence.[49] The traditional mayor-council form of government, with some adaptation to meet the differing emphases, could conceivably achieve either representativeness or executive leadership. The electoral ties inherent in such a structure, however, make the mayor-council structure a political one. In the search for the third value of nontechnical competence, reformers developed other structures that were frankly designed to weaken the control that citizens could exercise over the government. The reasoning behind this is derived from the collectivist argument that good public policy provides aggregate benefits for the whole, and such policy can be produced only if officials are shielded from the individualistic demands of citizens.

The structures that were developed by reformers, to eliminate the politics from city government, were the commission form of government and the city manager. The commissioners in the commission form are given responsibility for specific functional areas, but are not tied to any particular constituency. In recent years, the commission form has not been used as extensively as the city manager form. In the latter, a city administrator is appointed, either by the council or by the mayor. This city manager, then, is supposedly in charge of the day-to-day operation of the city and, since he is appointed, he is presumably not subject to constituency pressures. In addition to structural changes, the reform movement also produced other alterations in cities, for example, nonpartisan elections, at-large representation, and a civil service merit system.

These reformed governments were not only aimed at achieving the value of nontechnical competence; they were also aimed at the practical goal of destroying the centralized control of the urban party machines. The machines were viewed with alarm by political analysts and good government supporters because, as Greenstone and Peterson explain, they:

> . . . often provided large personal profits to individual racketeers, speculators, and businessmen. Basing their power on control of lower-class voters, the most successful members of the machine emulated their robber baron contemporaries in accumulating personal fortunes.[50]

Where these reforms were instituted, it appears that they did in fact weaken the party structure, although, of course, there were other forces that contributed to the decline in the number of urban party machines.

The extent to which a city is reformed has been shown to be related to citizen participation by affecting both the amount of participation that occurs and the kind of impact the participation will have. Greenstone and Peterson have argued that the effect occurs through the impact of the reforms on the resources of the mayor, the interests of the mayor, and the flow of inputs from citizens to the political system.[51] By destroying, or at least severely weakening, the party structure, the reforms removed a major political resource from the mayors. As Cole argues:

> . . . the decline of the urban machine has left the urban mayor with few (if any) vehicles for the amalgamation of sufficient political power with which to confront contemporary municipal problems.[52]

In those cities with reformed governments, the mayors lack the political resources to oppose the demands for citizen participation. In fact, as noted above, the reform mayors may well lack a stable organization, and mobilizing the citizenry via participation could be a basis for establishing such an organization. Therefore, mayors in reformed cities, lacking the resources to oppose participation, may have a definite interest in fostering such participation. On the other hand, mayors in those cities that still have strong party organizations have the resources to oppose participation and lack the interest to provide for participation.[53] In fact, if participation were to mobilize those citizens who had not been previously active in politics, the control of the party structure might actually be threatened.

Greenstone and Peterson also found that in those cities with strong parties, the flow of information necessary to mobilize the citizenry to demand citizen participation is limited. As they write:

> Centralized power in Chicago prevented opposition demands from flowing easily through the system. Newspapers and even politicians of opposite political persuasion did not give neighborhood groups their support, lest they antagonize the mayor needlessly. . . . In Philadelphia, and still more in New York, less concentrated political power enabled private welfare agencies, Republicans, reformers, and leading newspapers to support neighborhood groups seeking power for themselves.[54]

Ironically, in Los Angeles, which had the weakest party structure of the four cities, the flow of information was lower than in either Philadelphia or New York. Greenstone and Peterson explain this apparent anomaly by arguing that the very disorganization of the political structure meant that there were few channels through which demands could flow.[55]

These forces, according to Greenstone and Peterson, determined the impact of citizen participation in each of the four cities studied. They concluded that, in those cities with strong party machines, as might be expected, there was no redistribution of power. The stronger the reform movement, and, therefore, the weaker the party structure, the more power was redistributed. However, when the focus shifted to an examination of the distribution of material benefits, they discovered that the stronger the machine, the more efficiently and effectively were material benefits distributed.[56] The centralized party structure acted as a conduit for distributing benefits. In fact, parties have historically created and maintained their control through the distribution of such material goods. The lack of such centralized structures in reform cities hampered the dispersal of benefits. Once again, the point must be made that the goals of citizen participation may be contradictory in practice.

Cole found that reformed cities had less citizen participation structures, a pattern that he found to be especially striking when looking simply at whether or not a city has any participation program: ". . . over half those cities rated as most reformed have adopted no citizen participation program, whereas only about 27 percent of those cities rated the least reformed had adopted no participation program."[57] There is an obvious contradiction that defies easy resolution. Greenstone and Peterson found that it was more likely that citizen participation would result in power redistribution in reformed cities than in nonreformed cities; yet Cole found that reformed cities were less likely to have citizen participation programs. The contradiction cannot be explained away by the fact that the time frame or programs were different, for both studies focused on the Community Action Programs in the sixties. Some tentative explanations may, however, be posited.

Participation programs may be less likely in reformed cities for two reasons. In the first place, according to Kaufman, the predominant value premise of the reformed movement was nonpartisan competence.[58] The goal was to free decision makers from political demands and to allow them to make decisions on the basis of their technical expertise. To that end, the city manager form of government places responsibility for operational decision making in the hands of a manager who is appointed rather than elected. Not being subject to election, at least not in a direct sense, he may be less concerned with mobilizing citizen groups or with responding to citizen groups than would be a mayor, who needs an organizational base within the public to maintain his position. This aloofness of the manager from the citizens may discourage citizen participation.

A second reason why reformed cities may have less participation is the extent to which such cities are decentralized. For example, Greenstone and Peterson found in Los Angeles that, since reform groups had no local machine bosses to attack, they also had no incentive to mobilize community organizations. In other words, lack of a clear target may discourage organization.[59]

While there may be less motivation for participation to occur in reformed cities, there may be reason to expect participation that does occur to be successful in achieving redistribution of power. The tradition of reform includes a commitment to democracy and to distribution of power. The extreme concentration of power by the party machines was a primary motivation for the reform movement. Therefore, it might be expected that if citizen organizations did form in reformed cities, there would be support for distributing power to them. It may well be, then, that reformed cities have less citizen participation, but the citizens may get more out of whatever participation there is.

Another characteristic of the environment that may have an effect on the impact of participation is the size of the community. There is contradiction in the literature on the effect of community size. Austin and Cole both found in their studies of community action agencies that the larger the size of the city, the more citizen participation occurs.[60] Austin also found that six of eight community action agencies with less than 150,000 population had limited participation, but only two of nine cities with more than 150,000 had such limited participation.[61] In fact, he found that three of four cities with populations over 150,000 had adversary participation.[62] Similarly, Cole found that ". . . city size is an important predictor of the various types of participation programs"[63] His data indicated that 39 percent of cities with populations between 50,000 and 100,000 had no participation activity, while only 9 percent of cities larger than 500,000 had no such activity.[64]

Verba and Nie, on the other hand, discovered that "Participation is lower than average in places with a population under 10,000 and peaks in places with a population of 10,000 to 25,000."[65] This is congruent with the finding by Yin et al. that "the greatest success for all criteria, *program impact, community impact*, and *skill development*, was found for target populations between 5,000 to 20,000 citizens."[66]

Verba and Nie had developed an argument that may help to explain the diversity in the findings concerning the impact of size. They argue that size is not as important as the extent to which a community has developed characteristics that establish it as a well-defined unit–its "boundedness." They conclude that "as communities grow in size, and, more important, as they lose those characteristics of boundedness that distinguish the independent city from the suburb, participation declines."[67] Size is, therefore, often related to the degree of "boundedness" and may mask or confound the more important relationship. As further substantiation for this, Yin et al. also found that the degree of existing community identification determined the impact of citizen participation.[68] They found that communities with "clearly ascribed identities were considerably more likely to be successful in implementing citizen views."[69]

It appears, therefore, that the degree to which a community is an identifiable unit, and the extent to which its members have a sense of identification with that community, are important determinants both of the extent of participation in the community and the amount of impact the participation may have. The impact of size is apparently important only as it affects community type and community identity.

SUMMARY

Perhaps the most important conclusion to be drawn from this review of the determinants of citizen participation is that it is possible to identify factors that apparently do increase the impact of participation. Not all of these, however, are easily controllable by either citizens or officials designing a citizen participation program. For example, the degree of community identity cannot be easily manipulated, and neither can the structure of the target organization; yet, the structuring of the citizen participation, which to a large extent is concontrollable, is also important. The literature indicates that citizen committees or boards, which are given legal authority, have members elected by an identifiable constituency, and which have identificable power bases, are the most effective forms of citizen participation. It is also important to emphasize again that factors successful in creating one impact of participation may not result in other impacts. This knowledge might help in creating realistic expectations for what participation will produce.

It is also important to know that the structure of the target organization and the characteristics of the environment are important determinants of success. This may also help create more realistic expectations of impact, even if the optimum participation structure is established.

NOTES

[1] Robert K. Yin et al. *Citizen Organizations: Increasing Client Control Over Services* (Santa Monica, Ca.: Rand, 1973), p. 8.

[2] Ibid., pp. 14–15.

[3] Ibid., p. 16.

[4] David M. Austin, "Resident Participation: Political Mobilization or Organizational Co-Optation?" *Public Administration Review* 32 (September, 1972):412.

[5] Yin et al., *Citizen Organizations*, p. 17.

[6] Ibid., pp. 17–23.

[7] Ibid., pp. 17–19.

[8] Ibid., p. 20.

[9] Ibid., pp. 20–23.

[10] Ibid.

[11] *Citizen Participation in the American Federal System* (Washington, D.C.: Advisory Commission on Intergovernmental Relations, 1979), p. 171.

[12] Richard L. Cole and David Caputo, *Urban Politics and Decentralization: The Case of General Revenue Sharing* (Lexington, Mass.: Lexington Books, 1974), p. 115.

[13] Yin et al., *Citizen Organizations*, p. 25.

[14] Carl F. Johnson, *A Study of City-Wide Citizen Participation in Ten Cities, Part II* (Washington, D.C.: National Citizen Participation Council, 1975), p. 11.

[15] James J. Vanecko, "Community Mobilization and Institutional Change: The Influence of the Community Action Program in Large Cities," *Social Science Quarterly* 50 (December 1969):616.

[16] Yin et al., *Citizen Organizations*, p. 45.

[17] Ibid., p. 56.

[18] Aaron Wildavsky, *The Politics of the Budgetary Process*, 3rd ed. (Boston: Little, Brown, 1979), pp. 1–5.

[19] Yin et al., *Citizen Organizations*, pp. 57–58.

[20] Joseph L. Falkson, *An Evaluation of Policy Related Research on Citizen Participation in Municipal Service Systems: Overview and Summary* (Washington, D.C.: TARP Institute, 1974), p. 32.

[21] Carl J. Johnson, *A Study of City-Wide Citizen Participation in Ten Cities, Part I* (Washington, D.C.: National Citizen Participation Council, 1975), p. 34; Kenneth Clark and Jeanette Hopkins, *A Relevant War on Poverty* (New York: Harper & Row, 1968), p. 84.

[22] Philip Selznick, *TVA and the Grass Roots: A Study of Politics and Organization* (Berkeley: University of California Press, 1949), p. 237; Judith V. May, *Citizen Participation: A Review of the Literature* (Council of Planning Libraries, 1971), p. 40.

[23] Georgette Bennett-Sandler, "Citizen Participation in Policing: Issues in the Social Control of a Social Control Agency," *Journal of Voluntary Action Research* 7 (Special Issue, January-June 1978):19.

[24] Daniel A. Mazmanian and Jeanne Nienaber, *Can Organizations Change?* (Washington, D.C.: The Brookings Institution, 1979), pp. 21–24; 72–73.

[25] Yin et al., *Citizen Organizations*, p. 62.

[26] Ibid., pp. 62–64.

[27] Ibid.

[28] Ibid., p. 65.

[29] Ibid.

[30] Ibid.

[31] Paul E. Peterson, "Forms of Representation: Participation of the Poor in the Community Action Programs," *The American Political Science Review* 64 (June 1970):491–507.

[32] Johnson, *A Study of City-Wide Citizen Participation in Ten Cities, Part I*, p. 34; Clark and Hopkins, *A Relevant War on Poverty*, p. 84.

[33] Ibid.

[34] Johnson, *A Study of City-Wide Citizen Participation in Ten Cities, Part I*, p. 34.

[35] Daniel P. Moynihan, "Community Action Loses," in *The New Urban Politics: Cities and the Federal Government*, ed. Douglas M. Fox (Pacific Palisades, Ca.: Goodyear, 1972), p. 174.

[36] Richard L. Cole, *Citizen Participation and the Urban Policy Process* (Lexington, Mass.: Lexington Books, 1974), p. 106.

[37] May, *Citizen Participation*, p. 46.

[38] Ibid.

[39] Michael Aiken and Jerald Hage, "Organization Interdependence and Intra-Organizational Structure," *American Sociological Review* 33 (December 1968):915; Tom Burns and G. M. Stalker, *The Management of Innovation* (London: Tavistock, 1961), p. 209; Edward Harvey, "Technology and the Structure of Organizations," *American Sociological Review* 33 (April 1968): 258.

[40] Harvey, "Technology and the Structure of Organizations," p. 250.

[41] Ibid., p. 258.

[42] Aiken and Hage, "Organizational Interdependence and Intra-Organizational Structure," p. 915.

[43] Burns and Stalker, *The Management of Innovation*, p. 209.

[44] Martin L. Needleman and Carolyn Emerson Needleman, *Guerrillas in the Bureaucracy: The Community Planning Experiment in the United States* (New York: John Wiley & Sons, 1974), p. 163.

[45] Ibid., p. 164.

[46] Ibid., pp. 170–175.

[47] Ibid.

[48] Norman Fainstein and Susan S. Fainstein, "The Future of Community Control," *American Political Science Review* 70 (September 1976):920–921.

[49] Herbert Kaufman, *Politics and Policies in State and Local Governments* (Englewood Cliffs, N.J.: Prentice-Hall, 1963), p. 34.

[50] David J. Greenstone and Paul E. Peterson, "Reformers, Machines, and the War on Poverty," in *Cities and Suburbs*, ed. Bryan T. Downes (Belmont, Ca.: Wadsworth, 1971), p. 379.

[51] Ibid., p. 394.

[52] Cole, *Citizen Participation and the Urban Policy Process*, p. 58.

[53] Greenstone and Peterson, "Reformers, Machines and the War on Poverty," p. 391.

[54] Ibid., p. 394.

[55] Ibid.

[56] Ibid., p. 397.

[57] Cole, *Citizen Participation and the Urban Policy Process*, p. 57.

[58] Kaufman, *Politics and Policies in State and Local Government*, pp. 35–40.

[59] Greenstone and Peterson, "Reformers, Machines, and the War on Poverty," p. 394.

[60] Austin, "Resident Participation," p. 416; Cole, *Citizen Participation and the Urban Policy Process*, p. 43.

[61] Austin, "Resident Participation," p. 416.

[62] Ibid.

[63] Cole, *Citizen Participation and the Urban Policy Process*, p. 43.

[64] Ibid.

[65] Sidney Verba and Norman H. Nie, *Participation in America: Political Democracy and Social Equality* (New York: Harper & Row, 1972), p. 232.

[66] Yin, *Citizen Organizations*, p. 51.

[67] Verba and Nie, *Participation in America*, p. 247.

[68] Yin, *Citizen Organizations*, p. 50.

[69] Ibid.

8

MODELS OF PARTICIPATION

There is some evidence that citizen participation can have some of the impacts that it is expected to have; yet, the literature points clearly to the fact that the expected impacts are not always produced by participation. This should hardly be surprising. It is a confirmation of the basic argument of this book that differing expectations held, and differing structures created, are crucial determinants of the perceived success of participation. In addition, the literature review has pointed to other factors, such as environmental and target organization characteristics, that are also important determinants of the impact of citizen participation.

What is needed is a more rigorous and systematic effort to interrelate these factors into models of citizen participation impact. There is much, of course, that is idiosyncratic about participation experiences. Unique characteristics of individual leaders, particular communities, or other specific situational factors can be crucial determinants of success and failure, but the same could be said about any social or political experience. It is important to move beyond an analysis of the unique to an attempt to develop theoretical understanding of participation, which is why it is important to develop and test models of participation.

It is important to recognize, in this process of model building, that the same factors may not predict equally to the three expected impacts of participation. There is ample evidence in the literature to support the hypothesis that different factors are associated with the three goals of citizen participation. For example, Cole found that the most satisfied citizens were not in those Community Action Agencies that were rated the most powerful. He explained this finding by arguing that these citizens were forced into situations of conflict with their fellow citizens and with government officials. This increased conflict was a source of dissatisfaction with the participation experience.[1] In addition, Cole argued that citizen participation programs raised the level of citizen expectations to unrealistic levels. When the expectations were not met, dissatisfaction was the result. As Cole argues:

> . . . participants at the upper ends of the program continuum can be expected to display greater levels of hostility toward city hall for a reason similar to that often applied to citizens of modernizing nations. When the expectations of citizens are rapidly raised and gratification is not immediately forthcoming, so the theory would argue, they are likely to become frustrated, angered, and potentially hostile.[2]

Cole, therefore, indicates that there is a conflict in achieving the goals of power redistribution and improvement in citizen attitudes. The Community Action Agencies (CAAs), which were most effective in redistributing power, were not the ones in which the citizens were most satisfied. In fact, it appeared as though the power itself may have had a negative effect on their attitudes.

Another example of conflict between two goals of citizen participation came from the research by Greenstone and Peterson, who also examined Community Action Agencies. They found that reformed cities were more effective in redistributing power to the CAAs than were unreformed cities. They explained this by arguing that the reform ideology is supportive of power decentralization. Indeed, the focus of the reformers' efforts was the extreme concentration of power that was characteristic of the urban party machines. In addition, the machine's centralization of power was enough to block efforts to redistribute power. They found, however, that the reformed cities were less effective at efficiently distributing the material benefits of the War on Poverty than were the unreformed cities. To explain this, they argued that the centralization of the unreformed cities provided the structural mechanism to disburse the material benefits efficiently. In fact, machines had maintained themselves through such a process of distributing material goods. On the other hand, the lack of such a centralized structure slowed the process of distributing material benefits. In other words, the same centralization of power that blocked power redistribution acted as a conduit for distributing material benefits, presumably improving service delivery.[3]

These research findings give empirical support for the argument that different factors are determinative in predicting the different impacts of participation. The remainder of this book is an attempt to test this assertion further. This chapter will define the variables to be considered and will posit models of participation.

The next two chapters will test these models using two sets of data. One data set was gathered in 1978 by the Advisory Commission on Intergovernmental Relations and the International City Managers' Association. The data were gathered by mailing a questionnaire to each city with a population over 10,000 and to counties with a population over 50,000. There were 1,495 cities and 323 counties that responded. This data set includes questions on the attitudes of officials toward citizen participation, the numbers and types of participation structures established, the level of citizen activity and the impact of participation, as perceived by the official responding. The strength of these data is their comprehensiveness, although this data base has two significant limitations for the purposes of this study. In the first place, it relies totally on the perception of officials as an indicator of impact. Secondly, the data do not include many variables that, it will be argued here, are important in determining the impact of participation. Most importantly, it has no measures of the individuals participating, nor any information on the environmental context in which participation occurred.

As a result, this study will also utilize data gathered by the authors. These consist of case studies on the decision making processes used to implement the Housing and Community Development Act (HCDA) of 1974 in four cities. In the summer of 1975, the cities of Utica and Syracuse, New York, were examined, and in March and April 1976, Richmond and Norfolk, Virginia, were investigated. Since all four cities relied extensively on citizen advisory boards to meet the HCDAs participation mandate, by using a standardized questionnaire, an attempt was made to interview all the citizens on those boards. The goal of reaching the universe of advisory board members was not reached. In Syracuse, there were 33 citizens on the board, and 28 were interviewed. In Utica, the City Council appointed a board composed of 18 citizens. In addition, the mayor called a meeting to consider allocation of HCDA funds, and proclaimed that those who attended would be his advisory committee—28 people were listed as having attended. Of the total of 46 names on both lists, 34 were interviewed. The same dissension and suspicion in the city, which resulted in two boards being formed, also complicated the interview process. More discussion of the political situation in Utica will appear in Chapter 9. In Norfolk, 18 of 27 citizen board members completed the interview, and in Richmond 21 of 23 citizens responded. The response rates in percentages are as follows: Syracuse, 84 percent; Utica, 74 percent; Norfolk, 67 percent; Richmond, 91 percent. With the exception of Utica, where the internal conflict made some citizens unwilling to participate, there was no obvious bias in the pattern of response.

In each of these cities, the boards were to act as advisers to those government officials responsible for making decisions concerning the allocation of the community development funds. It was believed that the nature of the interaction between citizens and officials would be an important determinant of the impact of participation. Therefore, attempts were made to interview the government officials with whom the advisory boards interacted most closely. Eighteen government officials in Utica, and 24 in Syracuse, were interviewed. In Richmond, 20 officials were interviewed, and 29 were interviewed in Norfolk. With the exception of a few department heads in Utica, who refused to cooperate, it was felt that the goal of reaching those officials most involved with the HCDA process was achieved.

The respondents were asked a variety of questions intended to elicit perceptions of problem areas in: the cities, the workings of the advisory boards, the attitudes toward government, and personal characteristics. There was substantial overlap in the questions that were asked of the citizens and officials, in order to allow comparisons. In addition, each group of respondents was asked a set of questions specifically applicable to itself. All respondents were also encouraged to make additional comments or elaborate, if they so desired.

The methodology of the studies of the four cities is a combination of case study and structured interviews among the participants. As with any methodology, there are advantages and disadvantages. On the positive side, the case study approach allows for an in-depth examination of the implementation process in the cities. This means that information on the context in which participation occurred is available. Also, it is possible, in the process, to examine the participants at the individual level of analysis. Presumably, if participation has an impact, that impact should be perceived by these participants. Using a structured interview among the participants permits some standardization of the data. The disadvantage, of course, is that the case study methodology does not permit control of threats to internal validity. Another problem is the fact that the focus on only four cities limits the generality of the results. It should be noted that, since two sets of data are being used for testing hypotheses, it may be necessary to develop different operationalizations for variables in each data set. Therefore, in the following discussion of the models, operationalization of the variables will not be discussed thoroughly. A fuller discussion of the operationalization of variables will be included in the data analysis chapters. It should also be made clear that both sets of data are cross-sectional, which means that it is impossible to examine the dynamic aspects of the participation process. Attempts have been made, however, to measure dynamic aspects indirectly by asking the respondents to report their perceptions of change.

MODEL OF PARTICIPATION: POLICY IMPACT

It is hypothesized that there are three classes of variables that determine the impact of participation on policy: characteristics of the environment, characteristics of the target organization, and characteristics of the citizen participation structures. Impact on policy will be measured by the perceptions of respondents in both the ACIR data and the case studies. In addition, in the case studies, evidence on the change in policy to conform with citizen requests will be used to substantiate the perceptions.

Environmental Characteristics

As indicated in the last chapter, the context in which participation takes place can affect both how much and what effect citizen participation has. Studies by Cole, and Greenstone and Peterson, found relationships between the type of government structure and the amount of citizen participation and the impact it has.[4] Cole found that reformed cities have less citizen participation structures than do unreformed cities. This was explained by the fact that, as Kaufman argued, the reformed structure was created with the goal of increasing professional competence. As Sayre and Kaufman found, in a study of New York City, professionalism increases the power of bureaucracies in city government.[5] As Chapter 5 argues, citizen participation is often contradictory to decision making by bureaucrats on the basis of professional expertise. Therefore, it would seem logical to hypothesize that participation which occurs in reformed cities will be less likely to create changes in policy than that which occurs in unreformed cities. Further substantiation for this hypothesis can be found in the argument that in unreformed cities, government officials are tied directly to identificable constituencies via the electoral process and wish to cultivate citizen support to maintain themselves in office. The effects of this concern should also be felt to some degree by bureaucrats, who are at least legally accountable to the elected leaders.

Another aspect of the environment that is hypothesized to have an effect on the impact of participation is the amount of conflict that exists in the city. The organizational theory literature argues that organizations faced with a rapidly changing environment will attempt to adapt by adopting a flexible and open organizational structure and by developing resource bases.[6] Thus, it appears that the instability, which conflict may create, would act to increase the openness of the government to citizen participation. Nevertheless, it is argued here, that some conflict may make it difficult or impossible to achieve changes in policy. The conflict may well extend to disagreements concerning what policy changes would be desirable. While the governmental organizations may provide access to citizens in an attempt to mollify them, the lack of consensual demands may well stymie governmental actions—at least in the short run. This means that policy change would be minimal at best. It is hypothesized, therefore, that the greater the conflict in the environment, the less policy impact will be produced by citizen participation.

The literature also indicates that the value structure of the community would have an effect on the impact of participation.[7] The general support, of the concept of citizen participation, should provide those citizens who do participate with a power base to use in interactions with government officials. On the other hand, the support by the general public, for a particular citizen group or a particular issue that a citizen group espouses, should also provide that group with a power base. Unfortunately, neither data set used in this study includes measures on the attitudes of the general citizenry. Because of this, it will be impossible to test hypotheses concerning the effect of citizen attitudes on the policy impact of citizen participation.

Target Characteristics

The last chapter identified three characteristics, in the organizations that serve as targets for citizen participation, that are believed to increase the impact of participation. The first was the extent to which the target organization felt it needed to increase its resource base, and perceived citizen participation as a means of achieving that goal.[8] Secondly, it was argued that those organizations with an organic, as opposed to a mechanistic, structure would be more open to input from citizen participation. Such an organic model is expected to characterize organizations that deal with a rapidly changing environment.[9]

Unfortunately, neither data set provides measures for the degree to which the target organizations need to increase their resource base. The case study data provide only minimal, and not very satisfactory, indicators of the structural type of the organizations included. However, both sets of data do provide very clear measures for the third characteristics of the target organization that is believed to be important: the attitudes of the organizations' members toward participation. It is argued that these measures can act as acceptable substitutes for perception of need and structural type, since both of the other factors are believed to have an effect on participation by making the officials, who are the targets of participation, more willing to tolerate citizen input.

The attitudes of the officials are important because citizen participation is an interaction. Even if the participation is mandated, officials could (if they were opposed to it) stymie the efforts of participants by establishing purely symbolic participation structures, and by ignoring citizen requests transmitted by those structures. The willingness of officials to respond to participation seems to be an important prerequisite, if citizen participation is to have an impact on policies of government. It is, therefore, hypothesized that the more positive the attitudes of the officials toward citizen participation, the more that participation will have an impact on policy.

Organizational Characteristics

The third set of determinants of whether citizen participation will have an impact on policy are characteristics of the participation itself. The first such characteristic that would be hypothesized to increase the policy impact of participation is the existence of a citizen organization, for organizations provide a point of regularized contact between officials and citizens. Regularized contact makes it less likely that the officials would ignore the organization. In addition, an organization lowers the costs involved in officials responding to citizen demands for two reasons: first, such a regularized procedure is more easily integrated into the decision processes than is an ad hoc or intermittent contact, and second, an organization is more likely to facilitate establishing priorities among citizen demands than is a structure such as an open meeting. This makes it easier for officials to respond to those demands that the citizens themselves feel are most important. By making it more difficult for officials to ignore citizens, and yet by lowering the costs involved for officials to respond, organizations increase the likelihood that citizen participation will have an impact on policy. It is, therefore, hypothesized that citizen organizations will have a greater impact on policy than will public hearings. (It must be pointed out that policy impact is conceived here as creating policy change.) It may well be the case that public hearings are very effective in stopping governmental action, thus assuring maintenance of the status quo.

Certain characteristics of citizen organizations should increase their effectiveness. If the organizations are given some form of legal authority over the decision process, it should be hypothesized that they will have greater impact on policy than if no such authority were given. Since all of the citizen organizations in both data sets are solely advisory, it will not be possible to test this hypothesis. Nevertheless, there are other characteristics of the structuring of participation that can be tested; for example, one finding of the TARP study of eight municipal services was that, the earlier the participation occurs in the decision process, the greater the impact it will have.[10] This makes sense intuitively, since it appears difficult to change a plan, once it is presented as a *fait accompli.* Therefore, it is hypothesized that the earlier the stage of the decision process at which participation occurs, the greater the impact.

It is also hypothesized that, the greater the amount of access citizens have to the decision process, the greater their impact will be. Although, as hypothesized here, boards may have more impact than do public hearings, providing multiple structures for citizen access would make it possible for citizens to put greater pressure on officials. This, in turn, would make it more likely for the citizens to have an impact on policy.

Another resource of power is information. One weakness citizens frequently have is their inability to compete with government officials who have the time to develop expertise. Citizens might be expected to have a greater impact on policy decisions, if they had expertise equivalent to that of the officials with whom they deal. Such expertise could come from two sources. Citizens could have equivalent expertise because of the nature of their jobs. For example, in their study of the Army Corps of Engineers, Mazmanian and Nienaber found that two instances where citizen participation was effective involved college professors, in one instance, and a retired Corps engineer in another[11] and, in both cases, the participants had expertise. The other possible source of expertise is provision of professional staff support for the citizens.

Only limited information on the expertise of the citizens is available. The Syracuse, Norfolk, and Richmond boards were given staff support but did not have independent staff. The ACIR-ICMA data indicates whether or not staff assistance was given to citizen participants. It is, therefore, hypothesized that the provision of staff support increases the impact citizens have on policy.

The basic argument here is that there are three sets of characteristics that determine the degree to which participation will have an impact on policy: environmental characteristics, characteristics of the target organization (specifically the attitudes of the members), and characteristics of the participation structure (see Figure 8.1).

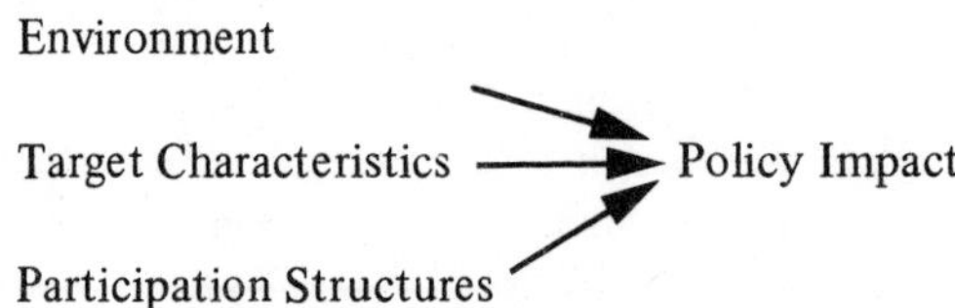

FIGURE 8.1. Determinants of Policy Impact

MODEL OF PARTICIPATION: POWER REDISTRIBUTION

Policy impact is not easily measured directly. Changes in policy may be the result of factors other than citizen requests; yet if the changes do conform with citizen requests, it seems justified to conclude that the citizens had an impact. It is more difficult to measure power redistribution, for several reasons. In the first place, there are two conceptions in the participation literature of what power redistribution is. One conception is that power redistribution is the inclusion, in the political process, of those people who have been previously excluded. This is the conception used by Greenstone and Peterson in their study of Community Action Agencies.[12] The other conception is the transferrence of legal authority from government officials to citizens. This is the conception used by Yin et al. in their study of citizen participation in HEW.[13] It should be pointed out that, in practice, including those not previously active may well be contradictory to transferring legal authority, for officials may feel uncomfortable about transferring authority to citizens with no experience or expertise. This reluctance may be due, not to the megalomania of the officials, but to their concern over how citizens who are inexperienced could possibly exercise authority wisely and responsibly. Officials, might, however, be willing to transfer authority if they feel citizens do have experience. Unfortunately, those with the experience or expertise that might make transferring authority more tolerable to officials are not likely to be those who were previous excluded. It is, therefore, unlikely (though not necessarily impossible) that broadly inclusive participation will be granted legal authority.

Another problem with measuring power redistribution is that of distinguishing it empirically from policy impact. The ability of citizens to achieve the services they desire from government is certainly what would normally be considered a form of power. To conclude, however, that policy impact is an indicator of power redistribution is to ignore the basic definition of power posited by Dahl; that is, the ability of A to get B to do something he would not otherwise have done.[14] A response, by officials, to a citizen request certainly does not indicate that citizens have the kind of causal control implied by Dahl's definition. For example, the acquiescence by the city's street department, to plow a street after a snowstorm, does not imply that power has been redistributed. Before it can be concluded that power has changed hands, citizens must be given legal authority to force the officials to comply, or officials must demonstrate, over time, that not only are they willing to respond to specific citizen requests, but that they are also willing to allow citizens to determine the basic direction of policy.

Neither set of data used in this study includes participation structures that have been granted legal authority. In addition, neither data set is longitudinal, which means that it is impossible to determine the extent to which citizen inputs determine the basic direction of policy. Therefore, this study will focus on the conception of power redistribution that is concerned with the extent to which those citizens, who were not previously involved in politics, were included in new participation structures. The four case studies provide such information on the members of the advisory boards. In this study, the measure of power redistribution will be the extent to which those boards included new participants.

It is argued that there are two classes of variables that will affect the extent to which citizen participation will result in power redistribution: environmental characteristics and target organization characteristics.

Environmental Characteristics

As indicated before, the nature of the city government affects the impact of citizen participation. Greenstone and Peterson found that reformed cities were more likely to have citizen participation in which power is redistributed. They argue that the basic thrust of the reform movement was the destruction of the centralized party structure and the distribution of that power to numerous civic organizations.[15] Power redistribution thus forms a basic part of the reformist ideology; however, reformed structures also attempt to maximize the value of expertise in their decision making. Power in such structures tends to rest with professionals and bureaucrats. A basic argument of this study is that citizen participation is contrary to the values of professional bureaucrats. It is believed that, when possible, they will attempt to limit access to those citizens who have demonstrated their ability and knowledge. Citizens who have previously been active could more directly demonstrate their competence. It is, therefore, hypothesized that, the greater the extent to which the city is reformed, the less the power redistribution.

It is also believed that the amount of conflict in the community will affect the extent to which power redistribution will occur—conflict is obviously a destabilizing influence. One organizational response to such an influence may be to insulate itself, but such a strategy may be impossible for political organizations. By their very nature, such organizations are forced to interact on a relatively constant basis with their constituency in the environment. In the case of citizen participation, governments are often mandated to include citizens. It is argued, therefore, that in such instances, officials will provide access to citizens, but will attempt to minimize the potential disruption that may result from participation in a conflictual environment. When possible, officials will provide access to those citizens who have demonstrated their knowledge of the governmental processes and their ability to play the political games. Since only those citizens who had been previously active could establish such a record, it is hypothesized that in a conflictual environment there will be less power redistribution.

Target Organization Characteristics

As previously indicated, the major measures of target organization characteristics, available in either data set, are indicators of the attitudes of the organizational members toward citizen participation. It is believed that these indicators are especially important, since government officials possess the resources to stymie participation, even if it is mandated. In general, it is hypothesized that the more positive officials are toward participation, the more successful citizen participation will be.

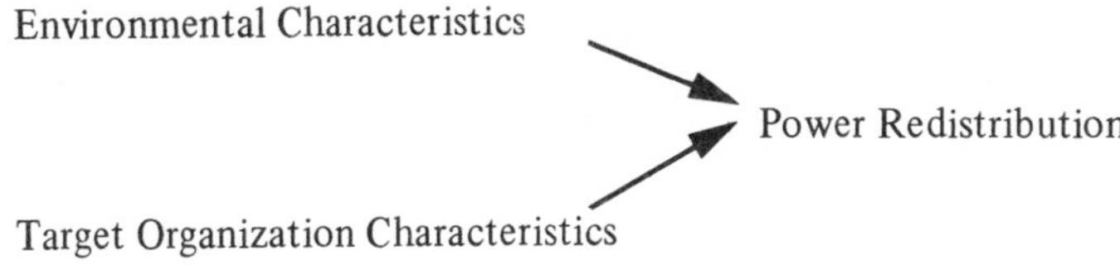

FIGURE 8.2. Determinants of Power Redistribution

In sum, the basic argument here is that there are two determinants that will decide the extent to which structures of participation will be established that will include those citizens who have not previously been politically active: characteristics of the environment and characteristics of the target organization. The relationship may be pictured schematically as in Figure 8.2.

MODEL OF PARTICIPATION: CITIZEN ATTITUDES

The third and final effect, which citizen participation is expected to have, is an increase in positive attitudes of the participants. Philosophers have consistently argued that participation in the affairs of state will create numerous positive political attitudes on the part of the citizen activists. Citizens are expected to become more trusting of government and to be more sure of their ability to have an impact on governmental decisions. In addition, the citizen participants are expected to be more satisfied with their lives in general, since participation is believed to increase their sense of self-fulfillment.

While philosophers have been relatively united on this argument, the empirical researchers have been far from agreement.[16] The review of the empirical literature indicated that, while Cole found that participation resulted in increased citizen trust, especially in those programs in the middle range of power and scope, other research concluded that no such relationship existed between participation and trust.[17] Some evidence has indicated that participation may increase efficacy, but the effect may only be felt toward those particular programs in which the citizens participate, rather than toward the government as a whole.[18] Even more negative findings were reported by TARP, which concluded that evidence on the impact of citizen participation on citizen attitudes was ". . . the weakest area of findings."[19]

There may be good reason for participation to have little impact on the attitudes citizens have toward the political system, for the basic attitudes of trust and efficacy are learned in a socialization process that begins in early childhood and continues throughout life. What is learned in that early socialization may be assumed to be relatively permanent and impervious to change due to a single, isolated phenomenon uch as participating on an advisory board. Any massive change may well require a longer term of experience.

Another reason why participation may not produce an increase in citizen trust and efficacy is the fact that the participation experience may be negative rather than positive. Participation is costly in terms of both time and effort and, it may invove citizens in conflict, which may make them feel stressful. Before such costs will be borne willingly, the citizens must feel that the benefits received will outweigh the costs. Whether or not such a favorable cost-benefit ratio is achieved, is a purely subjective calculation.

While the effect of participation on the political attitudes of citizens may be limited, research by Cole does indicate that impact can be felt in some cases.[20] It is hypothesized here that such impact will be dependent on three sets of variables: characteristics of the environment, characteristics of the participants, and characteristics of the target organization. The case study data will be used to examine these hypotheses.

Characteristics of the Environment

Cole argued that citizens were most trusting when they were active in those Community Action Agencies that he ranked as being between the two extremes of scope and influence.[21] He had expected that those in agencies with minimal influence and scope would be low in trust, since they would receive little from their efforts. However, he had expected that those in agencies ranked the highest in scope and influence would be the most trusting. One explanation he gave for the unexpected finding was that those agencies with the most scope and influence forced citizens unwillingly into situations of conflict with both government officials and their fellow citizens. This conflict was, he argued, considered stressful by the citizens and, thus, limited the extent to which participation could play a role in their becoming more trusting.[22]

Using this same logic, it is argued here that the amount of conflict in the environment will be one factor affecting the extent to which participation results in increased citizen trust and efficacy. In a highly conflictual environment, those citizens who are active would inevitably have to face conflict. The stress that results from this will limit the extent to which the participation experience will increase their trust. Since the conflict may well reduce the degree to which the citizens can successfully achieve their goals, it may also be the case that citizens will be less likely to feel themselves more politically efficacious. Therefore, it is hypothesized that the greater the conflict in the environment, the less citizen participants will report themselves to be trusting and efficacious.

Characteristics of the Participants

It was argued before that participation may have little impact on increasing the trust of citizens because the experience may be perceived to be negative. It is believed that the extent to which the experience was negative will depend, ultimately, on the extent to which citizens felt that the benefits outweighed the costs, an individualized, subjective calculation. Yet, it is believed that one indicator of the extent to which that calculation will be positive is whether the participants felt that they had achieved from participation what they expected. Presumably, the expectations of benefits motivated the citizens to be involved. If they received those benefits, it may be logical to argue that they were satisfied with the experience. It is hypothesized that this satisfaction, in turn, should make the citizens more trusting of the city government with which they dealt. This may not, however, have any impact on their attitudes toward other levels of government.

Characteristics of the Target Organization

A final factor that is believed to be an important determinant of the attitudes of the citizen participants is the attitudes of the officials with whom they interact. If the officials are either threatened by participation or are disdainful of it, the interaction between the officials and citizens may be expected to be strained, which may result in the citizens perceiving the participatory experience as negative. If the officials are supportive, however, the interaction should be less stressful and the citizen participants should develop more positive attitudes toward the city government. Again, it may not necessarily be the case that the positive attitudes will be generalized to other levels of government.

SUMMARY

There are three factors that are believed to determine whether citizen participation will have an impact on citizen attitudes: characteristics of the environment, the expectations of the participants, and the attitudes of the officials. Schematically, this model of participation appears as follows in Figure 8.3.

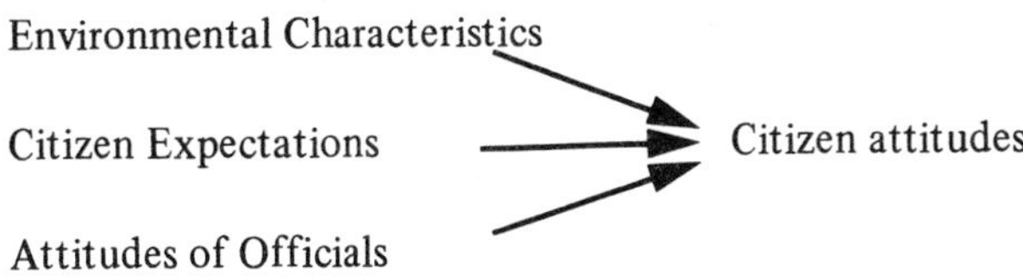

Figure 8.3. Determinants of Citizen Attitudes

As indicated, the next two chapters will test these hypotheses using two sets of data.

TESTABLE HYPOTHESES

Policy Impact

The greater the reformed structures of government, the less the policy impact.
The greater the conflict, the less the policy impact.
The more positive are the attitudes of officials toward citizen participation, the greater the policy impact.
Organizations create more policy impact than do hearings.
The earlier the stage at which citizens are given access to the decision process, the greater the policy impact.
The greater the amount of access given to citizens, the greater the policy impact.
The provision of staff support increases the impact citizens have on policy.

Power Redistribution

The greater the reformed structures of government, the less the power redistribution.
The greater the conflict, the less the power redistribution.
The more positive are the attitudes of officials toward citizen participation, the more the power redistribution.

Citizen Attitudes

The greater the conflict, the less trusting and efficacious are the citizens.
The more satisfied the citizens are with participation, the more trusting and efficacious they will be.
The more supportive the officials are of participation, the more trusting and efficacious the citizens will be.

NOTES

[1] Richard L. Cole, *Citizen Participation and the Urban Policy Process* (Lexington, Mass.: Lexington Books, 1974), p. 117.

[2] Ibid., p. 116.

[3] J. David Greenstone and Paul E. Peterson, "Reformers, Machines and the War on Poverty," in *The New Urban Politics: Cities and the Federal Government*, ed. Douglas M. Fox (Pacific Palisades, Ca.: Goodyear, 1972), p. 169.

[4] Cole, *Citizen Participation and the Urban Policy Process*, p. 51; and Greenstone and Peterson, "Reformers, Machines, and the War on Poverty," p. 165.

[5] Herbert Kaufman, *Politics and Policies in State and Local Governments* (Englewood Cliffs, N.J.: Prentice-Hall, 1963), p. 34; and Wallace Sayre and Herbert Kaufman, *Governing New York City* (New York: W. W. Norton, 1965), chapter 11.

[6] Michael Aiken and Jerald Hage, "Organizational Interdependence and Intra-organizational Structure," *American Sociological Review* 33 (December 1968):912–930; Tom Burns and G. M. Stalker, *The Management of Innovation* (London: Tavistock, 1961), pp. 120–121; Edward Harvey, "Technology and the Structure of Organizations," *American Sociological Review* 33 (April 1968):247–259.

[7] Judith V. May, *Citizen Participation: A Review of the Literature* (Council of Planning Libraries, 1971), p. 47.

[8] Ibid., p. 46.

[9] Edward Harvey, "Technology and the Structures of Organizations," *American Sociological Review* 33 (April 1968):250.

[10] Joseph L. Falkson, *An Evaluation of Policy Related Research on Citizen Participation in Municipal Service Systems: Overview and Summary* (Washington, D.C.: TARP Institute, 1974), p. 32.

[11] Daniel Mazmanian and Jeanne Nienaber, *Can Organizations Change?* (Washington, D.C.: The Brookings Institution, 1979), pp. 21–24; 72–73.

[12] Greenstone and Peterson, "Reformers, Machines, and the War on Poverty," p. 163.

[13] Robert K. Yin et al. *Citizen Organizations: Increasing Client Control Over Services* (Santa Monica, Ca.: Rand, 1973), p. v.

[14] Robert A. Dahl, "The Concept of Power," *Behavioral Science* 2 (July 1957): 201–215.

[15] Greenstone and Peterson, "Reformers, Machines, and the War on Poverty."

[16] For a review of classical arguments, see Carole Pateman, *Participation and Democratic Theory* (London: Cambridge University Press, 1970), chapters 1 and 2.

[17] Yin et al., *Citizen Organizations*, pp. 31–41.

[18] Ibid., p. 39.

[19] Falkson, *An Evaluation of Policy Related Research on Citizen Participation in Municipal Service Systems*, p. 33.

[20] Cole, *Citizen Participation and the Urban Policy Process*, pp. 114–117.

[21] Ibid.

[22] Cole, p. 117.

9

THE MODELS APPLIED: CASE STUDIES

With the exception of a few booming sunbelt cities, American cities in the mid-seventies shared some serious ailments. In the first place, their populations continued to decline as increasing numbers fled the noise, blight and fear of urban living and migrated to the greener pastures of suburbia. This left the cities with a decreased tax base with which to confront the very problems that had caused the migration. Aggravating the situation was the fact that those who remained in the cities were those who lacked the resources to leave: the young, the old, the poor, and the black. These are the groups who look most desperately to government for the provision of necessary social services. The total impact of these processes was to leave the cities with less resources to cope with increasing demands.

In the fact of this "urban crisis," Richard Nixon proposed the Housing and Community Development Act (HCDA) to help alleviate the physical blight. The act, which provided block grants to cities, was signed in 1974. Like most legislation of that period, this act contained a requirement that citizens be included in the process of implementing the program on the local level. To be eligible for funds, the act specifically required that cities must provide citizens with "adequate information" about the program, hold public hearings to elicit citizen views, and provide citizens "adequate opportunity to participate in the development of the application."[1] It must be remembered that these participation requirements were much less than those that had appeared in legislation in the sixties. This chapter is based on data gathered during 1975 and 1976 that focuses on the citizen participation processes used by Syracuse and Utica, New York, and Richmond and Norfolk, Virginia, to meet the participation requirements of this act. The New York cities were examined during the first year of the program and the Virginia cities in the second year.

OVERVIEW OF THE CITIES

The cities faced the urban crisis to varying extents. All were expecting declining populations and were thus concerned about tax bases, but there was little doubt that of the four, Utica was in the most desperate shape. The smallest of the four cities, with a population of approximately 82,000, it had once been a prosperous community with an economy based on textile mills. The mills, however, had moved to the south and nothing was moving in to take their place. The unemployment rate in 1976, the year after the study was done, was 12.05 percent. Politically, Utica had a mayor-council form of government, but did have some characteristics of reformed government. The elections were nonpartisan and the council was elected at-large rather than from districts. The mayor at the time the study was conducted was Edward A. Hanna, who had been elected on a populist platform, based on a direct appeal to the people. To symbolize his openness to the public, once elected he removed the door to his office and added the phrase "This government belongs to its people," to the city's stationery. His attacks on what he saw as the establishment, which included the City Council, resulted in political polarization in the city.

This polarization significantly affected the participation process used to implement the HCDA. Each of the City Council members appointed two citizens to an advisory board to draw up an application for HCDA funds. They produced a plan, but the mayor refused to recognize the legitimacy of the group, so the plan was doomed to failure. Meanwhile, the mayor established his own board by calling a public meeting and naming those who showed up his advisory board—the board was thus large and unstructured. While the mayor's office prepared the grant application, the mayor's group looked solely at housing problems. In addition to the two boards, four public hearings, various neighborhood meetings, and door-to-door surveys were used to meet the participation requirement.

When the mayor produced his grant application, the director of Utica Community Action, Inc. wrote to the County Department of Planning, which acted as a regional clearinghouse for the grant, to complain both about the mayor's plan and the process he used to produce it. Specifically, she complained about the lack of technical assistance given to the citizens. In addition, she argued that the public hearings were ineffective because Mayor Hanna had repeatedly stated that he would not be influenced by the hearings, and, she claimed, he abused those who spoke at the hearings. Mayor Hanna responded in defense of his actions and his program. Such acrimony and polarization may well be expected to affect the participation process in Utica.

Syracuse, by contrast with Utica, was not in such desperate condition. With a population of 183,000 in 1975, it had a diversified economy based on various manufacturing firms, including Carrier, General Electric and two automobile plants. The unemployment rate in 1976 was 8.93 percent.

The city had a typical unreformed government: mayor-council structure with partisan elections. Five of the nine councilmen were chosen from districts and four were at-large. At the time of the study, the mayor was Lee Alexander, the first Democrat after several years of Republican control.

In preparing the grant application in 1974, fifteen neighborhood meetings were held throughout the city, and in the second year of the program, ten neighborhood meetings were held. The meetings were publicized with posters, public service announcements, ads in newspapers, and with fliers that proclaimed in capital letters that Mayor Lee Alexander "invites" citizens to attend the meetings. A booklet outlining what suggestions were made at each of the meetings was printed, with the mayor's picture on the first page. The combined attendance at the ten meetings was estimated to be 400.

In addition, a Community Development Advisory Committee (CDAC) was established to act as liaison between citizens and the city government and to assist in drawing up plans for allocating community development funds. The committee was composed of 19 representatives from 14 neighborhoods and 18 at-large mayoral appointees. (When possible the neighborhoods chose their own representatives.) Finally, a pamphlet describing the second year community development process stated that "Formation of representative neighborhood organizations is encouraged."

All of this is in stark contrast to the experience Syracuse had with citizen participation under the community action programs in the sixties. The city's Community Action Training Center (CATC), sponsored by Syracuse University and, for a time by the Office of Economic Opportunity, was opposed by the mayor. According to Clark and Hopkins, he saw the community action program as a "competitive political base."[2] There were probably two main reasons for the change in the city's orientation to citizen participation. First, the CATC had dabbled with political mobilization by conducting a voter registration drive, which registered more Democrats than Republicans. This was obviously not viewed with pleasure by the Republican mayor. The HCDA program was not only aimed at political redistribution but, instead, focused on material distribution of federal resources. The second main difference was that Lee Alexander, as the first Democratic mayor after long Republican domination, could see the citizen participation process of the HCDA as a means of establishing a grass roots base of support.

In both Syracuse and Utica, the citizen participation became part of the political struggles. This was less the case in the two Virginia cities, which may be due to the fact that both cities had reformed city governments. Such governments, argues Kaufman, are formed to maximize the value of nonpartisan competence in the governing of cities.[3] Both cities had city manager forms of government and both had nonpartisan elections. Richmond retained one characteristic of a nonreformed structure—its 9 councilmen were elected from districts. In Norfolk, however, the entire council was chosen at-large.

Richmond had a population of approximately 233,000 at the time the study was done. Like Syracuse, it has a widely diversified economic base, including industry, and wholesale and regional trade. In addition, since Richmond is the state capital, 17 percent of the population was employed by government. The strong economic base may explain the low unemployment rate at the time of the study (approximately 5.08 percent), and the fact that, despite a large black population, racial relations had not been a major problem.

Richmond had had active and effective Model Cities and Community Action Programs and they were still factors that had to be considered in the city's decision making. In addition, the city had very distinct neighborhoods, which play an important role in city politics.

To meet the participation requirements of the HCDA in the first year of the program, Richmond relied on 14 neighborhood meetings, and one citywide public meeting. At the neighborhood meetings, questionnaires were handed out to determine citizen priorities for allocating the funds. In addition to the meetings, the city reconstituted and enlarged the city strategy team (CST) to act as a channel of citizen input for the preparation of the grant application. This team had been created to improve the city's decision making, by providing a forum where government officials from various agencies and various levels of government, as well as citizens, could examine the priorities of the city. The city strategy team had initially been composed of nine city officials and eight citizens appointed by the city council.

To reconstitute the CST for the HCDA process, 13 additional citizens were appointed, as representatives of neighborhood organizations and citizens groups, in areas where the HCDA funds might be targeted. Various city departments, for example the Department of Planning and Community Development and the Bureau of the Budget, were charged with making recommendations on the HCDA allocations to the CST. The plan produced by the CST differed little from that recommended by the planning staff; yet, in some instances, the CST was specifically ignored by the city manager, who made the final decision. For instance, the city manager threw out the CSTs request for funding curb ramps and added an allocation for street lighting in an area undergoing gentrification. In the second year, the CST was the sole vehicle for participation in the grant application process, but it had little to do, since commitments and guidelines made in the first year governed the allocations in the second year.

At the time of the study, Norfolk was the largest independent city in Virginia, with a population of 287,000. The city's location on an outstanding natural harbor has significantly affected its development—it is at the center of the world's largest naval concentration. This helps to explain both a low unemployment rate (6.15 percent in 1976), and the fact that the largest employment sector is government.

Norfolk has an image of a vigorous boom city, due in part to an ambitious urban renewal program, which has renovated much of the downtown area, in an effort to make the city a tourist and convention center. The rebuilding of the downtown has created some problems for the black population, since it meant the destruction of inner city housing occupied primarily by blacks; however, racial conflict was not a major problem.

In Norfolk, no structure existed that could be used to meet the participation requirements of the HCDA. Initially the city focused on publicizing the program through handouts, newspapers, meetings with neighborhood organizations, and an open forum. In October, the city council created a Citizen Advisory Commission (CAC) to provide further citizen input, and the council appointed the 24 members of the CAC on an at-large basis.

The community development plan was drawn up by the Community Development Committee, which was composed of representatives from the departments of Planning, Finance, Human Resources, Community Improvement, and Research, as well as the city manager. While the professional staff was drawing up the plan, the CAC was charged with establishing community goals. When completed, the grant application was given to the CAC for review and recommendations, but because of the exigencies of time, the CAC could do little to change it.

In the second year, the CAC began organization meetings early. It participated in citywide public meetings on the grant application, but it still was not involved in drawing up the second year plan. The CAC was not viewed as a programmatic body and, instead, was charged with completing studies of three of the goal areas identified during the first year. It did, however, review the plan, which again was drawn up the Community Development Committee and the City Manager, and this time, the CAC made specific comments on the HCDA allocation and succeeded in altering it.

Each of the four cities similarly established advisory boards, as vehicles for citizen participation in the grant application process, but the differences among the cities outweigh this similarity, for there was significant variance in the extent to which those boards were important in the HCDA decision making process. In Utica, the political maneuvering between the mayor and the council made the citizen participation on both boards meaningless—the mayor effectively controlled the decision making process. By contrast, the political situation in Syracuse and the mayor's desire to build grassroots support facilitated the participation process. The final plan reflected the citizen input: the HCDA money was distributed widely throughout the city so that all groups got a piece of the pie.

In Norfolk the impact of the citizens was minimal, although the requests by the CAC to make some changes in the second year plan were acceded to. The reason for the limited citizen impact could be traced to the reform mentality prevalent in the city. Expertise was seen as the most important basis for decision making, so the professionals drew up the grant application, while the citizens worked on reports that considered long-range goals for the city in nonspecific terms. Presumably, the experts would then determine the means to achieve these goals.

Richmond was also a reformed city, but it had active and organized neighborhoods whose representatives were given access to the City Strategy Team. As in Norfolk, the professionals had a major role in advising the CST. This may be one reason why the plan produced by the CST was so similar to that proposed by the professionals yet, the city manager felt free to make alterations in the plan as he saw fit.

While these vignettes may be useful in understanding the data analysis that follows, the primary focus is on attempting to identify general factors that explain the impacts of citizen participation, rather than on examining the unique characteristics of each participatory experience. The first hypotheses to be tested are those concerning the effect of citizen participation on policy.

POLICY IMPACT

There are three major categories of variables believed to affect the degree to which citizen participation can have an impact on policy: environmental characteristics, and characteristics of the targets and the structure of the participation. One measure of policy impact used here is perceptual. Respondents were asked about their perceptions of the impact that the advisory boards had on policy. (See Appendix A for the exact wording of the questions used.) Of course, since the responses are based on perception, they are ultimately subjective. A basic argument made here is that much of the beauty of citizen participation is in the eye of the beholder; thus, it is believed these perceptual measures are useful. In addition, the authors also ranked the cities on the basis of what they felt was the impact of citizens on policy, based on an examination of the control citizens had in the decision process, and the amount of control they had over the final decisions. Since the Utica plan was prepared totally by the mayor, that city was ranked 1, indicating the lowest citizen impact. The Norfolk board was seen as nonprogrammatic and could only comment on the finished plan; for that reason, Norfolk was ranked as 2. Richmond allowed citizens to participate with officials in drawing up the plan and it was, therefore, ranked third. Syracuse gave the citizens almost total control over the HCDA allocations and that city was ranked 4 or highest, in terms of impacts of citizen participation. Both the perceptual measure and this ranking will be used as dependent variables. It is believed that confidence in the findings will be increased if both measures produce similar results.

Environmental Characteristics

It is believed that the context in which participation occurs can affect what participation can accomplish. There were two specific aspects of the environment, which were hypothesized to affect the policy impact of citizen participation: the extent to which the city government is reformed, and the amount of conflict in the city. Reformed city governments are created to assure that decisions are made on the basis of expertise. It is, therefore, hypothesized that the more reformed the city government, the less citizen participation will result in policy impact. To test this hypothesis, the cities were rank-ordered on the basis of the extent to which their governments were reformed. Syracuse, with a mayor-council government, partisan elections, and half the city council chosen from the districts, was ranked as the least reformed. Utica was ranked second since, although it had a mayor-council form of government, the elections were nonpartisan and the council members were chosen at large. Richmond has a city manager form of government and nonpartisan elections, but had councilmen chosen from districts; thus it was ranked third. Norfolk was ranked fourth, since it had all of the characteristics of a reformed city government: city manager, nonpartisan elections, and a council chosen at-large. This ranking was then cross-tabulated with the perceptual indicator of policy impact. The relationship was extremely significant (Significance = .00) and the gamma coefficient was .64, which indicates a substantial relationship. The ranking on reform was also correlated with the rank ordering of the cities on policy impact. The Spearman's rho was .40. Since both tests produce substantial positive measures of association, it appears that, as hypothesized, reformed city governments lessen the degree to which citizen participation has an impact on policy.

The second environmental characteristic that was believed to affect policy impact was the amount of conflict in the environment. It was hypothesized that in a conflictual environment, officials would be likely to be bombarded with mutually exclusive demands. In such a situation, they will be unable to respond satisfactorily to all and thus will more likely avoid making any change. To measure the amount of conflict in the environment, respondents were asked to list those whom they perceive as being their opponents, when they attempt to achieve their policy goals. The perception of opposition was used to indicate conflict and the variable was dichotomized on the basis of those who listed opponents and those who saw no such opponents. This measure was then cross-tabulated with the indicator of perceived policy impact. The relationship was very significant (Significance = .00) and the gamma coefficient was .50. The cities were also rank ordered on the basis of their median scores on the conflict variable. This ranking was correlated with the rank ordering of the cities on policy impact. The Spearman's rho again was .40. Since both tests produce similar results, it appears that conflict does, in fact, lower the impact of citizen participation on policy.

Target Organization

The second determinant of policy impact was believed to be characteristics of the organization toward which the participation is targeted. It was argued that one of the most important factors is the attitude that the organization's members have of citizen participation, and it was hypothesized that the more supportive they are, the more the citizen participation will be effective in achieving policy impact. To measure the attitudes of the government officials, who in this study were the targets of participation, an index was created based on their responses to questions concerning what they saw as the benefits and problems of citizen participation. (See Appendix B for the questions and the construction of the index.)

The attitudes of officials could only have an impact on those citizens with whom they interact; thus, the analysis must be based on an examination of each city separately. The median attitude score of government officials in each city was calculated and the cities were then rank ordered, with the lower scores indicating low support. The result of that ranking was as follows: Utica = 1; Norfolk = 2; Syracuse = 3; Richmond = 4. In addition, the median score on the indicator of perceived policy impact was calculated for each city and the cities were also rank ordered on that basis, with the lower scores indicating low impact. The cities were ranked as follows: Norfolk = 1; Richmond = 2; Utica = 3; and Syracuse = 4. A Spearman's rho, calculated to determine the agreement between these two rankings, indicated that there was no relationship between these rankings. Using the rank order of impact developed by the authors, the Spearman's rho between attitudes and impact was .80. Since the two measures produce different results, no conclusive statement could be made about the relationship.

Organizational Characteristics

A third factor, which is believed to affect the extent of policy impact, is the structure of citizen participation. It was hypothesized that four characteristics of the structuring of participation affect the impact participation will have on policy: the type of structure used, the amount of access given to citizens, the effect of staff support, and the stage at which citizens are given access. There is not adequate information, in the case studies, to test three of these hypotheses. Since all four cities used both boards and hearings, no statement could be made about the relative effectiveness of these structures. There was also no way to test for the effect of staff support, since none of the four cities provided the citizens with independent staff. It was also decided that there was not adequate variance among the cities, in terms of amount of access, to rank the cities. In the first year process, Norfolk and Utica did little more than hold the two required public hearings, and establish boards. On the other hand, Richmond had 14 neighborhood meetings, as well as a board, and Syracuse had 15 meetings, and a board. In the following chapter, these three hypotheses will be tested using the ACIR data.

One hypothesis, which can be tested here, concerns the stage of the decision making process at which the citizens were admitted. Knowledge of the decision making process in each city was used to rank order the cities according to the stage of the process at which the citizens were given access. Utica was ranked the lowest, since the mayor controlled the planning process and citizens were only allowed to comment on the completed plan at a public hearing. Norfolk was ranked next since the professional staff drew up a plan and submitted it to the citizens' board for review. Richmond had several neighborhood meetings and, prior to the planning process, solicited the opinion of citizens by questionnaires. The board in Richmond was charged with drawing up the plan, although it was guided by suggestions from the professional staff. It was, therefore, ranked third. Syracuse started soliciting ideas from citizens in anticipation of the HCDA even before it was enacted. At extensive public hearings, citizen suggestions were elicited, aggregated by neighborhood, and forwarded to the citizens' board for approval. On this basis, Syracuse was ranked fourth. This ranking was then related to the ranking of the cities on impact. The Spearman's rho indicated no relationship between the stage of the decision process at which the citizens became involved and their perceived impact on policy. Using the ranking based on the authors' evaluation of the impact of citizens in each of the cities, the rankings would match perfectly.

Because of the contradictory results, it is once again impossible to make a conclusive statement about this relationship.

CITIZEN ATTITUDES

The second result expected from citizen participation is an improvement in the orientation of citizens toward their government. It is believed that by taking part in the activities of government, citizens would understand better the problems with which government must deal and, thus, would become less suspicious and more trusting of the government. Similarly, by becoming familiar with the government's activities, citizens should feel more confident of their ability to affect governmental actions.

It was hypothesized that three factors should affect the extent to which citizens become more trusting of the government, as a result of citizen participation: the amount of conflict in the environment, the citizen's own sense that citizen participation was a satisfactory experience, and the attitudes of the government officials with whom the citizens deal. The operationalization of conflict and of the attitudes of government officials was discussed in the previous section. To operationalize trust of both the local and national government, and of the sense of efficacy toward the local government, indexes were developed. (For the questions used to develop the indexes, see Appendix B.) Only one question was asked concerning efficacy vis-a-vis the national government, and it was used as a single indicator. All of these measures are static, in that they do not indicate change in levels of trust and efficacy as a result of participation. An attempt was made to estimate such longitudinal effects by asking the citizens if participation on the board had increased their confidence in government. To operationalize the citizens' sense that the participation experience was satisfactory, they were asked if they felt the time and effort spent in participating were worth it.

Conflict

None of the relationships between conflict, and feelings of trust and efficacy was significant and the gamma coefficients are only low to moderate (see Table 9.1). It is interesting to note, however, the direction of the relationships. As hypothesized, the greater the perception of conflict in the environment, the less likely citizens will feel a sense of trust or efficacy toward local or national government, and the less they are to feel that participation on the board has increased their confidence in government. These findings are of course weakened by the lack of significance.

TABLE 9.1

Relationship Between Conflict and Attitudes Toward Government

	Gamma	Significance	N
Trust of Local Government	–.30	.35	94
Trust of National Government	–.34	.15	96
Efficacy Toward Local Government	–.25	.21	86
Efficacy Toward National Government	–.23	.42	89
Increase in Confidence	–.28	.17	34

Satisfaction

Two of the relationships between the sense that the participatory experience was satisfactory and the attitudes of citizens toward government were significant (see Table 9.2). In both cases, the relationship is with feelings of

TABLE 9.2

Relationship Between Satisfaction and Attitudes Toward Government

	Gamma	Significance	N
Trust of Local Government	.51	.00	79
Trust of National Government	.004	.03	80
Efficacy Toward Local Government	.29	.51	73
Efficacy Toward National Government	.21	.49	75
Increase in Confidence	.20	.34	33

trust, although the relationships are of greatly differing size. The relationship between sense of satisfaction and trust on the local level is a a substantial .51 (gamma); yet, the relationship between satisfaction and trust of the national government is .004 (gamma). It appears that, while participating on the local level may be related to trust of the local government, that trust is not generalized to the national government. If the purpose of including participation requirements in federal legislation is to create a generalized feeling of trust toward government, that purpose is apparently not being achieved.

Two other points should be made about these findings. First, neither of the efficacy measures produced significant relationships and the gamma coefficients are low to moderate, which indicates that, although participation may be related to some attitudes toward government, it may not be related to all such attitudes. The second point may be even more disconcerting to the advocates of citizen participation. The relationship between satisfaction with the participation experience and the sense that that participation increased one's confidence in government is also not significant, and the relationship is low. These findings raise the specter that perhaps the participatory experience, regardless of how satisfactory it is, does not change attitudes, but rather tends to reinforce the existing political orientations of citizens. It may be that those who were previously trusting of the city government were more likely to view their participatory experiences positively, while those who were not trusting were likely to be dissatisfied with participation. As one Richmond government official pithily summed his feelings, "They [the citizens] always hated the government. Now they know why." In both cases, neither apparently saw the participatory experience as grounds for changing their confidence in government.

Of course, as argued in the previous chapter, participation on the board was only a short term experience when the study was done. Such an experience, perhaps, should not be expected to change attitudes developed from childhood. It is possible that a longer experience would result in some attitude change. As cautioned before, however, that experience would presumably have to be a positive one to create more citizen trust and efficacy—and participation is not always a positive experience, as the Richmond official's quote indicates.

Government Attitudes

A final variable, which was hypothesized to affect citizen attitudes, was the attitudes of government officials toward citizen participation. Again, this relationship will have to be at the level of the city, since government attitudes in one city cannot affect citizen attitudes in another city. To test this hypothesis, the cities were ranked on the basis of their median scores on the measures of citizen attitudes. These rankings were then compared to the ranking of the cities on the attitudes of government officials. The median scores on both trust and efficacy of the national government were so similar in all four cities that it was decided that any ranking would be meaningless; thus, only rankings on attitudes toward local government will be used. The rankings of the cities on trust of the city government, with low scores indicating low trust, are as follows: Utica, 1; Norfolk, 4; Syracuse, 3; Richmond, 2. The Spearman's rho between this ranking and the ranking of the cities based on the attitudes of government officials is .2, which indicates a low relationship. Once again, this may simply indicate that attitudes toward government are formed over a long time period and are not easily changed by interaction with government officials over a short period of time.

Examination of the two rankings raises other questions about this relationship (see Table 9.3). Utica and Syracuse are ranked the same on both the trust and government attitude rankings. The low Spearman's rho is due to the fact that Richmond and Norfolk are reversed on the rankings. Thus, although the relationship between attitudes and trust is a positive one in Utica and Syracuse, it is negative in Norfolk and Richmond. The two patterns cancel each other, resulting in a low measure of association.

One question must be asked: Why is the relationship negative in the Virginia cities? Some clues may be found by examining the cities separately. In

TABLE 9.3

Rankings of Cities on Officials' Attitudes and Citizens' Trust

	Support	Trust
Utica	1	1
Norfolk	2	4
Syracuse	3	3
Richmond	4	2

Norfolk, the citizens were evenly split between believing that participation on the board either had not increased their confidence in government, or had increased it only slightly. In Richmond, on the other hand, 41 percent of the citizens felt that the experience had had no effect on them, and 35 percent felt that the experience on the board had, in fact, decreased their confidence. It seems obvious that the Richmond citizens were both less trusting of the city government than were the Norfolk citizens, and felt that the experience on the board had either reinforced their feelings or made them even less trusting. This was so despite the attitude of the government officials.

Since it is hard to imagine that officials who are negative will create more trusting citizens, it is felt that sources of the lower trust in Richmond must be sought elsewhere. One factor which may explain the differences is what the citizens expected to achieve from participation on the board. In Norfolk, 89 percent of the citizens expected to receive either nothing or, at least, increased understanding of government. In Richmond, 38 percent expected to receive increased communication with government, presumably in the hope of effecting policy changes. It appears that the expectations of Norfolk citizens were low and easily satisfied, while the Richmond citizens may well have expected concrete results, which did not materialize. This, in turn, may be due to the way the citizens were recruited for the boards. In Norfolk the citizens were appointed at large by the city council, whereas in Richmond the citizens were appointed as representatives of particular groups. Ninety percent of the Richmond board members felt that they were acting as group representatives, compared to 56 percent in Norfolk. Since they were acting as spokesmen, the Richmond board members may have expected that they would achieve concrete goals, so when the goals were not produced, their confidence in government declined.

If this interpretation is correct, the implication is that the attitude of government officials may not be as important a determinant of citizen trust as is the citizens' own expectations of what will be produced by participation. This fact, of course, would greatly hinder the ability of government officials to establish participatory experiences that might increase the trust of citizens, regardless of how supportive the officials are.

The cities were also ranked on the basis of the median efficacy scores of the citizens. That ranking (with lower scores indicating lower efficacy) is as follows: Richmond, 1; Norfolk, 2; Utica, 3; Syracuse, 4. A Spearman's rho between that ranking and the government officials' attitudes is –.5, which indicates a substantial relationship, although in a direction opposite to that hypothesized. Examination of the rankings shows that the greatest disparity in the rankings occurred in Utica and Richmond. The previous analysis has given some indication of why citizens in Richmond may have been low in efficacy, but no explanation can be given for why the citizens in Utica ranked third in efficacy. It is also difficult to understand why the relationship is negative. It may be possible that, in those cities where the officials are not supportive, only the most efficacious citizens dare to become active—or the findings may be only idiosyncratic to these cities.

POWER REDISTRIBUTION

The final dependent variable to be examined is power redistribution. In this instance, it will be measured by determining the extent to which the participation mandates create an opportunity for those who have not previously been active in politics. Five questions on the survey concerned the extent to which the citizens had previously been active in politics. These questions were then combined into an index (see Appendix B). Two environmental characteristics (the amount of conflict and the amount of reform), and one characteristic of the target organization (officials' attitudes), were believed to affect the extent to which power redistribution would occur. The analysis has to be done at the aggregate level, since the question focuses on the total amount of change in a city. Therefore, the cities were rank ordered according to their median scores on the dependent variable. The result of this ranking, with the lower scores indicating less power redistribution, is as follows: Norfolk, 1; Richmond, 2; Syracuse, 3; Utica, 4. This rank ordering was then correlated with the rank orderings of reform, conflict, and officials' attitudes previously discussed. The Spearman's rho between the rank ordering of reform and power redistribution is -.80. This is a substantial relationship, indicating that the greater the reform, the less the power redistribution, which is contrary to the findings of Greenstone and Peterson.[4] It is consistent, however, with the earlier argument concerning impediments facing new participants in bureaucratic decision making.

An explanation for this may be found by examining the characteristics of reformed and nonreformed governments. Reformed governments are designed to make decisions on the basis of nonpartisan technical competence—in other words, expertise is the basis for decisions. When such governments are faced with mandates for participation, it may be only natural for them to include those citizens who have demonstrated competence in some way. Thus, of necessity, they will turn to those who have previously been active and already demonstrated their ability and/or expertise. In nonreformed governments, on the other hand, the officials must develop grassroots support to maintain themselves in office. While Riker may talk about the rationality of the minimum winning coalition in elections, elected officials feel more comfortable with as large a margin as possible.[5] They, therefore, may attempt to develop that needed support by involving as many people as possible through citizen participation.

The second environmental factor believed to affect power redistribution is the amount of conflict in the environment. It was hypothesized that government officials may try to insulate themselves from the instability caused by conflict in the environment. They may do this by not providing access to the citizens but, if participation is mandated, they will attempt to minimize the effect of conflict by providing access only to those with whom they feel the most comfortable. Then, they will turn to those citizens who have been previously active and demonstrated that they know how to play the game. The Spearman's rho between the rankings on power redistribution and conflict is -.80, indicating that there is, in fact, a substantial negative relationship between the amount of conflict in the environment and the amount of power redistribution.

Finally, it was hypothesized that the more the government officials were supportive of citizen participation, the more power redistribution would occur. This was expected to be so because, if officials were supportive, they would work to involve more citizens, or at least would provide access to those citizens who become active. Surprisingly, the Spearman's rho between the rankings of power redistribution and officials' attitudes is -.40. This means that, in those cities where the officials were less supportive, more new participants became involved. Once again, this is a finding that is difficult to explain. Perhaps, it indicates that the direction of causation is opposite to that hypothesized. Officials may be more supportive of citizen participation when they deal with citizens who have been previously active and are more knowledgeable about the processes of government. Alternatively, it may indicate that, regardless of their attitudes, officials may not be capable of mobilizing those citizens who have not been previously active.

SUMMARY

Before drawing any conclusions from this data analysis, some of these hypotheses will again be tested using a larger data base collected by the ACIR. To summarize, the data in this chapter have led to the following conclusions concerning the models of participation.

Policy Impact

The greater the reformed structures of government, the less the policy impact.
Substantiated

The greater the conflict, the less the policy impact.
Substantiated

The more positive are the attitudes of officials toward citizen participation, the greater the policy impact.
Not clearly substantiated

The earlier the stage at which citizens are given access to the decision process, the greater the policy impact.
Not clearly substantiated

Power Redistribution

The greater the reformed structures of government, the less the power redistribution.
Substantiated

The greater the conflict, the less the power redistribution.
Substantiated

The more positive are the attitudes of officials toward citizen participation, the more the power redistribution.
Not substantiated

Citizen Attitudes

The greater the conflict, the less trusting and efficacious are the citizens.
Substantiated

The more satisfied the citizens are with participation, the more trusting and efficacious they will be.
Substantiated

The more supportive the officials are of participation, the more trusting and efficacious the citizens will be.
Not substantiated

NOTES

[1] Housing and Community Development Act of 1974 (P.L. 93–415), Section 104 (a)(c).

[2] Kenneth Clark and Jeannette Hopkins, *A Relevant War Against Poverty: A Study of Community Action Programs and Observable Social Change* (New York: Harper Torchbooks, 1968), p. 153.

[3] Herbert Kaufman, *Politics and Policies in State and Local Governments* (Englewood Cliffs, N.J.: Prentice-Hall, 1963), p. 34.

[4] J. David Greenstone and Paul E. Peterson, "Reformers, Machines and the War on Poverty," in *The New Urban Politics: Cities and the Federal Government*, ed. Douglas M. Fox (Pacific Palisades, Ca.: Goodyear, 1972), p. 165.

[5] William H. Riker, *A Theory of Political Coalitions* (New Haven: Yale University Press, 1962), p. 32.

10

THE MODELS APPLIED: A SECOND TEST

The last chapter used data composed of both standardized questionnaires and case study analysis to test the three models of participation. These data, while permitting an examination of both general patterns, as well as the unique characteristics of each city, were limited since they were gathered in four cities only. This small number of cities limits the generalizability of the findings; thus, in this chapter, a second data set will be used in an attempt both to increase the generalizability and the validity of the findings of the last chapter.

The ACIR-ICMA data set used in this chapter is composed of responses to a questionnaire administered to budget officials in 1,818 cities and counties.[1] This large number of cities will provide greater confidence in generalizing the findings. In addition, these data provide information on the structuring of citizen participation that will permit the testing of some hypotheses which could not previously be tested. In some ways, these data are limited. For the purposes of this study, perhaps the most serious limitation is the fact that the data contain no information on either the attitudes or the characteristics of the citizens participating. This means that only the policy impact model can be tested with these data. A second limitation is that the data are based solely on the budget officials' perceptions of impact, which may, of course, bias the results. However, research by Stein et al., comparing these data to objective measures of budgetary change, indicates substantial overlap between the subjective measures and the actual change.[2]

The dependent variable is operationalized by seven measures (see Appendix C). One of the measures is the response by officials to the question of how many changes have been made in the budget process because of citizen participation. The other six measures are questions concerning the officials' perceptions of the impact of participation on the budget itself. Two of the questions focus on the effect of participation on dropping of a grant proposal or program. One question concerns the impact of participation on developing new proposals. Two questions focus on the transferring of funding from a grant to the general budget or vice versa. And, finally, one general question is asked about the impact of participation on the setting of budget priorities.

While the initial intention was to develop an index of impact, intercorrelations among the variables were low; thus, each is examined separately. This lack of relationship may have important theoretical implications. It has consistently been argued here that the dependent variables expected from participation differ to such an extent that different models of participation must be developed. The finding of low intercorrelation among the policy impact measures suggests that that dependent variable is itself diverse. This may mean that, while citizen participation may have an impact on policy in one way (for example, dropping proposals), it may not have an impact in another way (developing new proposals), and vice versa. This, in turn, would complicate the process of evaluating participation. Although participation may have one form of impact on policy, those involved may still not be satisfied, since the specific impact they expected did not materialize. This then suggests the importance of using these data to examine whether the effectiveness of participation varies across types of impact. It also becomes important to examine whether different environmental or organizational characteristics are related to the form of policy impact produced by participation. These questions will be examined in this chapter along with the hypotheses concerning policy impact that were posited in Chapter 8.

ENVIRONMENTAL CHARACTERISTICS

The amount of conflict in the environment was hypothesized to reduce the impact of citizen participation on policy. This was believed to be so because government officials would be bombarded with conflicting demands. Since they would be incapable of satisfying all, they would perceive no action as the easiest and safest route. In the ACIR data set, the measures used to operationalize conflict was a question that asked the officials how often controversies arise among citizen participants over the allocation of funds.

The relationship between the officials' perception of conflict and their perception of the impact of participation on the budget process is highly significant and produces a gamma coefficient of .55. This indicates a substantial relationship, but in a direction opposite to that hypothesized. The perception of conflict was also correlated with the indicators of impact on the budget itself. The results are shown in Table 10.1. With two exceptions, the relationships

TABLE 10.1

Effect of Conflict on Policy Impact

	Gamma*
Change in Process	.55
Dropping Grant Proposals	.31
Developing New Grant Proposals	.26
Transferring Funding to a Grant	.12
Transferring Funding From a Grant to the General Budget	.36
Dropping a Service or Program	.37
Setting of Priorities	.53

*Relationship is significant at the .05 level.

between budget impacts and perceived conflict are moderate. One exception is the relationship between conflict and the transferring of funding from the general budget to a grant, which has only a low relationship. Stein et al. find that in cities over 25,000, citizen participation has a negative impact when developing new grant proposals or transferring functions to the general budget. This is explained in terms of increased participation of the middle class in these cities and the desire to keep taxes down.[3] The positive relationships here indicate that, in the smaller cities, increased participation must still be having a positive relationship with new grants and transfers. The size of the city, a variable not studied here, may be an important environmental variable in affecting impacts of citizen participation. The other exception is the relationship between conflict and a setting of priorities in the budget, where there is a substantial relationship. In each case, the relationship is again opposite to that hypothesized.

The fact that the direction of the relationship is opposite to that hypothesized is especially perplexing because the data in the last chapter confirmed the hypothesis. Perhaps some explanation for this apparent contradiction can be found in the different measures used in the two sets of data. The measure of conflict used in the last chapter was a question which asked the citizens who they felt was opposing them. This indicator measured the citizens' perception of conflict. If they perceived opposition in the environment, they were less likely to perceive policy impact as a result of citizen participation. In these data, however, the measures of conflict are based on the perceptions of government officials. If the government officials perceived conflict, they were more likely to believe that citizen participation had an impact on policy. These findings may indicate that, when conflict arises, government officials do attempt to alter policy to resolve the conflict.

This finding would be consistent with James A. Thompson's argument that, in a turbulent environment, organizations are more likely to adopt flexible responses to external demands.[4] Yet, since the citizens were in disagreement over desirable policy changes, not all of them can receive what they want. Officials may have to pick among citizen demands, which would leave some citizens with nothing, or alternatively, officials may try to create a compromise between the competing demands. In either case, at least some citizens would be likely to be dissatisfied with the policy change that would result or they would believe that their participation had no impact. If this speculation is accurate, it would highlight, once again, how difficult it is to implement citizen participation in ways that will be satisfactory to all those involved.

TARGET ORGANIZATION CHARACTERISTICS

As with the data examined in the prior chapter, the ACIR data contain measures of only one aspect of the characteristics of the target organization: the attitudes held by government officials toward citizen participation (in this case, the budget officers). There were two indicators of the officials' attitudes on the questionnaire. One question asked officials if they believed that more, less, or the same amount of participation was desirable in the budget process. The assumption was that those officials who desired more participation were the most supportive of citizen participation. The second indicator was a question that asked the officials if they thought citizens attended public hearings to achieve special interests, or because they had a genuine concern about the budget process. It was assumed that officials who believed citizens only pursued special interests were negative toward participation.

Only two of the relationships between the official's desire for more participation, and the dependent variables, were significant. The two dependent variables that were significantly related were the measure of change in the budget process (gamma = .22), and the measure of change in budgetary priorities (gamma = .21). In each case, the more supportive the officials were, the less the change they perceived. This was opposite to the hypothesized direction, but it may be explained by the fact that those officials who are supportive of participation desire more participation because they see it as having little impact at the moment.

The second measure of officials' attitudes is significantly related to all but two of the dependent variables. The two significant relations are those with the measures of the impact of participation on transferring funding from a grant to a budget or vice versa (see Table 10.2). There is a significant, but low, relationship between the officials' attitudes and their perception of the impact of citizens on the development of new grant proposals. The other relationships are moderate

TABLE 10.2

Effect of Officials' Attitudes on the Impact of Policy

	Gamma*
Change in Process	.36
Dropping Grant Proposals	.20
Developing New Grant Proposals	.16
Transferring Funding to a Grant	.11**
Transferring Funding From a Grant to the General Budget	.04
Dropping a Service or Program	.25
Setting of Priorities	.39

*Relationships are significant at the .05 level unless otherwise specified.
**Not significant at the .05 level.

and in the expected direction: the more the officials see citizens pursuing their own special interests, the less likely they are to believe that participation has an impact on policy. It makes sense to believe that officials who see citizen requests as benefiting special interests would attempt to limit the impact of those requests on the budget, as these data indicate. This bears out the notion that professional bureaucratic budget officers strive for neutral competence and believe in a public interest, reacting negatively to the self-interested citizen. Based on this, it appears that the attitudes of officials do have an effect on the impact of citizen participation.

STRUCTURES OF CITIZEN PARTICIPATION

The final set of hypotheses deals with the ways the structures of citizen participation affect the amount of policy impact that results. It was hypothesized that citizen organizations would have more impact on policy than would public hearings. To test this hypothesis, the number of advisory boards in the cities was summed, as were the numbers of meetings on the citywide level and on the neighborhood level. These three measures were then related to the dependent variables. As Table 10.3 indicates, the number of advisory boards is consistently more strongly related to the dependent variables than is the number of meetings.

Boards were expected to have more impact than meetings because they are an on-going structure, which is both easier to fit into an organized routine and less easily ignored. Substantiation for the importance of the institutionalization of citizen participation can also be found in another relationship. Officials were

TABLE 10.3

Comparison of Impact of Boards and Meetings

	Boards*	Citywide Meetings*	Neighborhood Meetings*
Change in Process	.27	.15	.16
Dropping Grant Proposals	.33	.26	.25
Developing New Grant Proposals	.43	.35	.24
Transferring Funding to a Grant	.27	.22	.19
Transferring Funding From a Grant to the General Budget	.45	.26	.29
Dropping a Service or Program	.38	.22	.35
Setting Priorities	.34	.27	.23

*Gamma is the measure of association. Relationship is significant at the .05 level.

asked to categorize citizen participation in their cities, based on whether it was mostly informal or formal. These responses were then related to the dependent variables. As Table 10.4 indicates, there is a moderate relationship between the formality of citizen participation and its impact on policy—greater formality creates greater impact.

It was also hypothesized that the greater the access given to citizens, the greater will be their impact on policy. To test this hypothesis, a composite measure of access was created, composed of the number of meetings at both the city and neighborhood levels, and the number of advisory boards. As might be expected from examining the separate impacts of meetings and boards, this composite measure is positively related to the dependent variables (see Table 10.5). Access has the least relationship with the budgetary process and with transferring funding from the general budget to a grant.

These data also permit an examination of the extent to which citizens availed themselves of the structures of participation. The officials were asked to list the average number of citizens who attended the various kinds of hearings. These measures were then related to the dependent variables. The relationships show a remarkably consistent pattern of moderate relationships (see Table 10.6). This would indicate that the greater the citizen activity, the more impact participation has on policy.

This finding was confirmed by the relationship between the officials'

TABLE 10.4

Relationship of Formalization and Policy Impact

	Gamma*
Change in Process	.45
Dropping Grant Proposals	.27
Developing New Grant Proposals	.22
Transferring Funding to a Grant	.25
Transferring Funding from a Grant to the General Budget	.28
Dropping a Service or Program	.25
Setting Priorities	.37

*Relationship is significant at the .05 level.

TABLE 10.5

Relationship of Amount of Access and Policy Impact

	Gamma*
Change in Process	.23
Dropping Grant Proposals	.32
Developing New Grant Proposals	.41
Transferring Funding to a Grant	.24
Transferring Funding from a Grant to the General Budget	.42
Dropping a Service or Program	.40
Setting Priorities	.32

*Relationship is significant at the .05 level.

perceptions of the amount of citizen participation in the budget process and the policy impacts. As Table 10.7 indicates, there are very strong relationships between the perceived amount of participation and the dependent variables, with the strongest relationships being those with change in the budgetary process and the setting of budgetary priorities. The weakest relationship is with the transfer of funding to a grant. It appears, therefore, that the more participation is perceived by the officials, the more they believe that participation has an impact. Of course, it is possible that, if there is much citizen activity, the official simply assumes that participation is having an impact whether or not this is the case. Considering the close relationship, however, between perceived and actual changes in expenditure patterns as reported by Stein et al., it is concluded here

TABLE 10.6

Effect of Numbers Participating on Policy Impact

	Citywide Hearings*	Neighborhood Hearings*	Combined Hearings*	Hearings on Revenue Sharing*	Hearings on the Budget*	Community Development Hearings*
Change in Process	.40	.14**	.32	.30	.28	.21
Dropping Grant Proposals	.35	.27	.25	.09	.17	.34
Developing New Grant Proposals	.41	.36	.24	.24	.23	.47
Transferring Funding to a Grant	.24	.23	.12	.21	.25	.23
Transferring Funding from a Grant to the General Budget	.42	.25	.31	.22	.26	.33
Dropping a Service or Program	.28	.23	.29	.20	.27	.34
Setting Priorities	.41	.31	.36	.28	.28	.33

*Gamma is the measure of association. Relationship is significant at the .05 level unless otherwise specified.
**Not significant at the .05 level.

TABLE 10.7

Relationship of Amount of Participation and Impact

	Gamma
Change in Process	.76*
Dropping Grant Proposals	.41
Developing New Grant Proposals	.37
Transferring Funding to a Grant	.29
Transferring Funding from a Grant to the General Budget	.38
Dropping a Service or Program	.38
Setting of Priorities	.64

*Measure of association is gamma. All relationships are significant at the .05 level.

that the amount of participation does have an effect on the degree of impact that participation has on policy.[5]

A final hypothesis was that citizen participation will have more impact when the citizens are provided with staff support because the staff would provide them with expertise to facilitate communications with bureaucrats. The relationship between staff support and policy impact is shown in Table 10.8. It appears that there is a moderate positive relationship between the provision of staff and the policy impacts of participation.

TABLE 10.8

Relationship of Staff Support and Impact

	Gamma
Change in Process	.36*
Dropping Grant Proposals	.30
Developing New Grant Proposals	.32
Transferring Funding to a Grant	.22
Transferring Funding from a Grant to the General Budget	.28
Dropping a Service or a Program	.35
Setting of Priorities	.39

*Measure of association is gamma. All relationships are significant at the .05 level.

SUMMARY

This chapter has focused on a second test of the policy impact model, using a larger data set than that in the last chapter, in an attempt to increase the generalizability and the validity of the findings. This data set also permitted the testing of hypotheses about the effect of the structures of participation, which could not be tested previously due to the lack of variance in the four cities studied. In most cases, the hypotheses posited in Chapter 8 were confirmed. When bureaucratic attitudes were measured by a question concerning whether citizens are pursuing special interests when they attend budget hearings, these attitudes were related to policy impact in the expected direction. The more negative the attitudes (that is, the beliefs that citizens represented special interests), the less policy impact resulted from participation. In addition, the hypotheses concerning the structuring of participation were substantial. Organizations have more impact on policy than do hearings. Staff assistance for citizens also increases the policy impact of participation. In addition, it was found that the greater the amount of access given citizens, the greater the policy impact. Finally, it was found that the greater the amount of citizen participation, the greater the impact.

One hypothesis was not substantiated, and contradicted the findings of the last chapter. Conflict was hypothesized to decrease policy impact and in the four cities that was found to be the case. In these data, however, conflict was related to increased policy impact. This apparent contradiction may be explained by the differing perspectives of citizens and officials: citizens see less policy impact in the presence of conflict and officials see more.

Multiple dependent variables were used in this chapter because of low intercorrelations among the measures. Despite these low intercorrelations, only one slight discernible pattern was observed in the relationship between the independent variables and the various measures of policy impact. The independent variables did not predict as well to transferring funding to a grant from the general budget as they did to the other dependent variables. The reason for this may be found in the analysis done by Stein et al., mentioned above. Examining only the 590 surveyed cities over 25,000 in population, they found that citizen participation had a negative impact on transferring funding to a grant proposal. The negative relationship in that subset is obviously weakening to the overall positive relationship in the data as a whole. Stein et al. explain the negative relationship, in the larger cities, by arguing that these cities may have reached their "saturation point" in grant funding and can find no grants that they are not already using.[6]

The final chapter will focus on summarizing the major arguments of this study and the findings of both data analyses. In addition, it will consider the prospects for citizen participation in the future.

NOTES

[1] We wish to thank Dr. Bruce McDowell, at the Advisory Commission on Intergovernmental Relations, and especially, Professor Robert Stein, Rice University, for their help in obtaining this data set.

[2] Robert M. Stein, Elise Kornmayer, David John Gow, "Federally Mandated Citizen Participation: A Study of Municipal Budget Impact," paper presented at the Midwest Political Science Association Annual Meeting, April 25, 1980, p. 22.

[3] Ibid., p. 31.

[4] James A. Thompson, *Organizations in Action: Social Science Bases of Administrative Theory* (New York: McGraw-Hill, 1967), p. 21. See also Robert W. Kweit and Mary Grisez Kweit, "Bureaucratic Decision-Making: Impediments to Citizen Participation," *Polity* 12 (Summer, 1980):658.

[5] Stein et al., "Federally Mandated Citizen Participation," p. 22.

[6] Ibid., p. 31.

11

SUMMARY AND CONCLUSIONS

There is no more important topic in a democratic government than that of citizen participation. It strikes directly at the core of the structuring of the relationship between citizens and their government, a relationship that in a democracy is supposed to be uniquely close and interdependent. Although the United States was not initially designed as a democracy, there have been periods throughout its history when citizens have forced back the initial restrictions on citizen involvement in an attempt to make the government more democratic. In these periods, citizens were often aided and abetted by elected government officials who saw the new participants as a potential base of support, thus, the crises of participation were ended, at least temporarily.

The United States in the eighties is in the middle of another of these participation crises. This crisis began two decades ago in the midst of the moralist and reformist culture of the sixties. Demands for participation arose partly because of the demands of new groups to be granted access to the system, and partly because of the general alienation and disaffection of U.S. citizens with their government. As in past periods of crisis, the government responded, this time, but the response differed from those in the past. Prior reforms had been aimed primarily at the electoral process and more citizens were given the vote. Initiative and referenda made the vote a more integral part of the policy process.

In the current crisis, there were some reforms of the electoral process; for example, civil rights laws assured blacks their constitutional right to vote, and eighteen-year-olds were given the franchise. In reponse to reforms in the Democratic party, primaries became a more important part of the presidential selection process; yet, the major focus during this crisis became not the electoral process, but the bureaucracy. And, with the exception of Sunshine Laws, the reforms were aimed not only at reducing the barriers to participation, but at mandating that citizen participation become part of the decision-making process of the bureaucracy.

There are many problems in implementing these mandates for participation. One major source of problems is the expectations that accompany attempts at citizen participation, for in many cases, expectations are unrealistically high. Participation in some cases is considered a panacea to cure the ills of the polity, but it is simply a change in process. By this change in process, however, participation advocates claim that changes will occur in the distribution of power in society, in the attitudes of citizens toward their government, and in the type of policies produced by those governments. Instituting citizen participation does not guarantee that the expected effects of participation will automatically materialize.

Another problem caused by expectations is the very simple fact that different people want different things. A participation process may produce one of the expected outcomes, but not the one desired by at least some of those involved. The differing perspectives of citizens and officials provides an especially fertile ground for disagreements about effects of participation. This was illustrated by the differing relationship of conflict with policy impact, when viewed from the differing perspectives of officials and citizens. The problems of satisfying all are also aggravated by the fact that the goals of participation are at best vague and usually completely implicit: beauty is in the eye of the beholder. In a paraphrase of Lincoln, citizen participation can please some of the people all of the time, all of the people some of the time, but not all of the people all of the time.

A second source of problems in implementing the participation mandates is the structuring of citizen participation. The governmental structure is a republic. Although technology may exist to permit the government to function in a manner very close to the classical notion of democracy, there are few who would advocate such a change. The emphasis seems to be on providing increased points of access to citizens, but there is no agreement on how inclusive participation structures should be. If all cannot be included, how many should be and who should they be? And what is the responsibility of government, if citizens do not avail themselves of the access provided? In a reformulation of the chant of the sixties, what if you have a public hearing and no one comes?

Another problem of structuring is that of the legal authority given these new participation structures, be they hearings, advisory boards, interactive cable television hook-ups, or whatever. If these structures are given legal authority to direct the decision making of bureaucratic organizations charged with implementing policy, what then is the role of the elected executive who is presumably in charge of those bureaucrats and what is the role of the elected legislature that has presumably developed the policy which the bureaucrats are to implement?

This last point leads directly to the third source of problems in implementing participation. The bureaucracy is increasingly the focus of participation. The mandates that have proliferated, especially during the seventies, have required that the implementation of the federal grant programs on the local level must be accompanied by citizen participation. These mandates, which forced citizens into the implementation stage of the policy process, of necessity also forced them into the process of bureaucratic decision making. At least one reason for these mandates was the recognition that the power of bureaucracies was increasing due to their control of expertise and routine, and the belief that citizen participation was one way to control bureaucratic power and make it more accountable.

Yet, the bureaucracy is a particularly inhospitable context for citizen participation. The very expertise that lies at the base of bureaucratic power is antithetical to a decision-making process which responds to those who can claim no special qualification other than that they are the ultimate recipients of the policy outputs. The regularization and routine of the bureaucratic process is not easily compatible with the often chaotic process of citizen participation.

The major question then becomes: what can be achieved by citizen participation? The basic argument of this study is that, while citizen participation can achieve some of the goals expected of it, its success is not automatic, but contingent upon other factors. It is also argued that the three goals of participation differ to such an extent that different factors predict to each. Therefore, three different models of participation were posited, specifying factors that were believed to predict most effectively to the three goals of citizen participation: policy impact, citizen attitudes, and power redistribution. These three models were then tested with data gathered in four cities and the policy impact model was also tested using a broad-based data set gathered by the ACIR-ICMA.

For the most part, the data substantiated the hypotheses. There were, however, two major exceptions. The two sets of data provided contradictory findings of the relationship between conflict and policy impact. The citizens believed there was less policy impact when they perceived that they were opposed by others. This supported the hypothesis that less policy impact would occur in a conflictual environment. The government officials surveyed by the ACIR, however, believed there was more policy impact where controversies arose among citizens. The contradiction was believed to be due to the differing perspectives of the citizens and officials. The officials may try to respond to citizen demands when there is conflict but, since not all citizens can achieve all they desire in such an environment, the citizens do not perceive that their participation has had an impact. This again highlights the problems of pleasing everyone by citizen participation.

The second major exception was the effect of bureaucratic attitudes on the dependent variables. It was believed that positive attitudes toward participation would be an important determinant of whether citizen participation could achieve its expected goals. This was believed to be the case because bureaucrats, if opposed to participation, have resources that they can use to make it nothing more than a symbolic process. By the same token, they also have resources that they could use to facilitate that participation if they should so desire. Only slight substantiation, however, could be found for this hypothesis. The government officials surveyed by the ACIR, who thought that the citizens were searching for their own special interests, were less likely to perceive that participation had an impact on the budget than were those officials who thought citizens became active because of a genuine concern in the budget. This is given extra importance since the research by Stein et al. showed that their perceptions of impact, for the most part, accurately reflected the changes that occurred.[1] The data from the four cities, however, provided only weak and inconsistent support for the hypotheses concerning bureaucratic attitudes.

The lack of substantiation may be due to the fact that bureaucrats may actually lack the resources adequate to alter the impacts of participation. Opposition may not be important in a situation in which participation is mandated. Support may not assure that participants will change their attitudes toward government or will be motivated to get involved, when they had previously not been involved.

Yet another finding indicates that the bureaucracy is not an unimportant factor in determining the impact of participation. As hypothesized, citizen participation had less impact on power redistribution and on policy impact in those cities with reformed government structures. This is consistent with the study by Lineberry and Fowler who found reformed government to be less "responsive" to "the enduring conflicts of political life."[2] Such reformed governments are established to achieve a policy process based on expertise and nonpartisan competence. It may be that, in reformed cities, the political culture is such that citizen input is not as highly valued a part of the governmental process as it is in those cities where elected officials owe their jobs to easily identifiable constituencies. This would seem to indicate that, as they were intended to do, traditional political structures facilitate access by citizens, while reformed structures minimize that access to ensure that decisions are made by experts on the basis of expertise. This highlights the argument made here concerning the antithesis of bureaucratic decision making and citizen participation.

Another hypothesized relationship which was substantiated was that between the citizens' own individualized cost-benefit calculation and their trust and efficacy. There was evidence, however, that the direction of causation may be reversed. Those who saw, as worthwhile, the time and effort spent on participation were higher in trust and efficacy than were those who did not believe in the worth of participation. Yet, there was no relationship between the belief that the costs of participation were worthwhile, and the responses to a question that asked the citizens if they thought their confidence in government had increased as a result of their experience on the board. This might indicate that the participation on the boards simply reinforced the existing attitudes of the citizens. Those who were previously trusting and efficacious were more likely to view the participation process as worthwhile, while those who were low in trust and efficacy were not likely to see the time and effort as well spent. Of course, it is conceivable and it is an argument of proponents of citizen participation that long range trust and efficacy will result from citizen participation. Waving the magic wand of mandated citizen participation has not changed and probably could not change overnight years of antipathy. Over time, given some successes, attitudes may well change.

This finding, as well as the findings about the importance of both the amount of conflict in the environment and the governmental structure, points to another fundamental problem in implementing citizen participation. So much of the success of participation is dependent on factors beyond the control of either the citizens or the bureaucrats. Perhaps that is the reason why bureaucratic attitudes are not strongly related to the impact of participation.

There are some ways, however, that citizen participation can be structured to increase its impact. The ACIR data substantiated the hypotheses that were made concerning the importance of the type and number of participation structures used. Those data indicated that structured citizen advisory boards have more impact on policy than do public hearings. The total amount of access given the citizens is also positively related to policy impact, as is the extent to which the citizens avail themselves of that access. Finally, providing the citizens with staff support increases their impact on policy.

This means that, if the goal is to increase the impact of citizen participation on policy, there are means that officials can use to try to maximize that goal. But it must be kept in mind that, although policy change may occur by structuring participation in these ways, a change in citizen attitudes and redistribution in power may not necessarily occur simultaneously. The ACIR data did not permit testing for the effect of participation on citizen attitudes or power redistribution.

In sum, it appears that participation can produce some of the impacts expected of it. But, the effects are contingent on other factors, and only some of those factors can be manipulated by either the citizens or officials involved. This means, of course, that it is difficult to structure satisfactory citizen participation. This is not necessarily meant as a negative conclusion, for it is believed that major problems are caused by the fact that expectations of what will be produced by citizen participation are unrealistically high. It is argued that it is important and useful to develop more realistic expectations of what citizen participation can achieve and what other values, such as expertise, may have to be compromised to achieve participation. It also forces us to step back and take a broader perspective. In programmatic terms, the "War on Poverty" has generally been viewed as a failure. However, a positive footnote is often added, which credits community action with establishing an indigenous leadership corps. As participation opportunities continue to expand, it may be possible for more and more U.S. citizens to become effective participants in the democratic process.

This leads to the question of what the prospects are for participation in the future. Marc Grainer of TARP has argued that many bureaucrats believe that the current citizen participation crisis has been completed, or as he said, "The war is over." They believe that, he says, because the structures for participation in the bureaucracy have been put in place. There may be good reason for them to believe this, since the provision of structures in the seventies coincided with a period of relative citizen quiescence after the turbulent sixties. But the search for structures is only a single battle in a war to achieve the goals that people expect from participation. The succession of participation crises has made that clear.

It is possible that another series of battles will occur in the future. The United States is entering a period of scarcity, when the political system will be focusing efforts not so much on distributing the benefits of society, but on distributing its costs. Programs will be cut back or eliminated and conflict is almost inevitable in such a situation. Not only will citizens be likely to become more active to protect their interests, but bureaucracies will also be likely to try to mobilize citizen constituents to act as a power resource in the bureau's battles for scarce budgetary allocations. Citizen participation is, therefore, likely to increase in the future. Based on the findings in this study, that in turn may mean that participation will have more impact on policy. It does not mean, however, that citizens will become more supportive of government. In fact, this study has found that a conflictual environment is related to lower levels of trust and efficacy among citizen participants. Perhaps, a clearer recognition of the prospects as well as the problems of citizen participation will make both citizens and officials more understanding of and willing to bear the inevitable tradeoffs among the goals of participation. This is part of a long-term education process for both the governors and the governed. Citizen participation should not be viewed as an end unto itself, but as one of many means of bridging the gap between citizen and statesman.

NOTES

[1] Robert M. Stein, Elise Kornmayer, and David Gow, "Federally Mandated Citizen Participation: A Study of Municipal Budgetary Impact," paper presented at the Midwest Political Science Association, April 25, 1980.

[2] Robert L. Lineberry and Edmund P. Fowler, "Reformism and Public Policy in American Cities," *American Political Science Review* 61 (September 1967):715.

APPENDIX A: QUESTIONNAIRE ITEMS USED IN CASE STUDY ANALYSIS

- If you made an effort to change this law which you oppose, how likely is it that you would succeed? (Asked of both the city and national levels of government.)
- How much do you think you can trust the city government to do what is right?
- To what extent do you trust the government in Washington?
- If you have a serious complaint about poor services by the city, do you think you can get city officials to do something about it, if you contact them?
- Who are your usual opponents?
- Is the time and effort spent on the board worth it?
- Has participaton on the board increased your confidence in government?
- Many cities have experienced problems as a result of the federal government's policy of forcing local governments to increase citizen participation in decision making. What problems has it caused here?
- What have been the benefits to the citizens of this kind of citizen participation?
- What have been the benefits of this kind of citizen participation for city government?
- What do you believe is the purpose of fostering this form of citizen participation?
- How much effect do you think the board has had on policy making?
- Other than the board, what has the city done, if anything, to solicit citizen participation?
- During the last ten years have you ever done any of the following?
  - Worn a campaign button or gone to a political meeting?
  - Worked actively in a political campaign?

Contributed money to any campaign organization?

Contributed money to any civil rights organization?

Taken part in any nonviolent protest such as picketing, boycott, march, or sit-in?

APPENDIX B: QUESTIONS USED TO CONSTRUCT INDEXES

Trust of City Government

How much do you think you can trust the city government to do what is right?

Would you say the government in (city) is pretty much run for the benefit of a few big interests, or that it is run for the benefit of all the people?

Trust of the National Government

To what extent do you trust the government in Washington?

Would you say the government in Washington is run pretty much for the benefit of all the people or that it is run for the benefit of a few big interests?

Government Officials' Attitudes

Many cities have experienced problems as a result of the federal government's policy of forcing local governments to increase citizen participation in decision making. What problems has it caused here?

What have been the benefits to the citizens of this kind of citizen participation?

What have been the benefits of this kind of citizen participation for city government?

Citizens' Prior Political Activity

During the last ten years, have you ever done any of the following?

Worn a campaign button or gone to a political meeting.

Worked actively in a political campaign.

Contributed money to any campaign organization.
Contributed money to any civil rights organization.
Taken part in any nonviolent protest such as picketing, boycott, march, or sit-in.

Efficacy Toward the City Government

If you have a serious complaint about poor services by the city, do you think you can get city officials to do something about it if you contact them?

If you made an effort to change this law [which you oppose], how likely is it that you would succeed?

APPENDIX C: QUESTIONS USED FROM THE ACIR DATA

• There is generally (1) very little (2) a moderate amount of (3) a great deal of citizen participation in the budget process.

• (1) More (2) About the same level of (3) Less citizen participation would be desirable in the budget process.

• (1) Very few (2) A moderate number of (3) A substantial number of changes have been made in the budget process because of citizen participation. For each of the following pairs of sentences, check the one that best describes the situation in your local government:

Most participation is informal through phone calls and personal contacts with government officials.
Participation is usually through advisory committees, hearings, or other parts of the formal structure.
Most participants attend meetings only to seek additional funding for the special interests they represent.
Citizens attend hearings because of genuine interest in the entire budget.
Generally, citizen controversies rarely arise over allocation of funds.
Citizen controversies often arise over allocation of budget funds.

• Does your local government provide staff assistance to citizens to help them prepare for participation?

• How many of the following types of hearings does your local government conduct each year (exclude hearings that are held at the neighborhood or district level).

Combined hearings on the proposed use of revenue.
Sharing funds and on the regular budget.

Hearings (separate from regular budget hearings) on the proposed use of revenue sharing funds.

Hearings (separate from revenue sharing hearings) on the proposed budget.

Community Development Block Grant hearings.

- On the average, how many citizens attend each type of hearing?
- Are any of the four types of hearings held at the neighborhood or district level?
- How many are held at the neighborhood or district level?
- On the average, how many residents attend each type of hearing?
- Do representatives of citizens' organizations attend any of the hearings?
- Have grant proposals, developed by local government staff, been dropped because of citizen participation?
- Have new grant proposals been developed as a result of citizen suggestions?
- Has your local government transferred funding for a service or program from its general budget to a grant because of citizen participation.?
- Has your local government assumed the costs in its general budget for continuing a service or program funded through an expired grant because of citizen participation?
- Has your local government dropped a service or program funded through a grant when the grant expired because of citizen participation?
- Has citizen participation had a measurable effect on the setting of priorities within your local government's general budget?

BIBLIOGRAPHY

Advisory Commission on Intergovernmental Relations. *Citizen Participation in the American Federal System.* Washington, D.C.: U.S. Government Printing Office, 1979.

Alshire, Robert W. "Planning and Citizen Participation: Costs, Benefits and Approaches." *Urban Affairs Quarterly* 5 (March 1970):369–393.

Arnstein, Sherry. "Maximum Feasible Manipulation." *Public Administration Review* 32 (September 1972):377–90.

Austin, David M. "Resident Participation: Political Mobilization or Organizational Co-optation?" *Public Administration Review* 32 (September 1972): 409–420.

Bachrach, Peter. *The Theory of Democratic Elitism: A Critique*. Boston: Little, Brown, 1967.

Bachrach, Peter, and Morton Baratz. *Power and Poverty*. New York: Oxford University Press, 1970.

Berelson, Bernard,; Paul F. Lazarsfeld; and William N. McPhee. *Voting.* Chicago: University of Chicago Press, 1954.

Burnham, Walter Dean. *Critical Elections and the Mainsprings of American Politics.* New York: W. W. Norton, 1970.

Campbell, Angus; Philip E. Converse; Warren E. Miller; and Donald E. Stokes. *The American Voter.* Chicago: University of Chicago Press, 1960.

Cole, Richard L. *Citizen Participation and the Urban Policy Process.* Lexington, Mass.: Lexington Books, 1974.

Cole, Richard L., and David A. Caputo. *Urban Politics and Decentralization: The Case of General Revenue Sharing.* Lexington, Mass.: Lexington Books, 1974.

Dahl, Robert A. *A Preface to Democratic Theory.* Chicago: University of Chicago Press, 1956.

Falkson, Joseph. *An Evaluation of Policy Related Research on Citizen Participation in Municipal Service Systems: Overview and Summary.* Washington, D.C.: TARP Institute, 1974.

Fox, Douglas M., ed. *The New Urban Politics: Cities and the Federal Government.* Pacific Palisades, Ca.: Goodyear, 1972.

Friedan, Bernard J., and Marshall Kaplan. *The Politics of Neglect: Urban Aid From Model Cities to Revenue Sharing.* Cambridge, Mass.: MIT Press, 1975.

Gamson, William A. *Power and Discontent.* Homewood, Ill.: Dorsey Press, 1968.

Gerth, H. H., and C. Wright Mills. *From Max Weber: Essays in Sociology.* New York: Oxford University Press, 1958.

Greenstone, J. David, and Paul E. Peterson. *Race and Authority in Urban Politics: Community Participation and the War on Poverty.* New York: Russell Sage Foundation, 1973.

Hamilton, Alexander; James Madison; and John Jay. *The Federalist Papers.* New York: The New American Library of World Literature, 1961.

Hansen, Susan Blackwell. "Particip[illegible], Political Structure and Concurrence." *The American Political Science Review* 69 (December 1975):1181–1199.

Hummel, Ralph. *The Bureaucratic Experience.* New York: St. Martin's Press, 1977.

Johnson, Carl F. *A Study of City-Wide Citizen Participation in Ten Cities.* Washington, D.C.: National Citizen Participation Council, Inc., 1975.

Jones, Bryan D., with Saadia Greenberg and Joseph Drew. *Service Delivery in the City: Citizen Demand and Bureaucratic Rules.* New York: Longman, 1980.

Kasperson, Roger E., and Myrna Breitbart. *Participation, Decentralization and Advocacy Planning.* Resource Paper #25, Association of American Geographers, 1974.

Kweit, Robert W., and Mary Grisez Kweit. "Bureaucratic Decision-Making: Impediments to Citizen Participation." *Polity* 12 (Summer, 1980): 647–666.

Langton, Stuart, ed. *Citizen Participation in America.* Lexington, Mass.: Lexington Books, 1978.

——. *Citizen Participation Perspectives: Proceedings of the National Conference on Citizen Participation.* Medford, Mass.: Lincoln Filene Center for Citizenship and Public Affairs, 1978.

Lewis, Eugene. *American Politics in a Bureaucratic Age: Citizens, Constituents, Clients and Victims.* Cambridge, Mass.: Winthrop Publishers, 1977.

Lineberry, Robert L., and Edmund P. Fowler. "Reformism and Public Policy in American Cities." *American Political Science Review* 61 (September 1967): 701-716.

Lowi, Theodore J. *The End of Liberalism: The Second Republic of the United States.* 2nd ed. New York: W. W. Norton, 1979.

Marris, Peter, and Martin Rein. *Dilemmas of Social Reform: Poverty and Community Action in the United States.* 2nd ed. Chicago: Aldine, 1973.

Marshall, Patricia, ed. *Citizen Participation for Community Development: A Reader on the Citizen Participation Process.* Washington, D.C.: National Association of Housing and Redevelopment Officials, 1977.

May, Judith V. *Citizen Participation: A Review of the Literature.* Council of Planning Libraries, 1971.

Mazmanian, Daniel A., and Jeanne Nienaber. *Can Organizations Change?* Washington, D.C.: Brookings, 1979.

Mogulof, Melvin B. *Citizen Participation: A Review and Commentary on Federal Policies and Practices.* Washington, D.C.: The Urban Institute, 1970.

Mosher, Frederick C. *Democracy and the Public Service.* New York: Oxford University Press, 1968.

Needleman, Martin L., and Carolyn E. Needleman. *Guerrillas in the Bureaucracy: The Community Planning Experiment in the United States.* New York: John Wiley & Sons, 1974.

Nie, Norman H.; Sidney Verba; and John R. Petrocik. *The Changing American Voter.* Enlarged Edition. Cambridge, Mass.: Harvard University Press, 1979.

Pateman, Carole. *Participation and Democratic Theory.* Cambridge, Mass.: Cambridge University Press, 1970.

Pennock, J. Roland, and John W. Chapman, eds. *Participation in Politics.* New York: Lieber-Atherton, 1975.

Pennock, J. Roland. *Democratic Political Theory.* Princeton: Princeton University Press, 1979.

Pranger, Robert J. *The Eclipse of Citizenship: Power and Participation in Contemporary Politics.* New York: Holt, Rinehart and Winston, 1968.

Presthus, Robert. *The Organizational Society.* Rev. Ed. New York: St. Martin's Press, 1978.

Redford, Emmett S. *Democracy in the Administrative State.* New York: Oxford University Press, 1969.

Rosener, Judy B. "A Cafeteria of Techniques and Critiques." *Public Management* 57 (December 1975): 16–19.

——. "Citizen Participation: Can We Measure Its Effectivness?" *Public Administration Review* 38 (September/October 1978), pp. 457–463.

Sayre, Wallace S., and Herbert Kaufman. *Governing New York City: Politics in the Metropolis.* New York: W. W. Norton, 1965.

Schattschneider, E. E. *The Semi-Sovereign People.* New York: Holt, Rinehart and Winston, 1960.

Selznick, Philip. *TVA and the Grass Roots: A Study of Politics and Organization.* Berkeley: University of California Press, 1949.

Simon, Herbert A. *Administrative Behavior: A Study of Decision-Making Processes in Administrative Organization.* 3rd. Ed. New York: The Free Press, 1976.

Speigel, Hans B. C. *Citizen Participation in Urban Development.* Vol I. Washington, D.C.: NTL Institute for Applied Behavioral Research, 1968.

Stein, Robert M.; Elise Kornmayer; and David Gow. "Federally Mandated Citizen Participation: A Study of Municipal Budgetary Impact." Paper presented at the Midwest Political Science Association 1980 Annual Meeting, Chicago, Ill., April 25, 1980.

Steinman, Michael. "Low Income and Minority Group Participation in Administrative Processes: Mexican American Orientations to Health Care Services." *Urban Affairs Quarterly.* 11 (June 1976):523–544.

Strange, John H. "Citizen Participation in Community Action and Model Cities Programs." *Public Administration Review* 32 (October 1972):655–669.

——. "The Impact of Citizen Participation on Public Administration." *Public Administration Review* 32 (September 1972):457–470.

Thompson, James D. *Organizations in Action: Social Science Bases of Administrative Theory*. New York: McGraw-Hill, 1967.

Verba, Sidney, and Norman H. Nie. *Participation in America: Political Democracy and Social Equality*. New York: Harper & Row, 1972.

Warren, Roland L.; Stephen M. Rose; and Ann F. Bergunder. *The Structure of Urban Reform: Community Decision Organizations in Stability and Change*. Lexington, Mass.: Lexington Books, 1974.

Wilson, James Q. "Planning and Politics: Citizen Participation and Urban Renewal." In *Urban Renewal: The Record and the Controversy.* edited by James Q. Wilson, pp. 409–421. Cambridge, Mass.: MIT Press, 1967.

Woll, Peter. *American Bureaucracy*. 2nd ed. New York: W. W. Norton, 1977.

Yin, Robert K.; William A. Lucas; Peter L. Szanton; and J. Andrew Spindler. *Citizen Organizations: Increasing Client Control Over Services.* Santa Monica, Ca.: Rand, 1973. Report #R-1196–HEW.

Zurcher, Louis A., Jr. "The Poverty Board: Some Consequences of 'Maximum Feasible Participation'." *Journal of Social Issues* 26 (Summer 1970):85–107.

INDEX

ABOUT THE AUTHORS

MARY GRISEZ KWEIT has been an Associate Professor of Political Science at the University of North Dakota, Grand Forks, North Dakota, since 1978. Prior to that Dr. Kweit taught at the College of William & Mary and the University of Virginia.

Dr. Kweit has published and delivered papers in citizen participation, bureaucratic decision making, and political behavior. Her most recent book, coauthored with her husband, is *Concepts and Methods for Political Analysis.* She has been a citizen participant as a member of the Executive Board of her neighborhood organization. In addition, she has served as a consultant to state and local governments in the areas of citizen participation and economic development.

Dr. Kweit was a Phi Beta Kappa graduate of Carleton College and earned her M.A. and Ph.D. degrees at the University of Pennsylvania.

ROBERT W. KWEIT is Associate Professor of Political Science and Director of Master of Public Administration Programs at the University of North Dakota, Grand Forks, North Dakota. He has been at the University of North Dakota since 1976, after teaching at St. Joseph's College and Hamilton College.

Dr. Kweit has worked extensively in the areas of citizen participation, the bureaucracy and political activism and he has published and delivered papers in these areas. He has recently coauthored, with his wife, *Concepts and Methods for Political Analysis.* Professor Kweit has been a citizen participant as an Executive Board member of his neighborhood organization and is currently a vice-president of the Grand Forks Planning Commission. He has worked as a consultant to state and local government for citizen participation and community development.

Dr. Kweit is a graduate of Syracuse University and received his M.A. and Ph.D. at the University of Pennsylvania.